AF531706

Globalization, International Trade and World Welfare

Edited by

Abhilas Kumar Pradhan

2012

Icfai Books
The Icfai University Press

Globalization, International Trade and World Welfare

Editor: Abhilas Kumar Pradhan

© 2012 The Icfai University Press. All rights reserved.

No part of this publication may be reproduced, stored in a retrieval system, or transmitted in any form or by any means – electronic, mechanical, photocopying or other otherwise – without prior permission in writing from the Icfai University Press.

While every care has been taken to avoid errors and omissions, this publication is being sold on the condition and understanding that the information given in the book is merely for reference and must not be taken as having authority of or being binding in any way on the authors, editors, publishers or sellers.

Icfai Books, IB and IB logo are trademarks of the Icfai University Press. Any other product or corporate names, that may be registered trademarks, are used in the book only for the purpose of identification and explanation, without any intent to infringe.

First Edition: 2012
Printed in India

Published by

This book is published by IUP.
University Campus, Agartala-Simna Road,
P.O. Kamalghat Sadar, Agartala – 799210, Tripura (West)
E-mail: info@iupindia.org
Website: www.books.iupindia.org

Unless repugnant to the context otherwise, any reference to the words Icfai, Icfai Books, Icfai University Press shall be read and construed as IUP only. This book is not for sale in US and Canada.

ISBN: 978-81-314-2719-4

The views and content of this book are solely of the author(s)/editor(s). The author(s)/editor(s) of the book has/have taken all reasonable care to ensure that the contents of the book do not violate any existing copyright or other intellectual property rights of any person in any manner whatsoever. In the event the author(s)/editor(s) has/have been unable to track any source and if any copyright has been inadvertently infringed, please notify the publisher in writing for corrective action.

Contents

Overview

The first article "**International Trade and Global Development: An Overview**" is written by *Abhilas Kumar Pradhan*. The article states that the world community has benefited enormously from the globalization and trade openness. Though the developed countries have retained their competitive advantage over the developing nations, trade openness has helped the developing countries to achieve higher economic growth rate and consequently higher level consumer welfare. Offshore outsourcing activities by the developed nations have created ample employment opportunities in the developing nations. However, the benefits of globalization have still been limited to a particular section of the society. The fruits of globalization need to be translated effectively and uniformly to all sections of the society. Hence, due efforts should be taken to make the process of globalization more inclusive and pro-poor.

The next article "**Impact of Globalization on International Trade**" written by *Ishita Mukherjee* examines the impact of globalization on international trade. It says that the process of globalization has accelerated considerably since the mid-1980s. In the past three decades, digital revolution and substantial policy reforms by the national government have contributed to the process of globalization. Trade openness and interdependence between the national economies have provided ample opportunities for developing economies, but with several challenges. It says that the degree of globalization of any economy depends mainly on four major elements, human migration, international trade, movement of capital and the integration of financial markets. The article discusses the contribution of technology to the process of globalization and also addresses the benefits and costs aspects of global free trade for the participating countries.

The third article "**Globalization and the Benefits of Trade**" is written by *Robert L Thompson*. The article states that comparative cost advantages lead to trade among various nations. It says that when a country engages in international trade, its households' real purchasing power rises. Their incomes stretch further because they can obtain at lower cost the goods and services they have been buying. When a country opens its borders to free movement of goods and services, the market then provides the incentive to move the country's resources into their highest-value uses, thereby facilitating economic growth.

The following article "**Globalization and Inclusive Development**" sourced from *UNCTAD secretariat* highlights some policy issues that could contribute to promoting a more inclusive, pro-poor process of globalization. The article says the international community is currently facing two broad challenges: first, the growth trends in the area of international trade need to be actively maintained, so as to allow an increasing number of developing countries to reap the benefits of globalization, and second, there is a need to ensure that the process of globalization becomes more inclusive, so that it benefits countries and sectors of population that have been left out. Despite the impressive performance of developing countries as a whole in recent years, and the aggregate development progress achieved, many countries, in particular the least developed and other low-income economies have not been able to benefit from the propitious environment. In addition, many countries, especially the least developed countries and lower- and middle-income developing and transition countries have not been able to translate growth effectively into poverty reduction and broader human development. The paper identifies some of the main policy areas that need to be addressed in order to make the globalization process more inclusive.

The subsequent article **"World Public Favours Globalization and Trade but Wants to Protect Environment and Jobs"** sourced from *worldpublicopinion.org* describes the views of the world public on Globalization and Free Trade. The article says that support for globalization is remarkably strong throughout the world. The highest levels of support are found in countries with export-oriented economies like China, South Korea and Israel. The greatest scepticism about globalization is found in Mexico, Russia and the Philippines. Respondents in 14 countries were asked whether trade was good or bad for their economy. A majority replied that it was good. However, respondents around the world expressed concern about the effect of trade on the environment. The article reveals that there is a significant concern about the effect of trade on employment, especially in developed countries.

The sixth article **"Does Globalization Cause Inequality among Rich and Poor Nations?"** is written by *M Stephen Lucas*. The paper examines the impact of trade on rich and poor nations and determines if globalization is to be blamed for the international inequality of wealth. It says that inequity does exist, but it is not because rich countries are taking advantage of poor nations. When the rich nations get richer other factors are at work such as more efficient use of resources, which need stable, open governments and the infrastructure for improved social conditions. Many poor nations fail because the state fails, or with a large population growth rate, they have difficulties managing the allocation of their resources. It further maintains that several of the poorer nations do not want to open up to international trade due to the fear of losing their own identity, when in fact they are losing an opportunity for their people to move out of poverty. Many of the poorer nations which have an agrarian economy that is labour-intensive, without technology are changing over to industrial economy that is not as labour-intensive. During this transition, they will provide cheap labour markets for multinational corporations, and wages for these people will increase.

The seventh article "**Trade and Inequity: The Role of Economists**" is written by *Dean Baker*. The article maintains that the role of economists in trade debates is especially pernicious because there is no area of economics in which economists have been honest about what their models show. Besides consistently exaggerating the benefits that are predicted by standard trade models, they have ignored or downplayed the distributional consequences. By doing so, they have derided those who raise the question about the path of the recent trade policy. In this backdrop, the article focuses on three aspects: 1) trade creates winners and losers, and given current patterns of trade, the winners are likely to be owners of capital and highly educated workers, with the rest of the population ending up as losers, 2) it is possible to redistribute capital from the winners to the losers, and 3) there are trade barriers that come in the way of protecting workers in the most highly paid professions, such as doctors, lawyers and accountants. Eliminating these barriers would both increase economic efficiency and reduce inequality.

The eighth article "**Globalisation and Its Impact on Labor**" is written by *Robert C Feenstra*. The article discusses the potential impact of trade on wages, which is an issue of ongoing concern in Europe. Outsourcing or offshoring, continues to receive a good deal of attention in the United States, too. It talks about how free trade affects the productivity of firms. As productivity improves, it is expected that the gains are reflected in lower prices, and therefore higher real wages. It explains the impact of outsourcing on the economy in general, and workers in particular. Additionally, it also discusses how in the current scenario of international trade, technology plays a role in the wages between skilled and unskilled workers worldwide. Evidences from Canada, United States, Mexico and European countries about how the wages have been affected due to outsourcing activities, migration and Information Technology are provided in the article.

The next article "**Economic Effects of Globalization: Lessons from Trade Models**" is written by *Cristina Manteu*. The article maintains that during the period 1990-2005, the average growth of world trade of goods and services increased and continued to exceed world output growth.

Trade openness has thus increased significantly both in advanced economies and in major emerging market economies. In the article, the expected impact of globalization has been analyzed in the framework of textbook trade models, which include the Ricardian single factor model, the Hechscher-Ohlin-Samuelson two-factor model and the new trade models incorporating scale economies and monopolistic competition developed in the 80s. The article focuses on the findings of the more recent trade literature, namely the so-called "new" trade models incorporating firm heterogeneity. It reviews the implications of models developed to account for a distinguished feature of the present globalization process, the growing international fragmentation of production. Finally, it discusses some issues raised by globalization regarding economic policy, in particular, for a small open economy.

The tenth article "**International Migration, Economic Development and Brain Drain: Issues and Evidence**" is written by *Abhilas Kumar Pradhan.* The article discusses various issues and statistical findings related to international migration of skilled workers and its impact on global development and welfare. International labour migration is an integral part of the globalization process and economic interdependence among nations. Undoubtedly, it is beneficial both for the receiving and sending countries as it helps them in the process of their economic growth and development. However, policy measures are to be initiated both at the Government and corporate level to keep international migration at a socially acceptable level.

The succeding article "**Globalization and American Wages: Today and Tomorrow**" written by *L Josh Bivens* provides rough empirical estimates of the effect of integration on American wages and inequality. It says that global integration has at least two potential impacts on American wages. First, workers employed in industries directly in competition with low-cost imports from abroad can expect to see immediate job dislocation and/or downward wage pressures. Second, as relative prices change across industries, the return to factors of production, including different kinds of labour inputs, can be expected to change as well. It says that the impact of trade flows has increased the inequality of earnings by roughly 7%, with the resulting loss to a representative household (two earners making the median wage and working the average amount of (household) hours each year) reaching more than $2,000. This amount rivals the entire annual federal income tax bill paid by this household.

The next article "**Trade, Jobs and Wages: Are the Public's Worries about Globalization Justified?**" is written by *L Josh Bivens*. The article describes the increasing anxiety about globalization and its effect on their jobs and communities in the context of developed nations. Economists, policymakers and pundits maintain that trade is good for the economy, that the wider public is simply misguided about its benefits, and that politicians who sympathize with those concerned about globalization are pandering to special interests at the expense of the wider economy. It says that job losses are stemming from growing trade deficits; and downward wage pressure for tens of millions of American workers. First, trade creates new jobs in exporting industries and destroys jobs when imports replace the output of domestic firms. While job-loss caused by rising trade deficits is the most visible effect of globalization, its impact on wages is a concern to an even much larger number of workers. Even if trade flows begin to balance and there is less job-loss in the future, the integration of the US economy with those of its low-wage trading partners will pull down wages for many American workers, and will contribute to the ever-rising inequality of incomes in the US economy.

The final article "**Globalization and the Least Developed Countries: Issues in Trade and Investment**" sourced from *UNCTAD* says that some countries and people have not benefited from the process of globalization. Among them are many Least Developed Countries (LDCs), and a relatively large share of the population of the LDCs. Many LDCs have been marginalized in the world economy although they have undertaken far-reaching economic reforms. The article also suggests that LDCs need to increase investments related to the development of productive capacities (namely productive resources, entrepreneurial capabilities and production linkages) and also significantly step up investments which are related to productive capacities (especially in infrastructure and institutions).

1

International Trade and Global Development: An Overview

Abhilas Kumar Pradhan

The world community has benefited enormously from the process of globalization and trade openness. Free Trade has helped the developing countries to achieve a higher economic growth rate and consequently, higher level of consumer welfare. Offshore outsourcing activities by the developed nations have created ample employment opportunities in the developing nations. However, the benefits of globalization have still been limited to a particular section of the society. Therefore, trade policy must address the issues with respect to movement of natural persons, financial mechanism, foreign direct investment, etc., to make the globalization process more inclusive and pro-poor.

Introduction

Internationalization of the world economy has been rapid during the last two decades. Besides trade, there is now a greater flow of capital, skilled labor, information technology and better organization of the production process across the borders. Globalization of

© *The Icfai University Press. All rights reserved.*

the world economy offers both, challenges as well as opportunities to the developed and developing countries. Empirical evidence support that globalization has contributed significantly to the economic growth and development in many East Asian economies such as Hong Kong, the Republic of Korea, and Singapore. But not all developing countries have been proportionately benefited from the process. In fact, many developing countries have been rather sluggish to integrate with the world economy. The costs and benefits resulting from international trade depend on many crucial factors like the size of the country's home market, its natural resource base, and geographical position[1]. Trade theories say that nations benefit from international trade because of the division of labor, on one hand, and competition in the world markets, on the other. Producers of the home country produce more efficiently due to specialization and the emerging threat from foreign competition. Similarly consumer groups enjoy a wider variety of domestic and imported goods at relatively lower prices because of the presence of stiff competition[2]. In addition to this, a trading country benefits from the new technologies that spill over to it from its trading partners. These technological spillover effects are very important for developing nations because they give them a chance to follow suit with the developed countries in terms of productivity[3] and production process which ultimately leads to production efficiency and lower price, hence higher consumer welfare. However, on the flip side active participation in international trade also entails risks and challenges, particularly those associated with the strong competition in international markets[4]. For instance, a participating country may have the risk that some of its industries which are less competitive and adaptable would be forced out of business[5]. Similarly, heavy dependence on foreign suppliers may be considered unacceptable when it comes to industries that play a significant role in national security.

During the period 1980 to 2002, there has been a spectacular increase in the world trade volume: nearly a threefold increase[6]. Technological revolution and the resulting decline in the cost of transport and communication have led to greater integration of the global economy. Reduction of trade barriers both regionally and globally has accelerated the growth of international trade, hence increased global welfare. Four important globalization parameters such as; volume of international trade, human migration, flow of capital and the integration of financial capitals describe the extent to which countries have been globalized[7]. Various nations have been performing differently on the said globalization parameters. Globalization has provided ample opportunities both to the developed and developing economies, but with several challenges. The article sheds light on some of the issues related to international trade and global development both in the context of developed and developing countries.

Does Globalization and International Trade Address Inclusive Development?

In the past 20 years, the ratio of trade to GDP has increased in all major economies[8]. Again a retrospection into the past five years imply that many countries across the globe have been able to achieve around 5 to 6 per cent growth rate which has enabled some countries to make progress towards the Millennium Development Goals[9]. Undoubtedly, globalization has helped many developing countries in their aggregate development process; however several countries, particularly the least developed and low-income countries have not been able to reap the benefits of globalization in true sense. Though many lower and middle-income developing countries have received the benefits of globalization, they have not been able to translate the growth effectively and uniformly to all sections of the society. A major consequence of the globalization wave is rising income inequality both within and between countries[10]. Therefore, there is an urgent need to make the process of globalization more inclusive and pro-poor so that the benefits reach the population which has either been left out or neglected. Policy measures should be initiated with respect to eradication of poverty, reduction of unemployment and underemployment, access to housing, health, education and other social services to the marginalized communities[11]. To make the globalization process more inclusive and pro-poor, trade policy must address the issues with respect to movement of natural persons, financial mechanism that would boost the benefits of foreign direct investment, building up new productive capacity and foreign aid which is more inclusive[12].

How does the World Public View Globalization and Trade?

There is a general agreement among the people of the world that integration of national economies and International trade has benefited various economic groups and agents. The Globalization process has received remarkably strong support throughout the world. The Chicago Council for Global Affairs and *WorldpublicOpinion.org* conducted a survey in countries like India, the United States, Indonesia, France, Russia, Thailand, Ukraine, Poland, Iran, Mexico, South Korea, the Philippines, Australia, Argentina, Peru, Israel, Armenia and the Palestinian territories, and analyzed the attitude of the world public on various key issues and in most of the cases they found positive answers outweighing negative ones[13]. Though most of the polled viewed trade benefits, consumers and their national economy, respondents across the globe expressed their concern about the effect of international trade on environment. When asked for the reason, the public was of the view that trade stimulates growth and mass consumption which results in more industrial growth and ultimately higher level of pollution. They also reasoned that trade openness allows companies to evade environmental laws by making their presence in countries with more lax regulations.

The poll also revealed that there is a great concern about the effect of international trade on employment in more developed countries. Respondents in countries like France, The United States viewed trade as harmful to their workers and detrimental for creation of new jobs in their countries. However, people in the countries like Israel, Mexico, Thailand and China regarded trade to be good for job security and creation of new employment opportunities.

International Trade and Income Inequality

As the poor and developing countries open up to international trade, their per capita income rises. Free movement of goods and services, labor, capital and technology is expected to help poorer nations to achieve their socio-economic goals and objectives. However, empirical facts reveal that though international trade has enabled to achieve a higher per capita income in many developing countries, it has not addressed the distributional issues. Economic integration and International trade has widened the income gap between rich and poor nations. As per the study conducted by the *World Economic Outlook*, (It studied 42 countries for which data was available for the entire 20th century) the per capita output has increased, but that the distribution of income among countries has become more unequal than at the beginning of the century (IMF, 2005)[14].

According to the World Bank report (2005), many regions of the world, have 25% or more of their population living on less than $1 per day (people living on $1 per day, in developing countries and people living on $2 in medium economies are considered poor.)[15]. In 2003, 85 per cent of the world income was concentrated with the richest 20% of the world population; where as the poorest 20% received only 1.4 per cent of the world income[16]. Inequality among rich and poor nations not only exists in the form of income

Figure 1

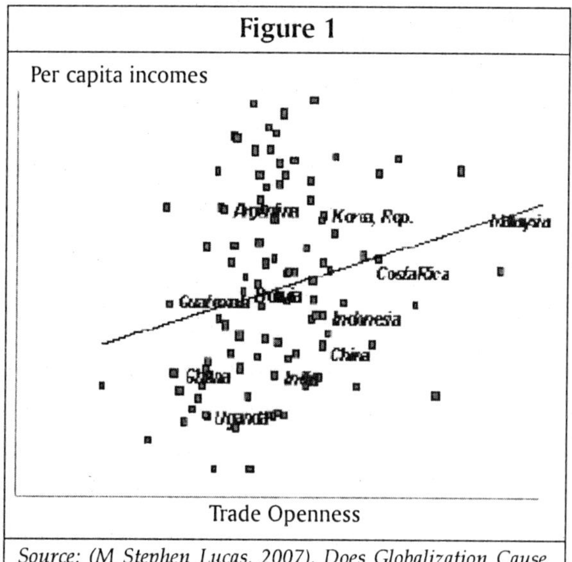

Source: (M Stephen Lucas, 2007), Does Globalization Cause Inequality among Rich and Poor Nations?

gap but it also makes its presence in terms of general living conditions of the mass (literacy, health, sanitation, etc.). Therefore, the aid packages from rich nations should aim at a more inclusive or pro-poor type of development.

Impact of Globalization on Productivity, Labor and Wage

Free trade improves productivities of firms and the expected gains are reflected in terms of volume production, lower prices, and therefore higher real wages. The impact of outsourcing or off shoring activities on the wage rates has received considerable attention in Europe and the United States. Similarly, international migration of skilled labor force, professionals and technical talents from developing nations to developed and affluent countries has also become a frequent topic of debate. Outsourcing activities have favored the wages of more skilled workers than the unskilled workers; hence there is a very uneven distribution of income in many countries across the globe[17]. Technology also plays a major role in describing the wage disparities between skilled and unskilled workers. Evidences from countries like Canada, the United States, Mexico and many European countries suggest that outsourcing activities have adversely affected their local wage rates and employment scenario. Particularly in the context of developed countries, there has been an increasing anxiety about globalization and its impact on their local jobs and community. The greatest benefit of globalization is that it has helped to increase the general wage rates and consequently higher purchasing power of the people in many low-income countries. For developing economies, globalization has created an environment for export-led economic growth and also new market places for the products that they produce more efficiently.

Internationalization and Global Development

Despite certain challenges and risks, the global community has benefited enormously from the globalization process. The world public has unanimously agreed that International trade has benefited both, the developing and the developed nations, though they have reaped the benefits of trade, disproportionately. Technological revolution and decline in the cost of transportation and communication has played a major role in the economic integration and emergence of global market places. In the presence of foreign competitors, it has now become possible for the domestic consumers to get a wide range of products at competitive prices, hence increased consumer welfare. Similarly, the domestic producers tend to produce more efficiently due to specialization and the presence of foreign competition. Due to free flow of labor, professionals and technical persons in developing countries also receive substantial amount of remittance income from their migrant workforce which make significant contribution to their national economies. The inflow of remittance income adds to their foreign exchange reserves and at the household level it helps in achieving higher standard of living and availing better education and healthcare facilities for the migrant family members. Similarly, developed nations also benefit from these migrant worker forces as they fill their supply shortages. Outsourcing activities by the developed countries have been proven to be very cost-effective.

The following tables provide information on the remittance income for various countries and hourly wage rates for selected occupations, in the US and India.

However, the trading direction indicates that, the developing countries export mainly labor-intensive products, whereas developed countries export capital-intensive products. Therefore, it is very natural that developed countries still retain

Table 1: Remittance Income

Country	Remittances in 2004 (in $ bn)
India	23
Mexico	17
Philippines	8.1
China	4.6
Pakistan	4.1
Morocco	3.6
Bangladesh	3.4
Colombia	3.1
Egypt	3.0
Brazil	2.8
Lebanon	2.7
El Salvador	2.5
Dominican Republic	2.3

Source: www.u21global.com

Table 2: Hourly Wage Rates for Selected Occupations, US and India, 2002-03		
Occupation	**Hourly Wage, US (in $)**	**Hourly Wage, India (in $)**
Telephone Operator	12.57	Under 1.00
Health Record Technologist/ Medical Transcriptionist	13.17	1.50-2.00
Payroll Clerk	15.17	1.50-2.00
Legal Assistant	17.86	6.00-8.00
Accountant	23.35	6.00-15.00
Financial Researcher/Analyst	33.00-35.00	6.00-15.00
Source: www.u21global.com		

their competitive advantage in the international trade. At the same time, it is also true that due to increased volume of labor-intensive products like clothes, carpets, etc., there has been increasing numbers of jobs and employment opportunities in the developing countries. The best part of international trade is the technological spillover effects from the developed trading partners to the developing trading partners. This provides huge opportunity to the developing nations to overcome their technological bottlenecks and in the process it helps them to catch-up with the developed nations. On the whole, globalization has stimulated the economic growth rates in various countries though the sharing of benefits seems to be uneven.

The Socio-Cultural Impact of Globalization

Globalization has also practical effects on a wide range of issues at social, geographical and political levels. In most of the developing countries, it has greatly influenced the general life styles of the people and it has affected the local culture, tradition and various socio-economic groups.

Conclusion

The world community has benefited enormously from the globalization process and trade openness. Though the developed countries have retained their competitive advantage over the developing nations, trade openness has helped the developing countries to achieve a higher economic growth rate and consequently higher level of consumer welfare. Offshore outsourcing activities by the developed nations have created ample employment opportunities in the developing nations. However, the benefits of globalization have still been limited to a particular section of the society. The fruits of globalization need to be translated effectively and uniformly to all sections of the society. Therefore, due efforts should be taken to make the process of globalization more inclusive and pro-poor.

(Abhilas Kumar Pradhan is a Faculty Member, Icfai Business School, Pune. The author can be reached at abhilas_p@ibsindia.org).

Endnotes

1 *http://www.worldbank.org/depweb/beyond/beyondco/beg_12.pdf2.*

2 Ibid.

3 Ibid.

4 Ibid.

5 Ibid.

6 Ishita Mukherjee: "Impact of Globalization on International Trade": The Icfai Universiy Press (2008).

7 Ibid.

8 Ibid.

9 UNCTAD Secretariat, (October 2007): "Globalization and Inclusive Development".

10 Ibid.

11 Ibid.

12 Ibid.

13 *(Worldpublicopinion.org)* "World Public Favors Globalization and Trade but Wants to Protect Environment and Jobs".

14 (M. Stephen Lucas, 2007): "Does Globalization 'Cause Inequality Among Rich and Poor Nations?"

15 Ibid.

16 Ibid.

17 Robert C. Feenstra, 2007 "Globalization and its Impact on Labor".

References

http://www.worldbank.org/depweb/beyond/beyondco/beg_12.pdf2

Ishita Mukherjee: "Impact of Globalization on International Trade": The Icfai Universiy Press (2008).

UNCTAD Secretariat, (October 2007): "Globalization and Inclusive Development".

"World Public Favors Globalization and Trade but Wants to Protect Environment and Jobs". *www.worldpublicopinion.org*

M. Stephen Lucas, (2007): "Does Globalization Cause Inequality Among Rich and Poor Nations?"

Robert C. Feenstra, (2007): "Globalization and its Impact on Labor". *www.u21global.com/PartnerAdmin*

2

Impact of Globalization on International Trade

Ishita Mukherjee

This paper examines the impact of globalization on international trade. Trade has been influenced by various factors to open up its dimensions worldwide both prior to globalization and post-globalization. The paper has shown some historical perspectives of global economic integration. Although the process of globalization started after World War II, it has accelerated considerably since the mid-1980s. In the past three decades, digital revolution and substantial policy reforms by the national governments have contributed to globalization. Economies have been encouraged to open up more and they have committed to stay open to international trade and investment. This was made possible by the crucial contribution of the GATT/WTO round of negotiations. Thus, greater openness and interdependence between national economies have provided wonderful opportunities for developing economies, but with several challenges.

Source: The Icfai Journal of International Business, Vol. III, No. 1, 2008. *© The Icfai University Press. All rights reserved.*

Globalization was a deep trend pushed by technology and right ideas, as much as anything else.

– Jeffrey Sachs

By virtue of exchange, one man's prosperity is beneficial to all others.

– Frederic Bastiat

Introduction

The term globalization refers to the increasing integration and interdependence among countries resulting from the free flow of trade, finance, ideas and people in a single global system. The World Bank defines globalization as "the growing integration of economies and societies around the world". The term also implies that changes in societies and the world economy have resulted from the dramatically increased international trade and cultural exchange. The British magazine *The Economist* recently likened globalization to a line from a John Lennon song, "Imagine there's no countries. It isn't hard to do". Clearly, globalization means different things to different people. "Today, capital is seen moving freely across the world. Internet technologies are creating global networks across national and international boundaries. Cultural influences are flowing across national and international boundaries" (Chang Yi-Jen, 2006).

One of the key effects of globalization is the increase of international integration in the market for goods, technology, finance, capital services and labor. An important indicator of the progress of globalization is the marked reduction in the difference in prices for both final products and factors of production, both within and among countries. Both this and its related effects are being felt by almost all nations of the world, most notably in countries where there exist open economies, like the ones in south-east Asia.

The term 'globalization' was first used by Levitt (1985) in "The Globalization of Markets". "Levitt used the term to characterize the vast changes that have taken place over the past two decades in the international economy—the rapid and pervasive diffusion around the world of production, consumption and investment of goods, services, capital and technology".

Defining Economic Globalization

Economic globalization is "a name for the process of integration, across frontiers, of liberalizing market economies at a time of rapidly falling costs of transportation and communications".[1] Globalization of the economy depends mainly on the following elements:

- The role of human migration;
- International trade;
- Movement of capital; and
- The integration of financial markets.

International trade and movement of capital across borders have long been considered to be the main elements of this integration. "While international trade is a very visible dimension of globalization, the WTO is definitely at the heart of global governance as a trade regulator".[2]

Indicators of Globalization

While a single statistics may not capture the exact extent of globalization, there are several other statistics providing its partial indication. A standard way to measure the extent of globalization is the ratio of a country's exports and imports, i.e., the country's international trade to its Gross Domestic Product (GDP) or Gross Net Product (GNP). By this measure, globalization has doubled on an average since 1950. Between 1965 and 1996, the growth in exports had been twice that of the growth in GDP. Hence, by 1996, the ratio of world trade to world GDP was roughly about 15% in developing countries and 40% in developed countries.[3] Between 1980 and 2002, while, world output had only doubled, there was a threefold increase in world trade. This upward trend in the ratio of world trade to world output has been visible since the end of the Second World War. The trend has accelerated between 1950 and 2000. However, prior to this, the ratio of world trade to world output had declined towards the end of the gold standard, as illustrated in Figure 1.

1 Martin Wolf (2004), Associate Editor and Chief Economics Commentator, *The Financial Times*; Special Professor, School of Economics, University of Nottingham.

2 WTO General, Pascal Lamy.

3 World Bank.

Figure 1: Volume of World Manufacturing Trade as a Ratio of World Manufacturing Output

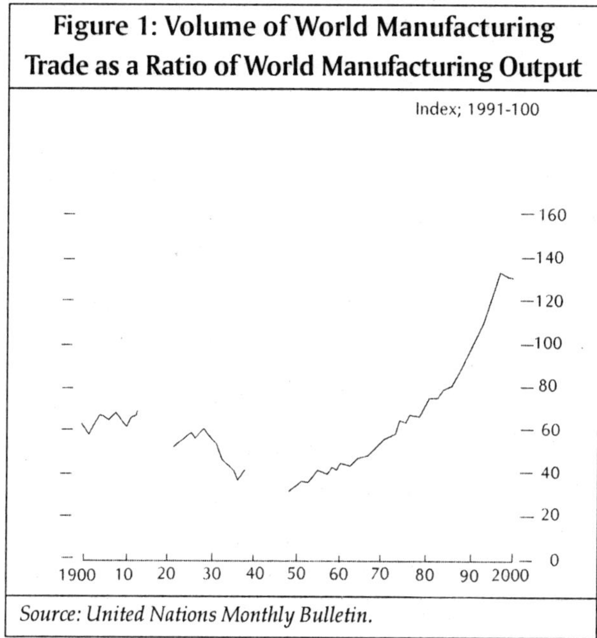

Source: United Nations Monthly Bulletin.

Thus, while the ratio of trade to GDP ratio increased in all major economies in the past 20 years, the scale of the increase has varied across regions. The ratio has risen by almost 10% in eastern European countries, the US and Japan, and by 15% in Europe and Latin America (Mark Dean and Maria Sebastia, 2002).

"In pursuing the objective of profit maximization and capital accumulation, major corporations across the world—specially those in North America and Europe as also in Japan in the far east—have been exerting their pressures and influence on their governments to facilitate this type of integration, made possible through the process of globalization, that is, the transnationalization of the world economy". There is no doubt that in recent decades, global economic integration is indeed accelerating at an unprecedented pace, and shows no signs of abating. The implications of this progress will be known for many years to come. The process has been going on for thousands of years, and history may provide us some guidance. A brief review of the historical process of globalization would help us understand the current context in which global economic integration is taking place and how similar or different it is from the past.

A Short History of Global Economic Integration

The process of global economic integration is hardly a new phenomenon. It was 2000 years ago, when the Romans first took the initiative of unifying their far-flung empire through a well designed transportation network along with a common legal system, currency and language. Hitchner (2003, p. 398) observed that "a citizen of the empire travelling from Britain to the Euphrates in the mid-second century would have found in virtually every town along the journey foods, goods, landscapes, buildings, institutions, laws, entertainment, and sacred elements not dissimilar to those in his own community". There is no doubt that this promoted trade and economic development.

At the end of the 15th century, explorers like Columbus and Vasco da Gama initiated trade through their voyages over vast distances. This paved the way for a thriving trade regime spread across continents. However, trade was limited to only a small set of commodities like spices, sugar, tobacco tea, silk, and precious metals. Subsequently, this form of trade came under the control of English and Dutch owned trading companies.

At the onset of the first world war, global economic integration took another major step forward. There was a significant expansion in international trade as well as the flow of financial capital and labor across borders. During this time, new technologies acted as a facilitator for this integration. With the opening of the Suez Canal, sail and railroads being replaced by steam and power, travel time costs between Europe and Asia were greatly reduced. Findlay and O'Rourke had indicated that trade expanded the variety of available goods both in Europe and elsewhere, and as the trade monopolies of earlier times were replaced by intense competition, prices converged globally for a wide range of commodities, including spices, wheat, cotton, pig-iron, and jute.

The post-First World War period mainly witnessed European countries, particularly Britain, as the center or core of the global trading system. The structure of trade during this period followed a 'core-periphery' pattern. Trade mainly took place in countries having an abundant supply of natural resources and land. While the flow of manufactured goods, financial capital, and labor was from the core to the periphery, natural resources and agricultural products flowed from the periphery to the core. An important exception to this fairly stable pattern was noticed in the course of the 19th century, when the US made a transition from the periphery to the core. In the US the share of manufactured goods increased from around 30% in 1840 to almost 60% in 1913. Government policies during this era brought about significant openness to trade. In Europe for example, a series of bilateral agreements ultimately reduced tariff barriers to trade.

Unfortunately, the great progress in international economic integration that was achieved during the 19th century was largely unraveled by the two world wars and the Great Depression in the 20th century. After the second world war, major powers like the US, the emergent Japan and western Europe undertook the intricate task of restoring international trade and monetary systems. However, the share of trade in global output reached the pre-First World War levels after several decades.

An important indication of this reintegration was the growth and development of intra-industry trade. Studies conducted by researches between the 1960s and 1970s revealed that a majority of the share of global trade occurred between those countries that had similar resource endowments and traded in goods of similar types, which were mainly manufactured products traded among the industrialized nations.

The integration after Second World War was supported by two factors, namely technological and political. The range of products to be traded internationally was broadened by technological advances that further reduced the costs of communication and transportation. In the political sphere, tariff barriers that increased dramatically during the Great Depression were lowered. Although there was a significant expansion in trade during the early post-World War period, recalling the exchange rate and financial crises of the 1930s, several countries adopted regulations that were aimed to limit the movement of financial capital across national borders.

From the above brief historical review, several conclusions can be drawn. The most important is the role of new technologies—a major factor supporting global economic integration, which had reduced the costs of communication and transportation. Another conclusion that can be drawn is that the extent of global economic integration has been mainly determined by national policy choices. For example, in the 19th century, integration was further brought forward by Britain as it embarked on free trade and free flow of capital.

Thus, the beginning of globalization can be traced to the post-Second World War period. However, the process saw rapid acceleration since the mid-1980s and this unprecedented speed as discussed was mainly driven by the above mentioned factors. These two important factors—(1) The contribution of technology and (2) The liberalization policies of governments, which have driven globalization are discussed next.

The Contribution of Technology to Globalization

Widespread technological revolution has resulted in a decline in the costs of transportation and communication. As a result it has become economically feasible for a firm to choose different locations for its different phases of production. This revolution thus led to greater integration of the world, i.e., globalization. It also facilitated the development of foreign trade among countries worldwide. Noted economist, Theodore Levitt, had once remarked "A powerful force drives the world towards a converging commonality, and that force is technology. The result is a new commercial reality—the emergence of global markets for standardized consumer products on a previously unimagined scale". This technological revolution played a very important role in the emergence of global marketplace. Between 1870 and 1914, technological improvements in steamships, railroads and the opening of water canals like the Suez Canal and Panama Canal brought about significant increases in global trade integration.

The first technological revolution started in the 19th century. With the advent of the steam engine, the cost of transporting goods became lower than before. In the later part of the 19th century, refrigeration helped in lowering the costs of ocean freight for perishable goods. This was followed by the second technological revolution in the mid 20th century that lowered the costs of transport and communication to a large extent. This was due to the falling transportation cost of airplanes, cars, ocean freights and telephone charges during this period.

The third and current phase of this revolution towards the end of the 20th century has been digital. The deregulation of telecom markets in several countries has lowered the costs of communication for long distances, and as a result, the access and exchange of information and ideas have become much easier than before. Moreover, the expansion of the Internet network worldwide has also lowered the costs of communication between trading nations.

Liberalization Policies of Governments and Trends in Trade

In the recent decades, global economic integration has been driven primarily by the liberalization policies of governments, which is in striking contrast to the initial episode of globalization towards the end of the 19th century—when technological development was a major factor behind this integration. This involved a sharp reduction in governmental barriers to trade in goods and services or in other words the liberalization of trade. As a result, the influence of non-tariff barriers such as export restraints, import quotas and import tariffs were being minimized to a large extent. Since the introduction of liberalization, trade has grown manifold owing to fewer restrictions. After the formation of the General Agreement on Tariff and Trade (GATT), the growth in the world economy had been sixfold. The world economic growth rate reached almost 5.2% in 2004 in spite of some initial downfall between 2001 and 2002. However, it increased again to 4.1% in 2003.

The *World Economic Outlook* released by the IMF in 2002, noted the following aspects related to global economic integration:

- Global integration in the late 19th century was driven mostly by technological developments, while, since the Second World War, integration was primarily driven by the liberalization of policies.
- Over the past three decades, trade and financial openness have increased in both developed and developing countries. While in the developing countries, trade openness increased sharply than financial openness, in the industrial nations, the increase in financial openness was greater compared to trade openness.
- The liberalization of trade policies in recent decades have brought about greater openness to trade as well as cross-border flow of capital, both in industrial and in developing countries.

Attempts to Institutionalize Trade

During the mid-90s, attempts were made towards institutionalization of international trade that would result in better coordination and cooperation among trading nations under a single umbrella of trade rules and regulations. The 1944 conference at Bretton Woods witnessed the creation of the two most important pillars of international economic relations, namely the International Bank for Reconstruction and Development (IBRD) and the International Monetary Fund (IMF).

International Trade Organization (ITO), later called the World Bank was created after the Second World War. It was considered as the third pillar. From 1946, the IMF and the IBRD opened up for business. In 1947, GATT was formed as a combined package of well-developed and acceptable trade rules and negotiations. Although plans such as ITO could not be met with much success, liberalization of trade and reduction in tariffs were achieved to a large extent under GATT, which existed for almost 50 years. However, GATT did not have an international standing like other international organizations like IMF or World Bank, as it was not an organization but merely a body of agreements. Towards the beginning of the 90s, international trade developed largely outside the purview of the GATT. Between 1947 and 1994, several regional trade blocs such as Association of South-East Asian Nations (ASEAN), European Union (EU) and The North American Free Trade Agreement (NAFTA) were created.

These trade blocs were setting their own rules for encouraging cooperative exchange among themselves and these were far outside the jurisdiction of the panel decisions under GATT. In the absence of any legal authority, the only function of GATT was to urge for the spirit of cooperation among member countries. Seeking to address these problems, the Uruguay Round of negotiations (1986-92) was launched under GATT. This was an important milestone in the history of multilateral trade negotiations. Besides promising lower trade barrier, the Uruguay Round broadened the scope of liberalization. It included industries such as textiles and apparel, which were initially protected traditionally. It also opened up trade in services, agriculture and intellectual property. Thus, the Uruguay Round of negotiations marked the beginning and the birth of World Trade Organization (WTO) and played a very important role in bringing about global integration. In 1994, GATT was transformed into WTO.

WTO and International Trade

A major role that was played by WTO in the liberalization policies of nations cannot be ruled out. There are several crucial ways through which WTO contributes towards globalization. It is the new international institution that outlines all the aspects of international trade. Moreover, it is the only decision-making body that settles international trade disputes and the only organization, on an international level, that deals with global rules of trade among nations. The four main objectives of WTO are as follows:

1. Enforcing rules for international trade;
2. Being a forum for monitoring trade liberalization;
3. Resolving trade disputes; and
4. Improving policy transparency.

Three different purposes are met by WTO rules to govern international trade. Firstly, the welfare of small and weak nations are protected against trade policy actions of large and powerful nations. Secondly, multilateral rules help the governments of nations in doing away with any interest group located domestically, and in seeking special favors. Finally, the tariff-binding rules of the WTO bring greater certainty to the international trading system and eventually help countries become more interdependent.

Regionalism and International Trade

The opening of world markets have been initiated through the growth of regional and bilateral trade pacts. These trade pacts have helped in removing barriers to trade and have further helped international trade to expand. This can be substantiated from the fact that more than 200 regional trades were taken into force between 1947 and 2000. Thus, regionalism has been an important factor behind the emergence of free trade and custom unions, and most countries worldwide have taken the initiative of becoming members of these regional trade agreements. As a result there has been an upsurge of international trade under regionalism. However, under the WTO regime, the question that arises is whether these regional trade groups actually hinder or help the growth of international trade.

Regional Trade Blocs and International Trade

In this era of globalization, there has been an emergence of significant trading ties among countries situated in the same regions. These multifarious trading blocs were formed at a time when international trade was progressing at an unprecedented pace. By definition, a trade bloc consists of a big free trade zone encompassed with single or multiple tax, tariff and trade pacts. The emergence of trade blocs reflected a rapid growth in international trade. Amongst the various trade blocs, the three largest have been NAFTA, EU and ASEAN. These trade blocs are localized to the areas of North America, Europe and south-east Asia respectively.

The first economic bloc was formed in 1834 and it was known as the German Customs Union (Zollverein), formed within the German Confederation. It was feasible for a country to register its membership with two or more different trade blocs, and if a country itself is more active, then it is categorized as a division of the less active regional bloc. For this reason, it is seen that Venezuela is a member of Andean Community as well as the member of Mercado Commun del Sur (Mercosur). Mercosur is a more dynamic trade block than the Andean Community. But at the same time, when compared to the Mercosur, in the Andean Community, Venezuela is more active. Hence, on the basis of this categorization, Venezuela is allocated to the Andean Community.

The various types of regional trade blocs are: NAFTA, Mercosur, the Andean Pact, ASEAN, European Community, European Free Trade Association (EFTA) (formed during the 1970s and 1980s) and, presently known as the European Union. Also, some other trading blocs are European Economic Area (EEA), Free Trade Area of the Americas (FTAA), the Asia Pacific Economic Cooperation forum (APEC) and the Trans-Atlantic Free Trade Agreement (TAFTA).

The European Union

The European Union, which is perhaps the world's largest trading bloc, consists of some principles for its member countries. It measures the performances of its associate nations. These performances are related to the economic growth and budgetary policies of its nations. Moreover, these doctrines are very essential for creating a base for European Union membership.

North American Free Trade Agreement (NAFTA)

The United States, Canada and Mexico had signed the NAFTA on January 1, 1984, and had agreed to phase out tariffs within a span of 15 years. NAFTA consists of a relatively integrated trade pact and maintains absolute autonomy of its members' governments. A significant outcome of NAFTA has been the steady movement of capital, technology and new job prospects in the three member countries of NAFTA and also in the direction of more productive uses. The main aim of NAFTA is to initiate the free flow of capital and investment among the member countries (i.e., the United States, Canada and Mexico), thereby promoting cross-border flow of trade among these countries.

The Effect of NAFTA

There has been a substantial increase in the US trade with Mexico due to the lowering of trade barriers. Moreover, trade with Canada also kept pace. Hence, the majority of all imports in the US are from Mexico and Canada[4].

According to a study conducted by Economic Policy Institute, the net job loss of 766,000 and the growing disparity of income in the United States can be directly attributed to the NAFTA agreement. However, the supporters of NAFTA have pointed out that the growth in trade has increased net job creation in the US, Mexico and Canada, and that in Mexico itself an increase in export activities has created more than half of the new jobs (Figures 2 and 3).[5]

The ASEAN

ASEAN comprises of more than a group of countries and has yearned for more integration.

"ASEAN negotiated a preferential trade arrangement within its membership in 1977, but serious progress in removal of barriers did not even get under way until 1987. As recently as 1989, the fraction of goods eligible for regional preferences was only on the order of 3%. It was not until January 1992 that the members proclaimed plans for an ASEAN Free Trade Area (AFTA) to be implemented by reduction of tariffs and non-tariff barriers in phases from 1993 to 2008" (see Frankel Jeffrey, 1997).

Regional trade blocs are important for the developing countries as they help in doing away with import substitution. The regional initiatives of emerging countries to become the members of trade blocs is a global phenomenon. NAFTA was completed in 1992 and ratified in 1993. Mercosur was inaugurated amongst the four countries in that division of South America situated east of the Andes (Argentina, Brazil, Paraguay and Uruguay) in 1991.

Trade blocs have to 'protect' the trade interests of their regions due to several reasons listed as follows:

- To establish some form of regional control regarding trade that fulfills the interests of nations within that region;

---

4 *Source: http://www.newsbatch.com/globalization.htm*

5 Ibid.

- To establish tariffs that protect intra-regional trade from 'outside' forces;
- To promote regional security and political concerns or to develop trade in such a way as to enhance the security in the region;
- To promote South-to-South trade, e.g., between Africa and Asia, and between Latin American countries; and
- To promote economic and technical cooperation among developing countries *(Malaysiaexports.com)*.

Figure 2: Job Creation during NAFTA Years

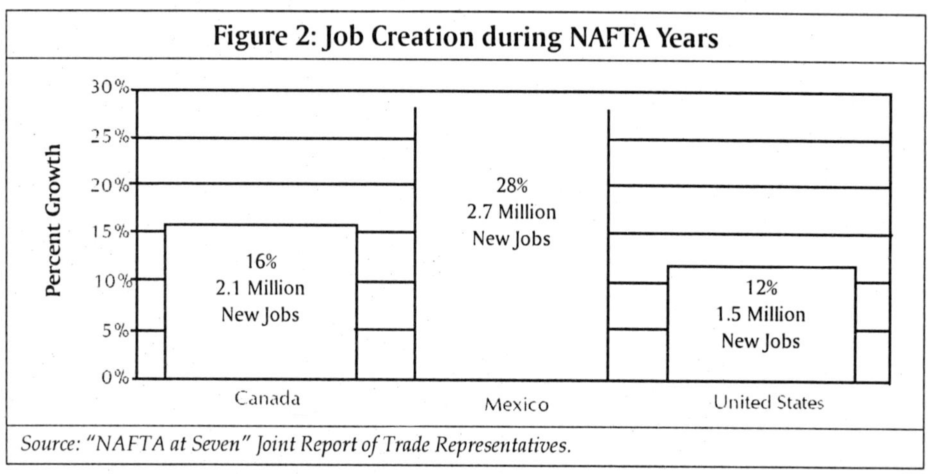

Source: "NAFTA at Seven" Joint Report of Trade Representatives.

Figure 3: Change in Real Wages in the United States during the 1990s

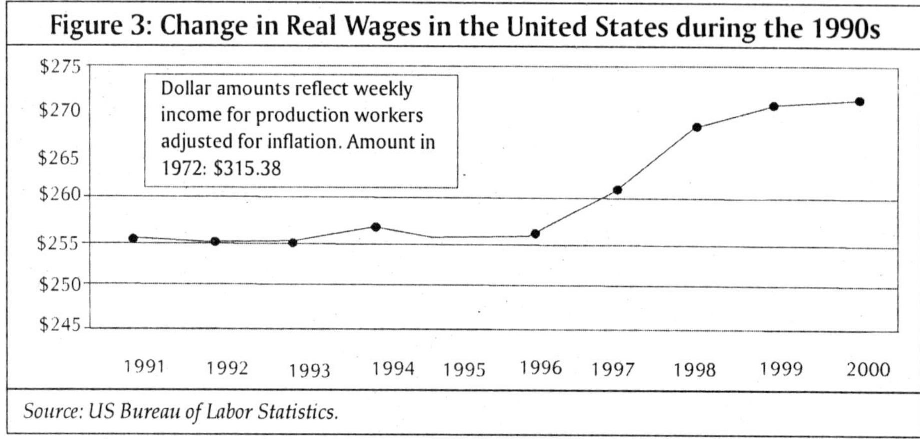

Source: US Bureau of Labor Statistics.

They also use several measures to restrain global competition as listed below:

- Import quotas (limiting the amount of imports into the country so that domestic consumers buy products made by their countries in their region);

- Customs delays (establishing bureaucratic formalities that slow down the process of the imported products entering the domestic market);
- Subsidies (government financial assistance towards sectors of the home economy so that they have an influx of capital);
- Boycotts and technical barriers; and
- Bribes and voluntary restraints.

(Source: http://ucatlas.ucsc.edu/trade/subtheme trade_blocs.php)

Since the early 1990s, cross-border trade in goods and services has been rapid both among member countries of ASEAN and the rest of the world. In recent years, this growth has been quite rapid. Between 2002 and 2005, exports from ASEAN countries grew by 70% and the share of exports in GDP from ASEAN countries grew by 70%.[6]

Impact of Globalization on Local Core Sectors

Impact on Agriculture

Globalization has revolutionized world agriculture. Millions of farmers, traders and processors of agricultural products are now able to instantly access better information on markets and about new techniques of production. All these have been made possible by innovations in information and communication technologies. In industrialized economies, fresh produces are delivered to supermarkets by aircraft from almost anywhere. The social culture and business of industrialized countries have been influencing developing countries in a major way. Moreover, developing countries have embarked in Structural Adjustment Programs (SAP), that would facilitate their trading relationships with other nations (Peter Robins, 1999).

With a view to take advantage of the benefits in innovations from globalization, vital reforms in the rules governing international trade in goods and services have become a necessity. There is no doubt that these changes affect every country's economy and the societies within these countries. In the Uruguay Round of negotiations that culminated into the formation of WTO in 1995, a specific agreement was made on reforms related to trade in agricultural products. As a result, member countries of

6 Labor and Social Trends in ASEAN 2007, Integration, Challenges and Opportunities, International Labor Office Regional Office for Asia and the Pacific.

WTO committed to reduce government support for agricultural sectors, and increase their export competitiveness and market access. To regulate trade in agriculture, many other agreements existed between nations, prior to the signing of the WTO agreement on agriculture. It therefore becomes mandatory to modify the previous agreements as these were in conflict with the new rules under WTO.

On July 1, 1995, The agreement on agriculture under WTO came into effect, and covered agricultural products. However, the items excluded marine products and forest products.

The three main objectives of the agreement are: (1) increasing export competition; (2) reducing domestic support; and (3) increasing market access. The main assumption behind the objectives were that production would become more efficient if the protective measures distorting international trade like tariffs, subsidies and quotas were removed. This would enable the producers to become more competitive and gain larger market share. A review of the agreement had begun in the 1990s and 2000.

The following are the results of the negotiations (Peter Robins):

- Agreement on agriculture;
- Domestic support and export subsidies;
- Agreement on sanitary and phytosanitary measures; and
- Ministerial decision concerning least-developed and net food-importing developing countries.

Thus, the negotiations made a concerted move towards the objective—more market orientation with respect to agricultural trade.

The other important issues have been:[7]

- Provisions were made for encouraging the use of less trade-distorting domestic support policies for maintaining the rural economy;
- Some flexibility in the implementation of commitments were made possible by the introduction of tightly prescribed provisions; and
- The concerns of net-food importing countries and least-developed countries have been addressed including the specific concerns of developing countries.

7 *http://www.wto.org/english/docs_e/legal_e/ursum_e.htm#aAgreement*

Impact on Labor

Mobility of labor is an important aspect of contemporary globalization. However, it can be said to have been compared unfavorably with globalization in the earlier periods i.e., in the later half of the 19th century. "The fundamental difference between the two phases of globalization is in the sphere of labor flows" (Nayyar, 1992). Between 1870 and 1914, around 50 million people (forming one-eighth of Europe's population in 1900) had moved out of Europe. Among them two-thirds had gone to the US and the other one-third to Australia, Canada and other places (Nayyar). During this time, people had the freedom to travel throughout Europe and even overseas without a passport. Until the First World War began, very few legislative or political barriers impeded the process of international migration. Moreover, they could also settle in new countries without much formalities or bureaucracy. "The international exchange of people was more important than the international exchange of goods" (Livi-Baci Massimo, 1993). Eventually, after the First World War, more restrictions were imposed on immigration. Thus, although labor migration is not totally absent in contemporary globalization, the scale may not be at par with that of the earlier phases of globalization. Table 1 compares the rates of net migration for the period 1870-1914. It is evident that the post-World War rates for immigration for both the US and Canada are about half of what they were in the earlier times. However, during 1970-80, the net migration of labor in North America and Europe was around 4.5 which was not far less from the rate of 5.4 during 1870 to 1910. It is noteworthy to know that labor mobility has become a factor of significant importance in capital mobility. In 2001, developing countries received overseas remittances from their migrant workers abroad amounting to a huge $72.3 bn, which was equivalent to 42% of their total FDI inflows. India alone (which ranked number one) received $10 bn, Mexico was second with $9.9 bn, followed by the Philippines with $6.4 bn (Ghosh Santanu, 2003).

Table 1: Net Migration Rates for the US/Canada and Europe

	1870-1910	1950-60	1960-70	1970-80	1980-85
US and Canada	+5.4	+2.7	+2.3	+4.0	+2.8
Europe	-2.6	-0.8	–	+0.5	+0.1

Source: Dean Baker et al., (1998:12). This source draws its data on the post-war period from Livi-Baci (1993:37-46), which makes a reference to net period from Livi-Baci (1993:37-46).

The Changing Role of Developing Countries in Global Trade

By looking at the pattern of international trade over the past ten years, it can be observed that the pattern of global trade has been changing in favor of greater trade and openness between the developed and developing countries. Although the developed countries have been trading mostly amongst themselves, the share of exports to the developing countries have increased by almost 2% between 1985 and 1995.[8] Moreover, trade has also increased among developing countries, although developed countries are still their main trading partners and major markets for exports. Moreover, the developed countries are major sources of imports for developing countries. During the period 1980-1990, the terms of trade of most developing countries were deteriorating as the prices of primary goods (like coffee and cocoa) had fallen relative to the prices of manufactured goods. Primary goods formed a large share of exports of the developing countries. The developing countries were proactive in their response to these changes, and to improve their terms of trade, they increased the share of manufactured goods in their list of exportable items. These manufactured goods were mainly labor intensive like clothes and carpets. The manufacture of such labor intensive goods facilitated the creation of jobs in the developing countries. In comparison, the nature of manufactured goods that the developing countries imported have mostly been knowledge and capital intensive, like machineries and transport equipment. It is in these goods that developed countries still retain their competitive advantage.

Empirical evidences have suggested that economic growth in the economies of the countries in East Asia like the Republic of Korea, Singapore, Hong Kong and China has increased significantly due to globalization. For example, globalization has provided opportunities for export growth, and this in turn has created jobs for millions of people. Initially those who were employed into low-productivity agriculture have now been absorbed in higher-productivity manufacturing. This has fuelled employment creation and economic growth.[9]

Tables 2 and 3 provide data on the annual growth rate in GDP in the ASEAN region between 2000 and 2007 and the data on total employment during the period 1990-2006 respectively.

---

8 World Bank Report, 1997.

9 Labor and Social Trends in ASEAN 2007 Integration, Challenges and Opportunities, International Labor Office Regional Office for Asia and the Pacific.

Table 2: Annual Growth Rate in GDP (2000-2007)

ASEAN	2000	2001	2002	2003	2004	2005	2006	2007
Brunei Darussalam	2.9	2.8	3.9	2.9	0.5	0.4	3.7	2.6
Cambodia	8.4	7.7	6.2	8.6	10.0	13.4	5.0	6.5
Indonesia	5.4	3.6	4.5	4.8	5.1	5.6	5.2	6.0
Lao PDR	5.8	5.7	5.9	6.1	6.4	7.0	7.3	6.6
Malaysia	8.9	0.3	4.4	5.5	7.2	5.2	5.5	5.8
Myanmar	13.8	11.3	12.0	13.8	13.6	13.2	7.0	5.5
Philippines	6.0	1.8	4.5	4.9	6.2	5.0	5.0	5.4
Singapore	10.0	-2.3	4.0	2.9	8.7	6.4	6.9	4.5
Thailand	4.8	2.2	5.3	7.0	6.2	4.5	4.5	5.0
Vietnam	6.8	6.9	7.1	7.3	7.8	8.4	7.8	7.6
'Plus 3' Countries and India								
China	8.4	8.3	9.1	10.0	10.1	10.2	10.0	10.0
Republic of Korea	8.5	3.8	7.0	3.1	4.7	4.0	5.0	4.3
Japan	2.9	0.4	0.1	1.8	2.3	2.6	2.7	2.1
India	5.3	4.1	4.3	7.2	8.0	8.5	8.3	7.3

Source: IMF, World Economic Outlook Database, September 2006.

Table 3: Employment in the ASEAN Region (1990-2006)

ASEAN	1990	1995	2000	2002	2003	2004	2005	2006
Brunei Darussalam	107	–	146	–	–	–	–	–
Cambodia	–	4,932	5,275	6,400	6,948	7,496	–	–
Indonesia	75,851	80,110	89,838	91,647	90,785	93,722	94,948	95,177
Lao PDR	–	2,167	–	2,490	2,537	–	2,740	–
Malaysia	6,685	7,645	9,322	9,543	9,870	9,987	–	10,442
Myanmar	15,221	16,817	–	–	–	–	–	–
Philippines	22,532	25,698	27,775	30,251	31,553	31,741	32,875	33,185
Singapore	1,537	1,702	2,095	2,017	2,034	2,067	2,267	2,444
Thailand	30,842	32,573	33,001	34,263	34,677	35,711	36,302	35,931
Vietnam	30,286	34,590	38,368	40,162	41,176	42,316	–	–

Contd...

Contd...

'Plus 3' Countries and India								
China	6,39,090	6,80,650	7,20,850	7,37,400	7,44,320	7,52,000	–	–
Republic of Korea	18,085	20,416	21,158	22,170	22,139	22,557	22,856	23,151
Japan	62,610	64,560	64,430	63,310	63,130	63,300	63,560	63,820
India	–	2,90,048	3,31,383	–	–	3,47,764	–	–

Note: India: 1995 column shows data for 1994; Brunei Darussalam: 2000 column shows data for 2001.

Source: ILO, Key Indicators of the Labor Market (KILM) 4th Edition, Table 2; ADB, Key Indicators, 2005; National Statistical Office Data.

Table 4 provides data on employment by major economic sectors in the recent years.

Table 4: Employment by Major Economic Sectors in the Recent Years

ASEAN	Agriculture	Industry	Services	Other
Brunei Darussalam	1.4	21.4	77.2	0.0
Cambodia	60.3	12.5	27.2	0.0
Indonesia	44.0	18.0	38.0	0.0
Lao PDR	82.7	8.7	8.6	0.0
Malaysia	14.8	30.1	52.5	2.6
Myanmar	62.7	12.2	25.1	0.0
Philippines	37.0	14.9	48.1	0.0
Singapore	–	29.5	69.6	0.9
Thailand	42.6	20.2	37.1	0.1
Vietnam	57.9	17.4	24.7	0.0
"Plus 3" Countries and India				
China	46.9	22.5	30.6	0.0
Republic of Korea	7.7	18.1	74.2	0.0
Japan	4.4	27.9	66.4	1.2
India	54.0	20.0	26.0	0.0

Note: Years represented include: (2006) Republic of Korea; (2005) Indonesia, Japan, Philippines, Singapore, Thailand; (2004) Cambodia, China, India, Malaysia, Vietnam; (2003) Lao People's Democratic Republic; (2001) Brunei Darussalam; (1998) Myanmar.

Source: ILO, Key Indicators of the Labor Market (KILM) 4th Edition, Table 4a; National Statistical Office Data.

Thus, almost all developing countries that have been actively engaged in globalization have enjoyed certain benefits. However, these benefits have come with new challenges and risks. The costs and benefits of globalization has been a debatable topic worldwide.

Global Free Trade – Benefits and Costs

The following is an outline of the major benefits of unrestricted trade for participating countries:

- Better and increased access for domestic producers to a larger global market.
- A greater and better variety of imported goods being enjoyed by consumers and that too at very low prices.
- Efficiency is achieved by domestic producers who can produce more efficiently due to their international specialization. Moreover, the producers become more efficient because of pressure from foreign competition.
- Production equipments that are imported are technologically more sophisticated than those produced domestically. Thus, there is a 'spill over' of new technologies from the country's developed trading partner, and developing countries benefit the most from these technological 'spill overs'. As a result they get the chance and opportunity to catch up more quickly with the developed countries and become productive at par with them.

In the earlier phases of global integration, there were several economies which were isolated from the integration. This is because these economies were politically imposed. Today, these countries aspire to enjoy the above mentioned benefits by integrating themselves with the global system of trade.

The aforementioned benefits also come with certain risks for countries which actively participate in international trade. These are mostly those countries facing intense competition in the international markets. As a result, the businesses of certain less adaptable and competitive industries of a country may be withdrawn. This is a potential risk that a may country face. Moreover, the heavy reliance on foreign capital and suppliers is generally not acceptable for industries that have a crucial role in a country's national security. For example, governments of several countries ensure the food security of the nation in case there is a shortage or cut in food imports during warfare.

By introducing quotas, governments often reduce certain imports. They may also make imports less competitive and more expensive by imposing tariffs. Such protectionist policies may prove to be economically risky for a country as domestic producers will continue to produce inefficiently with high costs. This may eventually lead to economic stagnation. Thus, ensuring the competitiveness of key industries internationally should be considered as an alternative to protectionism, to achieve economic efficiency. Factors such as the availability of natural resources in a country, the size of its domestic market and geographic location also influence the costs and benefits of international trade. For example, countries with rich endowment of natural resources such as oil tend to trade more. Trade is less in countries having large domestic markets. Finally, there are certain countries whose geographical location may be either favorable or unfavorable for it to participate in international trade. In spite of these risks, several countries have chosen to globalize their economies.

Conclusion

The world is coming closer with free trade, which is considered as a pillar of globalization. Globalization is driven by the technological revolution in transport and communications. An important outcome of this revolution is the development of cross-border flow of trade between countries. Greater dependence and openness provide plenty of opportunities to national economies. However, there are several challenges which these economies need to address. While, globalization has brought about increased rewards for economies with good economic governance, it has also raised the costs for those with poor economic governance. The East Asian crisis in the 1990s has clearly demonstrated that while the flow of financial capital into an economy is quicker and faster than before, it can also be withdrawn quickly if investors lose confidence on the governance of that economy.

In the present scenario, the trend is towards free trade among all countries of the world, driven primarily by international trade. International trade, as an outcome of competitive liberalization, is also considered as an engine of growth. The benefits of international trade for an economy are manifold. National income enhances, and this in turn stimulates economic growth and welfare of a country. Moreover, international trade also brings out more choice and variety of products for a trading country. However, the path traversed by international trade has moved from a narrow and restricted view of mercantilism to a wider view of global trade having no restrictions. This has certainly increased the welfare of nations as a whole. Moreover, the reduction of trade barriers has enhanced the growth of trade, both regionally and globally. Hence, for the benefit of all trading countries across continents, the focus has now shifted to making global trade more flexible. Thus, it goes without saying that globalization is made more meaningful by cross-border trades and the absence of trade barriers.

(Ishita Mukherjee is a Senior Research Associate, Icfai Research Center, Kolkata. The author can be reached at ishita@ibsindia.org).

References

1. Chang Yi-Jen (2006), "Indigenous Peoples' Sustainable Development", Association of Aboriginal Comradeship, Taiwan.
2. Findlay, Ronald and Kevin H O'Rourke (2007), *Power and Plenty: Trade, War, and the World Economy in the Second Millennium*, Princeton University Press, p. 592.
3. Frankel A Jeffrey (1997), "Estimated Effects of Trading Blocs" (Chapter 5) in *Regional Trading Blocs in the World Economic System*, p. 388, ISBN paper 0-88132-202-4.
4. Ghosh Santanu (2003), "Dil Hai Hindustani for Indians Abroad", *www.indian express.com*, April 3.
5. Hitchner Bruce (2003), "Roman Empire", in Joel Mokyr (Ed.), *The Oxford Encyclopedia of Economic History*, Oxford University Press, Oxford, England, Vol. 4, pp. 397-400.
6. Levitt Thodore (1985), "The Globalization of Markets", in Kantrow A M (Ed.), *Sunrise...Sunset: Challenging the Myth of Industrial Obsolescence*, pp. 53-68, John Wiley and Sons, New York.
7. Livi-Baci Massimo (1993), "South-North Migration: A Comparative Approach to North American and European Experiences" in OECD, *The Changing Course of International Migration*, Paris, pp. 37-46.
8. Mark Dean and Maria Sebastia-Barriel (2002), *UN Monthly Bulletin of Statistics.*
9. Nayyar Deepak (1997), "Globalization: The Game, the Players and the Rules", in Satya Dev Gupta (Ed.), *The Political Economy of Globalization*, pp. 13-40, Kluwer Academic Publishers, Boston.
10. Peter Robins (1999), "Review of the Impact of Globalisation on the Agricultural Sectors and Rural Communities of ACP Countries", a study commissioned by the Technical Centre for Agricultural and Rural Cooperation (CTA) (May).

Bibliography

1. Anderson K (2000), "Globalization, WTO, and Development Strategies of Poorer Countries", (Chapter 2), in Yusuf S, Evenett S and Wu W (Eds.), *Local Dynamics in an Era of Globalization,* Oxford University Press, London and New York.
2. Anderson K (2002), "International Trade and Globalization", *International Trade and WTO.*
3. Kindleberger C P (1975), "The Rise of Free Trade in Western Europe, 1820-1875", *Journal of Economic History*, Vol. 35, No. 1, pp. 20-55.
4. NPR (National Public Radio), (2006), Bernanke's Long View of Globalization.
5. Reddy Y V (2001), "Globalization and Trade in South Asia", *International Trade and WTO.*
6. "Regional and Multilateral Trade Regimes", *http://namun.sa.utoronto.ca.NAMUN*—Shaw Peter.
7. "The Role and Function of Regional Trade Blocs", *http://ucatlas.ucsc.edu/trade/subtheme_trade_blocs.php*
8. Trade Blocks, The Icfai University Press.

3

Globalization and the Benefits of Trade

Robert L Thompson

Globalization involves increasing integration of economies around the world, from the national to the most local levels, thereby promoting international trade in goods and services and cross-border movement of information, technology, people, and investments. This article examines the benefits and costs to the US and other countries.

Since the conclusion of World War II in 1945, international trade has been greatly facilitated by agreement among trading countries on a set of rules for international trade, known as the General Agreement on Tariffs and Trade (GATT). These rules were developed through a series of eight "rounds" of international trade negotiations between 1947 and 1994. Through these negotiations, export subsidies were banned on everything but agricultural products, and import tariffs on manufactured goods were reduced to inconsequential levels. As a result, trade in manufactured goods has grown rapidly, achieving an unprecedented level of specialization and exchange among countries.

Developments in Ocean shipping have also facilitated the latest wave of globalization, e.g., larger and faster vessels and containerization of their cargoes.

Source: Essays on Issues, No. 236, March 2007 (www.chicagofed.org). *© 2007, Federal Reserve Bank of Chicago. Reprinted with permission.*

These developments, combined with state-ofthe-art logistics, have significantly lowered the cost of international transactions. Multinational firms now engage in just-in-time sourcing through global supply chains. Deregulation and increasing competition have further reduced costs of international transportation and telecommunications. Overbuilding of fiber optics capacity among countries during the dot-com boom in the 1990s also contribute to today's historically low prices of international telecommunications.

At the end of World War II, most countries imposed barriers to free movement of capital across their international borders. These barriers have been largely eliminated among high-income countries and have been significantly lowered in middle-income countries, too. Billions of dollars of funds can move instantaneously among countries at the touch of a computer key.

Why Trade?

Why do countries engage in international trade anyway? The US, for instance, engages in such trade to obtain goods and services that some other countries can produce at relatively lower cost than it can in exchange for goods and services that the US can produce at lower cost than the other countries can. If everything cost the same to make in every country, there would be no basis for international trade.

When a country engages in international trade, its households' real purchasing power rises. Their incomes stretch further because they can obtain at lower cost the goods and services they have been buying. The country as a whole benefits, too. When a country engages in international trade, it can produce more Gross Domestic Product (GDP) from its land, labor, and capital because it is not using them to produce things that other countries can produce at lower resource cost. When a country opens its borders to free movement in and out of goods and services, the market then provides the incentive to move the country's resources into their highest-value uses, thereby facilitating economic growth.

Globalization has created the environment in which export-led economic growth can reduce poverty by bidding up wages in low-income countries. As poor people's incomes rise, they gain purchasing power and become better markets for the products that others produce more efficiently. This has happened over and over again, particularly in Asia.

At the end of World War II, Japan, Korea, Taiwan, and most other East Asian countries were very poor and their wage rates were very low. Japan's early post-war manufacturing exports were cheap in both price and quality; however, Japan's manufacturing industries developed and matured over time. Japan's wage rates were bid up by this export-led growth to the point that it could no longer compete in the production of the low-end labor-intensive products, and their manufacture moved to South Korea and Taiwan to take advantage of cheaper labor there. As South Korea's and Taiwan's wage rates were bid up, the jobs moved to Southeast Asia and, more recently, the coastal provinces of China.

Now we are reading press reports of labor shortages in coastal China, which mean that employers in labor-intensive industries there are having to pay higher wages to get labor. Jobs in labor-intensive industries are starting to move into the interior of China and on to India, where wage rates are lower. As each place loses competitiveness in labor-intensive industries, it moves up to more sophisticated and higher quality manufactured products. As the labor-intensive sectors move to take advantage of cheaper labor elsewhere, they leave behind a significant reduction in poverty in each country they depart.

As wages and incomes have risen in each country in succession, that country has become a better market for products in which the United States is competitive. For example, Japan, South Korea, and Taiwan became the best markets for midwestern corn and soybean products as people there gained the purchasing power to include more animal protein in their diets. Globalization made it possible for them to experience the broad-based, export-led economic growth that increased their purchasing power. While Asia has a huge population, parts of which are still growing rapidly, high numbers of people alone do not create market opportunities. It takes purchasing power along with large populations to translate need into effective market demand.

The current Doha Round of the World Trade Organization's (WTO) negotiations is putting special emphasis on using trade to accelerate economic development in presently low-income countries. Out of the world's 6.5 billion inhabitants, about half live on less than $2 per day, and 1.25 billion live on less than $1 per day. People with so little purchasing power do not represent market opportunities. The objective of the Doha Round is to create a trading environment in which broad-based economic growth can occur in the presently low-income countries. Those countries confront the highest barriers to their exports in the very products for which they have a comparative advantage. These products include those made by labor-intensive manufacturers, such as textiles, apparel, and footwear, as well as crops that do well in the tropics, such as sugar, rice, and cotton.

Opponents of globalization often assert that opening up international trade will drag our standard of living down to that of low-wage developing countries. They have it exactly backwards. The objective is to accelerate broad-based economic development that brings wage rates inlow-income countries up closer to ours. In the process, this will provide people in those developing countries with the purchasing power that will create better markets for products we produce more efficiently, and the development of better markets will, in turn, create more jobs here in the sectors in which we have a comparative advantage.

Dynamic Change in Competitiveness

Countries' competitive positions change all the time. No economy stands still. New mineral deposits are found, and others are depleted. Some countries' populations grow, while those of others decline. Research may find new technologies that provide a greater advantage to one country than another. New technologies can completely wipe out previous industries. How many buggy whip manufacturers can you find in the US today?

It is normal for a new, high-tech product, e.g., the silicon chip or the personal computer, to go through a life cycle. When first introduced, production of a new product takes a lot of skilled labor. However, once the product's launch has been successful and a large market develops, its production can be mechanized and carried out by much less skilled labor than was required at the outset. It is not unusual for manufacturing to move at this stage to another country with abundant supplies of less skilled, and therefore lower-wage, labor. This can happen in a relatively short span of time. As such "commoditization" occurs, whoever can produce the product at lowest cost, while meeting the quality standards and delivery schedule of the buyer, will get the sale.

Today, industries rise and fall and rise again in other countries at a very rapid rate. What is clear, however, is that one of the great benefits of globalization is the manner in which it increases wage rates and purchasing power in previously low-income countries. This has happened over and over again in the past half century.

Any time an employer closes up shop in a community—large or small—it is traumatic to the community and to the individuals involved. Plant closings get high-profile coverage in the media. It is reported that 55,000 American jobs are moving overseas each quarter. One could easily get the impression from the media that all of our jobs are moving offshore. Not to understate the traumatic impact on the individuals and communities concerned, when put in perspective, the problem is not nearly as large as it appears in the media.

The United States has a well-functioning labor market and a very mobile work force. No one expects any longer to stay in a single job throughout a career. Every three months about 7 million Americans change jobs, and over 400,000 new jobs are created in the United States. The US unemployment rate is very low by international standards, and there are large numbers of undocumented workers in jobs that most Americans don't want. Economic theory tells us that when trade liberalization occurs, the gains of the gainers exceed the losses of the losers, and the country as a whole ends up better off. It does not say there are no losers, but it does say that because the gains of the gainers exceed the losses of the losers, it should be possible to compensate the losers for their losses and still end up with a net gain to society as a whole.

If a country is to reap the potential benefits from globalization—increases in both consumer purchasing power and potential GDP—adjustment must be allowed to occur. The market must be allowed to reallocate resources (land, labor, and capital) from the sectors that have lost competitiveness to sectors that can compete. However, such adjustment is neither costless nor painless. It hurts people who have specialized skills that are salable only in the sectors that are in decline. It also hurts people who have made investments in specialized machinery and factories that are not useful in producing other things than those they were designed to produce.

A well-functioning labor market, such as that of the United States, is essential to facilitate adjustment as smoothly and painlessly as possible. However, even with a well-functioning labor market, change can be costly in both monetary and emotional terms. Changing one's line of work often requires retraining, which may involve significant expenditure. There is also the matter of providing income for the family during the period of training. Changing jobs may require a physical relocation, which involves both the financial cost and the emotional cost of leaving family and friends behind and starting over in a new community. Older people may simply not feel they have enough working years left to incur the costs associated with starting over in another line of work or place.

Firms that lose their competitiveness are likely to have undepreciated specialized capital equipment that still has productive life left in it and must be written off as a loss. Investors in the business suffer capital losses. In the farm sector, a loss in competitiveness can also precipitate a drop in land values.

It is natural that people who are comfortable in their present situation—workers and investors alike—try to avoid adjustment. People in this situation often see themselves as being singled out for unfair treatment, being asked to accept losses in the value of their skills or investments. In our democratic system, it is also normal for politicians to do everything they can to "protect" jobs in communities that they represent, especially just before elections. As former Congressman Tip O'Neill said many years ago, "All politics is local." Further, no politician wants to see the number of voters in his or her district decline.

The Cost of Protectionism

When barriers to imports from lower-cost suppliers are erected, all of the country's consumers of that product are forced to pay more. In effect, they are taxed on their consumption of that good or service. The country's residents are asked to accept a lower per capita gross national product as a result of wasting some of the country's resources producing things that another country can produce at lower resource cost. Each job "saved" may end up costing consumers hundreds of thousands of dollars per year. The cost of providing the protection is diffused across all consumers of the products, while the benefits accrue to a relatively small group.

Great creativity is shown in the protectionist arguments used by leaders and advocates of industries that have lost their competitiveness. As a last resort, many petitioners for protection from lower-cost imports make the case that we need to protect a given industry because in a time of war it would be essential to have production capacity in that sector inside our country.

Labor groups often argue that it is unfair for them to have to compete with "cheap labor" in less developed countries. But that is exactly the point. In industries that are inherently labor-intensive, there is no way we can be competitive, and bidding up wages (reducing poverty) in presently low-income countries is what economic development is all about. Unless they can sell us the products that use their most abundant, and therefore lowest-cost resource—their labor—their wages will never rise. And they will never become good markets for the products in which we have a comparative advantage.

Sometimes an industry that has lost its competitiveness is granted "temporary" protection from lower-cost imports to give it time to update its technology or modernize its facilities. However, one has great difficulty finding examples of industries ever willingly giving up this protection. More often than not, the assistance is used as a subsidy to keep producing in the same manner as always, with no adjustment occurring. Delaying adjustment in this way usually makes it more costly later on. This appears to be the case in many parts of the US textiles and steel industries. This is also the situation in some parts of the agricultural sector, e.g., sugar, rice, and cotton, which have received the largest production subsidies and/or highest import protection.

It is not uncommon for industry leaders to argue that the cost per American consumer of protecting domestic production of a certain good is small. This may be true for a single product; however, if protection is provided to one industry, others will demand it. If a country provides protection across a broad range of goods and services, its citizens lose twice. Their incomes are lower because the country forgoes potential GDP when it allocates its resources inefficiently. And what income they receive has smaller purchasing power because they have to pay more for the protected goods and services that they could have obtained at lower cost.

Trade Adjustment Assistance

Recognizing that the gains of the gainers exceed the losses of the losers from trade liberalization, the US Congress has institutionalized Trade Adjustment Assistance as a means of compensating the losers. Compensation to losers from trade liberalization is granted out of a sense of equity or fairness to facilitate adjustment of labor or investment out of a declining industry. This may involve retraining workers who lose their jobs and buying out the undepreciated value of investments in specialized machinery and facilities that cannot be used for other purposes.

Compensation may also be justified if imports of cheaper goods had not occurred previously because an otherwise uncompetitive industry had used its political connections to secure government subsidies and protection from imports. In this case, a buyout or some other form of compensation may be necessary to neutralize that industry's political opposition, which might prevent trade liberalization from occurring and block the rest of a country's residents from reaping the benefits of freer trade.

Conclusion

Overall, the world has benefited enormously from globalization. However, because the adjustment required to attain the benefits of increased globalization can be costly to individuals, it is appropriate that society as a whole, which stands to benefit, shares in the costs of those who lose as a result of globalization through such means as Trade Adjustment Assistance. The current round of WTO trade negotiations, the Doha "Development" Round, provides an opportunity to exploit trade liberalization to bid up wages and reduce poverty in low-income countries. This would make the world a safer and more just place, while creating larger potential markets. I will look at the implications of globalization for rural America in an upcoming issue of this publication.

(Robert L Thompson, Gardner Chair in Agricultural Policy, University of Illinois at Urbana–Champaign, and visiting scholar, Federal Reserve Bank of Chicago.)

4

Globalization and Inclusive Development

This note highlights some topical policy issues that could contribute to promoting a more inclusive, pro-poor process of globalization. The issues selected aim to take advantage of the window of opportunity that has opened up as a result of the last five years of unprecedented economic growth. The international community currently faces two broad challenges: first, the current growth trends need to be actively maintained, so as to allow an increasing number of developing countries to reap the benefits of globalization; and, second, there is a need to ensure that the process of globalization becomes more inclusive, so that it benefits countries and sectors of the population that have been left out. A number of issues that require policy attention are highlighted, including aspects relating to trade policy, regional integration, new and innovative financial mechanisms, building productive capacity, the global value-chain, the promises and perils of commodities, climate change and environmental concerns and opportunities, and the role of aid, including aid for trade.

Source: United Nations Conference on Trade and Development (www.unctad.org). © UN. Reprinted with permission.

I. Introduction: The Promise of Globalization

1. The world economy has experienced unprecedented growth in the past five years. This has allowed many developing countries to make significant economic progress, achieving on average 5-6 per cent growth. In 2006, only two of 132 developing countries recorded falling real income, compared to seven countries in the period 2000-2005 and 13 in the half decade before that. Millions of people have been lifted out of extreme poverty and many developing countries have also been able to make some progress towards achieving the Millennium Development Goals.

2. This dynamic growth in developing countries has been stimulated by an intensification of globalization in the form of trade and investment flows. Since 1995, world merchandise trade has been growing at an annual average rate of 7.5 per cent. A distinguishing feature in the emerging pattern of globalization is the increased role played by developing countries: real exports of developing economies nearly tripled between 1996 and 2006, while those from the G-7 rose by only 75 per cent. Asia clearly dominated the picture, with transition economies and Latin America coming in second, and Africa showing exactly the same increase as the G-7. In terms of imports, the expansion in different regions was much closer. Overall, the share of developing countries in global trade increased from 29 per cent in 1996 to 34 per cent in 2006.

3. A related development has been the sustained rise in South-South exchanges. For example, South-South merchandise trade is estimated to have expanded from US$ 577 billion in 1995 to US$ 1.7 trillion in 2005. This resulted in a concomitant increase in the South-South share of world merchandise exports to 15 per cent in 2005, compared to 11 per cent in 1995. During the last two decades, the shares of a number of emerging economies in international merchandise and services trade have grown considerably.

4. Another interesting feature of the current expansion is the boom in commodity demand and prices. Common factors responsible for the price increases include the rapid pace of industrialization in the South, especially in China, but also in India and other emerging developing countries, and increased demand for biofuels. The rise in commodity prices has generated surpluses for many commodity-producing

developing countries and has led to significant and prolonged improvements in their terms of trade.

5. These developments have helped some countries make progress towards the Millennium Development Goals. As noted in the *Millennium Development Goals Report 2007*, worldwide the number of people in developing countries living on less than $1 a day fell to 980 million in 2004, down from 1.25 billion in 1990. The proportion of people in extreme poverty fell from nearly a third to 19 per cent. Indeed, if current trends continue, most regions will achieve the goal of halving the proportion of people living in extreme poverty. There has also been progress towards many other goals, such as improving education, with primary-school enrolment growing from 80 per cent in 1991 to 88 per cent in 2004, most of this progress having been achieved since 1999. Not surprisingly, much of this progress is due to significant advances made by countries of the South and south-east Asian countries in recent years.

II. The Qualification: The Benefits of Globalization have not yet Reached All

6. Despite the impressive performance of developing countries as a whole in recent years, and the aggregate development progress achieved, many countries, in particular the least developed and other low-income economies, have not been able to benefit from the propitious environment. Despite the recovery in 2003-2007, the per capita growth rates in Africa (3 per cent on average) and the developing countries of America (3.5 per cent) were only half that in East and South Asia (6.3 per cent). Moreover, some countries have not been lifted to the same extent by the economic recovery and continue to rely on exports of lowvalue-added primary commodities. These countries have suffered from worsening terms of trade, highly volatile world prices and a decline in their share in world trade. For example, the export share of the 50 Least Developed countries (LDCs), fell from 2.5 per cent in 1960 to about 0.5 per cent in 1995, and has since hovered around this level, though the improvement in commodity prices helped raise their share to 0.8 per cent in 2006.

7. In addition, many countries, especially the least developed countries and lower- and middle-income developing and transition countries, have been unable to translate growth effectively into poverty reduction and broader human

development. For example, despite its recent recovery, the proportion of people living in extreme poverty in sub-Saharan Africa (which includes 34 of the 50 LDCs), remains very high, decreasing only from 46.8 per cent in 1990 to 41.1 per cent in 2004. Given the rapid population growth, this has meant that the number of people living on less than $1 a day has actually been increasing, and is only now beginning to level off. Even in some of the faster-growing developing economies, some segments of the population continue to be excluded from the benefits. Poverty has been increasing in western Asia, for example, and continues to fall only slowly in Latin America and the Caribbean.

8. One of the disconcerting consequences of the new wave of globalization is therefore the rise of inequality, both within and between countries, be they developed or developing. Today, the richest 2 per cent of the world's adult population owns more than half of global household wealth. The bottom half, in contrast, barely owns 1 per cent[1].

9. The international community now faces two broad challenges. First, the current growth trends need to be actively maintained, so as to allow a growing number of developing countries to reap the benefits of globalization. This means addressing potential downside risks such as global imbalances, disturbances in financial markets, further increases in energy prices and the slow development of alternative technologies, and the potential reversal of commodity prices. Second, there is a crucial need to ensure that the current process of globalization becomes more inclusive. While economic growth has touched more economies than ever before, many developing countries continue to be left out. Also, even in countries that have benefited as a whole, there are communities or sectors of the population that have not been included.

10. This note is concerned with this second challenge. In concrete terms, promoting inclusive development requires the reduction of poverty, unemployment and underemployment; bringing lagging countries into global knowledge systems and global value-chains; and ensuring that marginalized communities have access to housing, health, education and other social services, are able to exercise their civic, civil and political rights and are able to expand their "capacities and capabilities"[2].

---

1 See "Inclusive globalization" in the United Nations Development Programme's *Annual Report 2007*.

2 Sen, Amartya (2000), *Development as Freedom*, New York: Knopf.

III. Policy Response: Much more can be done to Promote Inclusive and Pro-Poor Globalization

11. This section identifies some of the main policy areas that need to be addressed in order to make the globalization process more inclusive. There is evidence to suggest, especially in Africa and LDCs, that the recent trends in global growth have not generated the level of employment that will help reduce poverty. The International Labour Organization (ILO) estimates that worldwide unemployment stands at about 200 million people, rising to one third of the global workforce if the definition is broadened to include those who are underemployed[3]. The problem of jobless growth in commodity-dependent economies, for example, requires policy attention. In other areas, unemployment or underemployment is more related to falling productivity, or lack of productive capacity. In LDCs, for example, where the labour force is expected to increase significantly over the next few years,[4] falling farm size and increasing population growth is making it harder for agricultural workers to make a living. Low levels of investment and innovation in agriculture fuel a vicious cycle of poverty, prompting rural dwellers to look for work in the urban and nonagricultural sector, where there are, however, very few employment opportunities.

12. Moreover, what is ultimately desired is not just employment per se, but rather employment that pays sufficiently well and that allows people to enjoy more fulfilling lives. The following broad policy areas are therefore worth considering.

A. Access is Important, but Trade Policy must Increasingly Address Other Issues

13. Further liberalization of trade in goods and services through the Doha round offers an important opportunity to allow more countries to benefit from trade. If it delivers on its "development agenda", the round may begin to correct existing imbalances in the trading regime. Agriculture continues to be the linchpin of the negotiations, but as many middle-income countries have already become producers and exporters of manufactured goods, the Doha round must also result in significantly enhanced and additional real market access for developing countries' exports in these sectors.

---

3 Sachs, Ignacy, "Inclusive development strategy in an era of globalization", ILO Working Paper No. 35, Geneva, May 2004, p. 4.

4 See *The Least Developed Countries Report 2006* (UNCTAD/LDC/2006).

14. Other important areas for discussion include the need to liberalize trade in services, including the Mode 4 movement of natural persons. This would have a very large and positive impact in developing countries, in part because of the sheer size of the services economy. It has been estimated, for example, that welfare gains from liberalizing the movement of workers could amount to US$156 billion a year if developed countries increased their quota for the entry of workers from developing countries by 3 per cent. Another study has projected annual gains of some US$200 billion if a temporary work visa scheme was adopted multilaterally.

15. Policy attention should also be directed to the increasing application of non-tariff barriers, both as instruments of protection and for regulating trade. The nature of the non-tariff barriers most often applied has changed: measures intended to protect local consumers have increased, while measures meant to protect local producers have declined. In many developed countries, regulatory policy now focuses on protection of the environment, public health and safety, and often includes higher standards for the domestic market than existing international standards. These regulations may help promote higher prices for exporters from developing countries, but they may also open avenues for protectionist abuse and also entail greater compliance costs than would otherwise be the case. Some domestic subsidies that are currently allowed may have distorting effects on trade.

B. Regional Integration as a Stepping Stone to Markets and Multilateral Alliances

16. In addition to further liberalization of trade in the multilateral system, further progress can also be achieved through strategic regional integration. South-South investment and trade is emerging as a major new force in the world economy, with potentially far-reaching implications. For example, South-South agreements can achieve rapid boosts in production, consumption and trade at the regional level, as well as helping to underpin the position of developing countries in South-North agreements.[5] Other promising areas which may require policy attention at the regional level include trade and transit facilitation, transport infrastructure, investment projects in energy and water supplies, projects in industrial development and research and

5 See *Trade and Development Report, 2007* (UNCTAD/TDR/2007).

development, and shortcomings in the international financial system. These initiatives are often too costly and risky for an individual developing country but may be viable if several countries pool their resources.

C. Developing New and Innovative Financial Mechanisms

17. In addition to seeking ways to boost the benefits of foreign direct investment, policy attention needs to be directed to uncovering innovative and new financial mechanisms to help mobilize domestic and global resources. These include improving access to capital for small enterprises and the poor by reducing the costs of asymmetric information and by mainstreaming products such as micro-insurance and microfinance. There is a need for continued exploration of other new instruments that can potentially boost the pool of finance, including from new capital-surplus countries. The growth of some forms of South-South investment may help to bring about a more inclusive globalization, while more information is needed on the implications of increased portfolio investment to developing countries.

18. Ensuring that developing countries participate more equally in global credit markets is another area where a strategic policy approach is needed. The cost of capital in global markets is typically much lower than the costs that are charged to developing-country entrepreneurs. Policy attention needs to be paid to the search for new mechanisms to improve market information and to reduce the high transaction costs that can create barriers to viable business plans.

19. Another issue for discussion is the potential for a global monitoring and coordinating mechanism to reduce the likelihood and costs of financial crises caused by systemic vulnerabilities in the global financial markets. These can have particularly devastating effects on the poor, who lack financial resilience.

D. Building Productive Capacity

20. In order to participate fully in the global economy, developing countries must first have productive capacity and become more competitive. In part, this is an issue of the natural resources with which a country is endowed, but increasingly in the modern global economy it is also a question of created advantages relating to infrastructure, human capital, skills, resources and knowledge. The crucial lack of adequate transport, telecommunications and energy infrastructure in many developing

countries requires a range of policy responses including public-private partnerships, foreign direct investment and domestic resource mobilization.[6] One of the challenges for improving inclusion is that mechanisms to recoup the costs of investment in essential infrastructure and utilities can be disproportionately damaging to the poor, so that new approaches for financing and service provision may be required.

21. Skills development and training is another important ingredient to help create a more inclusive global economy. Both in the agricultural and nonagricultural sectors, policy attention is needed to help introduce new productive techniques, investment in innovation and research and development, better entrepreneurial skills, and management and marketing training. The extent to which skills and technology can be boosted through mechanisms such as foreign direct investment, global knowledge partnerships, public-private initiatives and even migration policy, is yet to be fully addressed by developed and developing countries.

E. Creating Synergies through the Global Value-Chain

22. There can be important synergies between modern, large-scale enterprises (often producing for export) and local, small-scale enterprises, but these will not always occur automatically and may need to be directly addressed through industrial policy. This is most apparent in some of the newly dynamic economic sectors such as tourism. It is not always obvious to local communities how they can fit effectively into the global value-chain. However, some service sectors, particularly those with long and cross-cutting production processes, offer many possibilities for domestic enterprises to participate more fully if the enabling policies are in place. Promoting beneficial linkages through procurement and employment may require proactive public policies in addition to the adoption of corporate social responsibility policies and practices by enterprises and industrial organizations.

F. The Promises and Perils of Commodities

23. Commodity-dependent economies are historically more likely to be excluded from the benefits of globalization than economies with a more diversified resource base. Out of 144 developing countries, 86 depend on commodities for more than half of their export earnings. In the past, falling and highly volatile prices for key

[6] See *Economic Development in Africa: Reclaiming Policy Space* (UNCTAD/ALDC/AFRICA/2007).

commodities have made this dependence particularly problematic, but today the current boom in commodity prices created by new demand in the emerging economies has opened up new opportunities for commodity-rich countries[7]. Policy issues that are attracting the attention of the international community include: the need to find new approaches to investment that are more advantageous to host countries; how to improve the transparency and accountability of international revenue payments in the sector; and the related need for recipient Governments to use their revenues wisely and in ways that lead to a more equitable distribution to the poor. Moreover, commodity-dependent countries are looking for ways to diversify more into upstream and downstream activities related to the commodities sector, such as distribution and higher value-added processing activities; in addition to diversifying beyond the commodities sector.

G. Climate Change and Environmental Concerns and Opportunities

24. Growing concerns about climate change, biodiversity and the environment are being reflected in a number of policy measures aimed at developing and developed countries alike. There may be a re-thinking of industrial policy, with particular implications for developing countries, for example, whether the traditional trajectory from agriculture through manufacturing to the services economy needs to be followed slavishly, or whether they can leapfrog to a cleaner and greener diversified economy. In other areas, the search for new cleaner technologies can have positive implications for developing countries, if, for example, increased research and development leads to approaches or tools that reduce the costs of providing infrastructure services for remote or distant communities. Other opportunities that are opened up also require a positive policy response from many developing countries, in gearing up to the high certification standards required in organic agriculture, for example; or in enhancing their branding and marketing of high-value biodiverse products.

H. Aid Must be More Inclusive

25. In recent years, donor countries have been increasingly focusing their official development assistance on emergency aid and social services such as education and health. Recent UNCTAD research argues that these important contributions need to be supplemented by a more strategic approach that recognizes that long-term

---

7 See *World Investment Report 2007* (UNCTAD/WIR/2007).

sustainability requires donor investment in productive capacities, including knowledge, science and technology, and enterprise development[8].

26. One example on the global radar screen – aid for trade – could be a promising approach for pro-poor and more inclusive economic development. Despite the increase in market-access opportunities, the participation in global markets of many developing countries can be hampered by supply constraints or lack of infrastructure. Aid-for-trade could help to address these problems. The pledges offered by the leaders of developed countries now need to be realized, once an appropriate framework for identifying and implementing the most effective policy levers has been agreed.

27. Policy attention needs to be directed to finding the most critical areas where the resources generated through aid-for-trade could be most effectively deployed. Assessment at the level of individual countries and sectors is needed in order to identify and prioritize the most important areas where aid, rather than private investment, is most appropriate. It is likely that these will be characterized by aspects of public goods, transaction costs, asymmetric information, risk and uncertainty. Transport costs, for example are an increasingly important element in competitiveness. Landlocked countries experience transport costs as a barrier that can be three times as large as the tariff barriers they face in developed countries; but even countries with good port and harbour facilities may face a disproportionately heavy cost in meeting stricter international safety and security standards. Capital requirements are often too high for the Governments of developing countries, and the public-good aspects of much infrastructure are such that the market alone is unlikely to provide what is needed. Another important area where aid-for-trade is likely to be effective concerns the financing of research and development: an activity that can be critical if LDCs are to increase innovation, productivity and value-added in agricultural and other sectors. Even in developed countries, research and development is costly, risky and characterized by uncertainty, and is frequently funded in part, if not in full, by public rather than private investment.

IV. Conclusion

28. This paper has highlighted some topical policy issues that could contribute to promoting a more inclusive, pro-poor process of globalization by taking advantage

---

8 See *The Least Developed Countries Report 2006* (UNCTAD/LDC/2006).

of the window of opportunity that has opened up has a result of the last five years of unprecedented economic growth. A more measured and coherent approach is needed to ensure that the benefits generated by globalization are more widely shared, and so can help to reduce the gap between those who have benefited and those for whom the benefits have not yet been forthcoming.

5

World Public Favors Globalization and Trade but Wants to Protect Environment and Jobs

Though the support for globalization is remarkably strong throughout the world, people across the globe expressed their concern about the effect of international trade on environment and jobs.

Majorities around the world believe economic globalization and international trade benefits national economies, companies, and consumers. But many think trade harms the environment and threatens jobs and want to mitigate these effects with environmental and labor standards.

The Chicago Council on Global Affairs and *WorldPublicOpinion.org,* in cooperation with polling organizations around the world, conducted the survey in countries representing 56 per cent of the world's population: China, India, the United States, Indonesia, France, Russia, Thailand, Ukraine, Poland, Iran, Mexico, South Korea, the Philippines, Australia, Argentina, Peru, Israel, Armenia and the Palestinian territories.

This is the fifth in a series of reports based on the global poll's findings that analyze international attitudes on key issues. Not all questions were asked in all countries.

Source: http://www.worldpublicopinion.org/pipa/pdf/apr07/CCGA+_article.pdf. Reprinted with permission.

Support for globalization is remarkably strong throughout the world. Seventeen countries plus the Palestinian territories were asked if "globalization, especially increasing connections of our economy with others around the world, is mostly good or mostly bad" for their country. In every case positive answers outweigh negative ones.

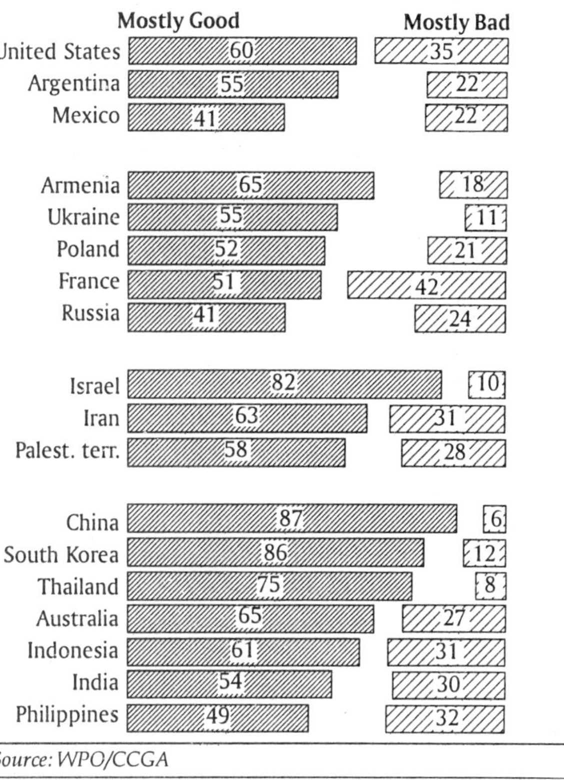

Source: WPO/CCGA

The highest levels of support are found in countries with export-oriented economies: China (87%), South Korea (86%) and Israel (82%). Positive answers fall below 50 per cent in only three countries, though such responses outweigh negative replies by wide margins. The greatest skepticism about globalization is found in Mexico (41% good, 22% bad), Russia (41% good, 24% bad) and the Philippines (49% good, 32% bad). In the United States, 60 per cent think globalization is mostly good and 35 per cent call it mostly bad.

There is an even stronger consensus around trade's positive impact on national economies. Respondents in 14 countries were asked whether trade was good or bad for their economy. In all of them, majorities reply that it is good. The highest levels of approval are in China (88%), Israel (88%), South Korea (79%), and Thailand (79%). The highest negative views, though still held by minorities, are found in the United States (42%), France (34%), Mexico (27%) and India (27%).

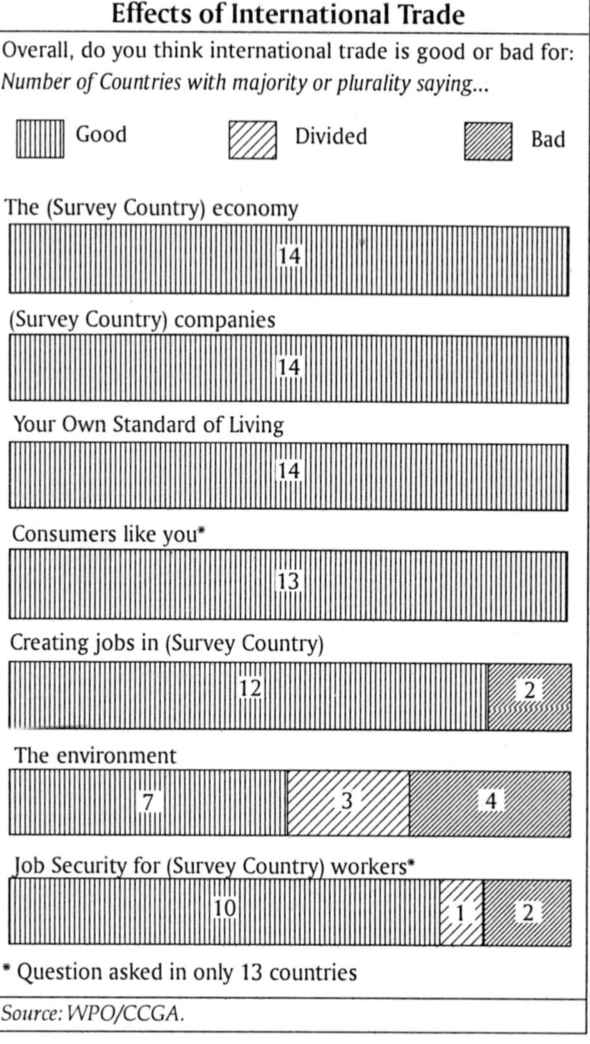

Majorities say trade benefits their country's companies in all the countries asked. Israelis (86%), Chinese (78%) and South Koreans (78%) again top the list of those saying trade is "good" for their country's companies. The highest percentages of negative replies are found in the United States (45%), France (43%) and Russia (34%).

Most of those polled also believe trade benefits consumers. Majorities (ranging from 56 per cent to 77 per cent) express positive views in all but one country, Argentina, where 46 per cent think trade is good for consumers (31% bad). A majority of the French are also positive (61%), though France has the largest percentage expressing negative views (38%). A strong majority of Americans also believes trade is good for consumers (70%).

Attitudes about whether trade is good or bad for "your own standard of living" follow a similar pattern. Majorities in all but three countries express positive views. Once again, the most enthusiastic are the Israelis (74%) and the Chinese (73%). Americans are also positive (64%). The three exceptions are: Argentina (good 42%, bad 30%), Russia (good 45%, bad 19%), and France (good 50%, bad 44%).

Trade and the Environment

Respondents around the world express concern about the effect of trade on the environment. In four countries, the idea that trade is bad for the environment is the most common view: France (66% bad, 29% good), the United States (49% bad, 45% good), Argentina (46% bad, 27% good), and Russia (44% bad, 25% good). Opinion is divided in Armenia (36% bad, 37% good), Mexico (41% bad, 41% good), and South Korea (49% bad, 47% good).

In none of the countries polled do large majorities believe trade helps the environment. Those most optimistic about trade's environmental impact are the Chinese (57%), Israelis (56%) and Palestinians (53%).

There are several reasons why people may think that trade harms the environment. Some may believe that it stimulates growth and consumption, resulting in more factories and cars and ultimately more pollution. Others may assume that by opening domestic markets to foreign goods, trade allows companies to evade environmental laws by moving to countries with more lax regulations.

One way to mitigate the potentially negative impact of trade on the environment is to require minimum environmental standards as part of trade agreements.

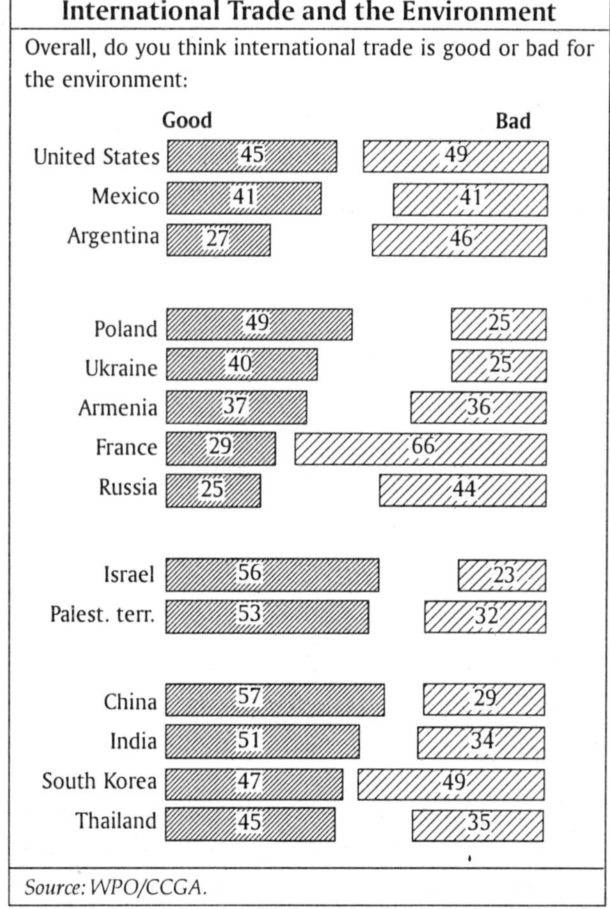

Source: WPO/CCGA.

Critics say, however, that including environmental standards in trade agreements hurts the developing world by raising costs and discouraging investment.

Nonetheless, the publics in developing as well as developed nations show strong support for such standards. Large majorities in all 10 countries asked—ranging between 60 per cent and 93 per cent—say that trade agreements should include "minimum standards for protection of the environment." Those in favor include two of the world's largest developing economies: China and India. The Chinese favor environmental protections by 85 per cent to 8 per cent and the Indians endorse them by 60 per cent to 28 per cent.

Trade and Labor

There is significant concern about the effect of trade on employment, especially in more developed countries. Eighty per cent of French respondents believe trade has a negative impact on job security in their country and 73 per cent think it is also bad for the creation of jobs there. In the United States, 67 per cent consider trade harmful for US workers' job security and 60 per cent call it detrimental for job creation. In Argentina and South Korea, respondents are divided about whether trade helps preserve jobs, though they tend to say trade is good for creating jobs.

In the other countries polled, majorities view trade as positive for job creation while majorities or pluralities think it is good for job security. Israelis, Mexicans and Thais are those most positive that trade helps create jobs (74% each). The largest majority saying trade is good for job security is in China (65%) while Indians (49% good, 37% bad) and Russians (43% good, 32% bad) are among the more skeptical.

Anxiety about trade's impact on labor is also expressed in a question about foreign policy goals. Respondents in seven countries were asked to judge the importance of possible foreign policy goals, including "protecting the jobs" of their country's workers. In all seven countries, majorities gave this goal the top rating of "very important:" Armenia (84%), Australia (83%), the United States (76%), China (71%), South Korea (68%), Thailand (66%), and India (54%).

Concerns about the effect of trade on jobs has prompted labor leaders in developed countries to insist that trade agreements include labor standards that would require signatory governments to comply with international labor standards, such as prohibiting child labor and allowing workers to form labor unions. They argue that such standards would prevent a "race to the bottom" by companies that move to countries without minimal worker protections in search of lower costs.

As in the case of environmental standards, those opposed say that adding labor protections to trade agreements would hurt developed countries by raising costs and discouraging investment.

Respondents in developed countries, not surprisingly, overwhelmingly support including labor standards in international trade agreements, including nine out of ten respondents in the United States (93%), Israel (91%), Argentina (89%), and Poland (88%).

But adding labor protections to trade agreements also receives strong support in many less developed countries that are known for low-cost labor markets. In China, 84 per cent favor them as do majorities in Mexico (67%), India (56%) and the Philippines (55%).

This is contrary to the widespread assumption that laborers in developing countries would oppose the imposition of higher standards because they desire the competitive advantages derived from lower labor costs. It is possible that the requirement of higher standards is attractive because it generates outside pressure to improve working conditions in their countries.

Complying with WTO Rulings

While respondents around the world tend to support international trade as an engine of economic growth, they are less enthusiastic about the World Trade Organization (WTO), which was founded in 1995 to enforce trade rules and resolve international trade disputes among member states. Most countries lean toward compliance with adverse rulings by the WTO, but there is substantial variation.

After being told that the WTO was "established to rule on disputes over trade treaties," respondents in eight countries were asked: "If another country files a complaint with the World Trade Organization and it rules against [survey country], as a general rule, should [survey country] comply with that decision or not?"

The US public, despite its reservations about international trade, shows the highest support for obeying WTO decisions. Seventy-three per cent of Americans endorse compliance. This is a slight increase from 2004, when 69 per cent favored compliance. American views about compliance with WTO decisions are consistent with the support they have shown in this and other polls for strengthening multilateral institutions.

Majorities in two other countries also endorse compliance with WTO rulings: China (58%) and Mexico (53%). Mexican support is up 5 points since 2004.

Modest pluralities favor obeying WTO decisions in three countries. These include India (37% yes, 29% no), Thailand (34% yes, 17% no) and Ukraine (40% yes, 12% no). In all three countries, substantial minorities say "it depends" or "not sure."

South Korea is the only country where a majority opposes complying with adverse WTO decisions (52% no, 37% yes). But while opposition to compliance has remained unchanged since 2004 (52%), support has dropped 11 points from 48 per cent. South Koreans have suffered adverse WTO rulings regarding their ship building and computer chip industries in recent years. The WTO has also forced South Korea to open up its market to rice imports.

Armenians tend to oppose compliance (35% no, 26% yes), though many Armenians (38%) are uncertain, saying it depends or don't know. Filipinos are divided (48% yes, 49% no).

Globalization and Trade: Results by Country

Americas

Argentina

Graciela Romer y Asociados, December 2006

Although some blame globalization for the economic collapse of 2001, Argentines tend to believe it benefits their country and their economy. However, they are skeptical about the effect of international trade on individuals and the environment. Fifty-five per cent of Argentines say that globalization, "especially the increasing connections of our economy with others around the world," is "mostly good" for their country, while just 22 per cent say it is mostly bad and 23 per cent do not offer an opinion.

Like most other publics polled, majorities of Argentines say that international trade overall is good for the Argentine economy (65%) and Argentine companies (61%). There is less agreement about whether it is good for Argentines themselves. Forty-six per cent of Argentine respondents think that trade is good for "consumers like you"—the lowest number among all countries polled—but 31 per cent say it is bad for them (23% do not answer). Argentines are the least confident of the publics polled about whether international trade is good for their "standard of living:" 42 per cent say it is, while 30 per cent say it is bad. A modest majority of Argentines (53%) sees international trade as good for creating jobs in Argentina, but they are divided on whether trade is positive or negative for "job security for Argentine workers" (38% good, 39% bad, 23% no response). These doubts about whether workers benefit from trade may be why Argentines strongly support including "minimum standards for working conditions" into trade agreements (89%). Argentines are doubtful that international trade is good for the environment: 46 per cent think that it is bad and 27 per cent think it is good. Nine in 10 Argentine respondents (90%) want environmental protections to be part of trade agreements.

Mexico

Center for Economic Research and Teaching (CIDE)/Mexican Council of Foreign Relations (COMEXI), July 2006

Mexicans tend to view globalization and international trade as positive for Mexico, though they have mixed feelings about its effects on the environment. While the most common view is that globalization is "mostly good" for Mexico (41%), about one in four (26%) volunteers that it is equally good and bad and one in five (22%) says that it is "mostly bad." Mexicans are positive about international trade. Majorities also see trade as positive for the Mexican economy (59%) and their own standard of living (53%). Two-thirds (66%) believe it is good for Mexican companies and nearly three-quarters (74%) say it is good for creating jobs in Mexico. Sixty-seven per cent agree that countries signing international trade agreements should be required to maintain "minimum standards for working conditions." When asked whether international trade is good or bad for the environment, Mexicans are divided, with equal numbers saying it is good (41%) and bad (41%) and one in five (19%) declining to answer. Three out of four Mexican respondents (76%) say trade agreements should require countries to maintain "minimum standards for the protection of the environment." A majority (53%) believes that Mexico should generally comply with adverse World Trade Organization decisions, about a fifth (21%) say it should not and 18 per cent say it depends.

United States

Chicago Council on Global Affairs, July 2006

Most Americans believe that globalization is beneficial for the United States, though they tend to think that international trade is bad for American jobs and the environment. Sixty per cent say that the globalization, "especially the increasing connections of our economy with others around the world" is "mostly good" for the United States, while 35 per cent say it is "mostly bad." Modest majorities of Americans see international trade as good for the US economy (54%) and for American companies (52%), though these majorities are smaller than in the other countries polled. Substantial majorities, however, feel that trade is good for consumers like themselves (70%) and for their own standard of living (64%). Americans are second only to the French in their belief that trade hurts employment. A majority believes that international trade is bad for "creating jobs" in the United States (60%) and bad for the "job security" of American workers (67%). An overwhelming majority (96%) of Americans sees "protecting the jobs of American workers" as a very (76%) or somewhat (20%) important foreign policy goal. This concern about job is reflected in their very strong support for including "minimum standards for working conditions" in trade agreements (93%). Slightly more see trade as bad for the environment (49%) than see it as good (45%). Nine in 10 Americans (91%) want countries that sign trade agreements to be required to maintain environmental protections. A large majority of Americans believe that the United States should comply with World Trade Organization rulings made against their country: three-quarters (73%) say that the US government should comply with WTO decisions "as a general rule" and only one-fifth (22%) say it should not.

Asia

Australia

Lowy Institute, July 2006

Most Australians view globalization favorably and believe that protecting Australian jobs should be a foreign policy goal. Sixty-five per cent say that globalization is "mostly good" for the country, while only one quarter (27%) say that it is "mostly bad." Australians also agree nearly unanimously (98%) that protecting the jobs of Australians workers should be an important foreign policy goal, including 83 per cent who say it should be "very important."

China

Chicago Council on Global Affairs, July 2006

The Chinese are among the most enthusiastic about the benefits of globalization and trade. Nearly nine in 10 (87%) Chinese believe that "the increasing connections of our economy with others around the world" is mostly good for China, the largest majority in the 18 countries asked. The Chinese are also the most positive about the effects of international trade, with very large majorities saying it is good for China's economy (88%) and Chinese companies (78%) and also good for the Chinese people's standard of living (73%) and for Chinese consumers (69%). This positive attitude about trade extends to its effect on Chinese jobs: about seven in 10 say trade is good for creating jobs in China (73%) and for the job security of Chinese workers (65%). Nine in 10 Chinese respondents (92%) say that "protecting the jobs of Chinese workers" is a very (71%) or somewhat (21%) important foreign policy goal. Nearly as many (84%) think that "minimum standards for working conditions" should be part of international trade agreements. Unlike most other publics, the Chinese tend to believe international trade is good for the environment (57%) while only 29 per cent say it is bad. Nonetheless, more than four in five Chinese respondents (85%) support requiring trade agreements to include environmental protections. The Chinese public supports China's compliance with adverse rulings from the World Trade Organization: 58 per cent believe that China should comply with these decisions as a general rule, while 19 per cent say it should not and 16 per cent believe it depends on the situation.

India

Chicago Council on Global Affairs, July 2006

A majority of Indians believe globalization benefits their country and think international trade is positive for their economy and the environment. Asked whether globalization and the "increasing connections of our economy with others around the world" are "mostly good" or "mostly bad," Indians say good by a margin of 54 per cent to 30 per cent. International trade is seen as good for India's economy (64%) and for Indian companies (59%). Majorities believe that trade is good for "consumers like you" (61%) and somewhat fewer agree that it is good for "your own standard of living" (54%). Fifty-six per cent of Indian respondents think international trade is good for creating jobs in India but a third of them (32%) say it is bad. About half (49%) say trade is good for Indian workers' job security (37% bad). More than eight in ten Indians (84%) believe that protecting domestic jobs is an important foreign policy goal, though they are less likely than other publics to say it is very important (54%). Contrary to the popular perception that people in developing countries oppose labor standards to gain an edge in the global labor market, majorities say international trade agreements should require countries to maintain minimum standards for working conditions (56%) and for protection of the environment (60%). Indian attitudes about whether their country should obey adverse World Trade Organization rulings are mixed: 37 per cent believe it should comply as a general rule, 29 per cent say it should not, and 21 per cent feel it depends.

Indonesia

Lowy Institute, July 2006

Most Indonesians believe that globalization has a mainly positive effect on their country. Asked whether globalization, "especially the increasing connections of our economy with others around the world," is mostly good or bad for Indonesia, 61 per cent believe it is mostly good. Only 31 per cent feel it is mostly bad.

Philippines

Social Weather Stations, November 2006

Filipinos tend to think globalization is good for their country, though they are among the most skeptical of the publics polled. The Philippine public also divides over whether their government should comply with World Trade Organization rulings. Although only half of Filipinos think globalization is good for their country, positive attitudes outnumber negative ones by a margin of 49 per cent to 32 per cent (20 per cent decline to answer). A majority of respondents (55%) think "minimum standards for working conditions" should be part of trade agreements, while just 30 per cent believe they should not be required. Asked if the Philippines should "as a general rule" comply with adverse decisions made by the World Trade Organization, Filipinos are again equally divided: 48 per cent believe it should and 49 per cent believe that it should not.

South Korea

East Asia Institute, July 2006

Most South Koreans believe that globalization is good for their country and that international trade has mainly positive effects, except on the environment. Nearly nine in 10 South Koreans (86%) say that globalization is "mostly good" for their country, the largest majority after the Chinese. Very few (12%) take the opposite view. Nearly eight in 10 Koreans (79%) see international trade as good for South Korea's economy, for Korean companies (78%) and for creating jobs in the South Korean economy (60%). Attitudes are slightly less positive about trade's effect on individuals: 68 per cent agree that international trade is good for "consumers like you" and 56 per cent believe it benefits "your own standard of living." Only a bare 51 per cent majority thinks trade is good for South Korean workers' job security, while 47 per cent disagree. Protecting domestic jobs is considered an issue that should be one of South Korea's important foreign policy goals by nearly all respondents: 97 per cent, including 68 per cent who say it is very important. South Koreans are divided about international trade's effect on the environment: 49 per cent say it is bad and 47 per cent good. They also believe South Korea should not "as a general rule" comply with adverse World Trade Organization rulings by a margin of 52 per cent to 37 per cent. Ten per cent say it depends. Armenia is the only other country among the seven countries asked about this that tends to favor noncompliance.

Thailand

ABAC Poll Research Center, September 2006

Thais generally view globalization favorably and believe that international trade is beneficial for their country's economy, companies, and for both workers and consumers. Three-quarters (75%) of respondents in Thailand call globalization "mostly good" for their country and only 8 per cent say it is "mostly bad." Most Thais also think international trade is good for their economy (79%) and for Thai companies (70%). Strong majorities also say trade benefits individual Thais: 65 per cent say it helps consumers in their country and raises their standard of living (59%). About three out of four say international trade is good for creating jobs in Thailand (74%) and nearly two out of three say it helps keep Thai jobs secure (64%). Domestic job security is viewed as an important foreign policy goal: 85 per cent say that "protecting the jobs of Thai workers" should be a very (66%) or somewhat (18%) important foreign policy goal. Thais are less convinced that trade is good for the environment, though this is the most common view by a margin of 45 per cent to 35 per cent. Seven out of ten (69%) say "minimum standards for protection of the environment" should be included in trade agreements. Thais have somewhat mixed opinions about what their government should do if the World Trade Organization rules against it on a complaint: 34 per cent say it should comply as a general rule, while 17 per cent say it should not and 25 per cent believe it depends. One quarter (24%) decline to answer.

Middle East

Iran

WorldPublicOpinion.org, December 2006

Most Iranians see globalization as positive for their country. Asked whether globalization, "especially the increasing connections of our economy with others around the world," is mostly good or mostly bad for Iran, a significant majority (63%) says that it is mostly good. Less than one third (31%) believe that it is mostly bad.

Israel

Tami Steinmetz Center for Peace Research/Evens Program for Conflict Resolution and Mediation, November 2006

Israelis are among those most positive about the benefits of globalization and international trade. More than four in five Israelis (82%) see globalization as "mostly good" for Israeli; just one in 10 see it as "mostly bad." International trade is also viewed favorably. Very large majorities believe it is good for the Israeli economy

(88%) and Israeli companies (86%), the largest percentages among the publics polled. About three-quarters also see trade as positive for Israelis themselves: 77 per cent say it is good for "consumers like you" and 74 per cent say it is good for "your own standard of living." Three out of four Israelis see international trade as good for creating Israeli jobs (74%), and a majority believes it is also good for Israeli job security (63%). An overwhelming majority (91%) says countries should be required to accept "minimum standards for working conditions" under trade agreements. Israel is one of the few three countries where a majority (56%) thinks trade is good for the environment; only a quarter (23%) say it is bad. Nonetheless, nine out of 10 (93%) Israelis also think trade agreements should include minimum standards for protection of the environment.

Palestitnain Territories

Palestinian Center for Public Opinion, October 2006

Most Palestinians believe that globalization and international trade are good for their economy in general and for Palestinians themselves. They also are one of the few publics that think trade is good for the environment. Fifty-eight per cent say that globalization, "especially the increasing connections of our economy with others around the world," is mostly good for their economy, while only 28 per cent say it is mostly bad. Palestinians also consistently see international trade as being positive for their economy (70%) and for Palestinian companies (67%). Similarly, Palestinians agree that trade helps their own standard of living (62%) and consumers like themselves (57%) as well as being good for job creation (62%) and for job security (57%). Fifty-three per cent of Palestinian respondents view international trade as a positive influence on the environment, while one third (32%) sees it as negative.

Europe

Armenia

Armenian Center for National and International Studies, December 2006

A majority of Armenians view globalization favorably and feel that international trade has a positive impact on their economy and on individual well-being. Sixty-five per cent of Armenians say that globalization is "mostly good" for Armenia, while fewer than one in five (18%) believe it is "mostly bad." Three-quarters (75%)

of Armenian respondents view international trade as good for the economy and 64 per cent view it as good for Armenian companies. Somewhat smaller majorities believe that international trade is good for Armenians themselves: 60 per cent say it is positive for their standard of living and 56 per cent believe it is good for them as consumers. A majority (61%) of Armenians think international trade helps job creation in Armenia. Only a slim majority, however, thinks it is good for job security for Armenian workers (52%) while a quarter say it is bad (24%). Domestic employment is an important issue for Armenians: 94 per cent say "protecting the job security of Armenian workers" should be an important foreign policy goal, including 84 per cent who say it is very important. Most (79%) also think "minimum standards for working conditions" should be part of trade agreements. Attitudes about international trade's effect on the environment are mixed: 37 per cent believe it is good, while 36 per cent say it is bad, and 27 per cent decline to answer. Nonetheless, four out of five Armenians (82%) think environmental protections should be incorporated into trade agreements. Armenia is one of only two publics (along with South Korea) where the most common view is that their government should refuse to accept adverse rulings from the World Trade Organization: 35 per cent say Armenia should not comply while only 26 per cent think that it should and 24 per cent say it depends.

France

Efficience 3, March 2007

The French (along with the Americans) are among those most skeptical about the benefits of international trade. While a slim majority of French respondents believe that globalization is positive for their country, they tend to be more negative than others about its impact on workers and the environment. Fifty-one per cent of the French say that "the increasing connections of our economy with others around the world" is "mostly good" for France while 42 per cent say it is "mostly bad"—the largest percentage among the 18 countries asked. Although 64 per cent believe that international trade is beneficial for the French economy, 34 per cent say it is bad (34%) and while 55 per cent think trade is good for French companies, 43 per cent believe the opposite. Majorities say international trade is positive for individual well being, though large numbers disagree. Sixty-one per cent say trade is good for consumers like themselves (38% say bad) and fifty per cent think it is good for their own standard of living (44% say bad). Most French respondents, however, agree that international trade is bad for labor. Four out of five (80%) say that trade harms job security in their country and three out of four (73%) think it has a negative impact on domestic job creation—the highest percentages among the 13 publics polled. The French are also the most likely to say that international trade hurts the environment: two-thirds (66%) believe it is bad for the environment, and less than three in 10 (29%) say it is good.

Poland

CBOS, September 2006

Poles tend to believe that globalization is positive and that international trade is good for their economy and the environment. A slight majority (52%) of Poles say that globalization, "especially the increasing connections of our economy with others around the world," is mostly good for their country, while 21 per cent believe it is mostly bad and 27 per cent decline to answer. Large numbers of Poles see international trade positively: more than three-quarters say it is good for the Polish economy (76%) and Polish companies (77%). Polish respondents also believe that individuals benefit from international trade. Seventy per cent say it is good for consumers like themselves and 59 per cent see it as good for their own standard of living. While a large majority (71%) sees trade as positive for "creating jobs in Poland," only a small majority (53%) believes it is good for "job security for Polish workers," while 21 per cent say it is bad and 26 per cent are unsure. Nearly nine in 10 respondents (88%) say "minimum standards for working conditions" should be required under trade agreements. Poles believe international trade is good for the environment by a margin of 49 per cent to 25 per cent, though 26 per cent decline to answer. But an overwhelming 90 per cent majority still says environmental protections should be required under trade agreements.

Russia

Levada Center, September 2006

Russians are lukewarm about globalization's benefits although they tend to be positive about the effects of international trade. Forty-one per cent of Russians say that globalization is "mostly good" for their country, the smallest proportion among the 18 countries polled. Only one quarter (24%) say it is "mostly bad," however, and more than one-third (34%) declines to offer an opinion. Two-thirds (66%) believe that international trade is good for Russia's economy, and a slight majority (51%) feels it is good for Russian companies, though a third (34%) say it is bad. About three in five (59%) think that international trade benefits consumers like themselves (22% disagree) and 45 per cent say that it helps their own standard of living (19% disagree and 36% are unsure). Russians also tend to see international trade as positive for Russian workers: 52 per cent believe it is good for "creating jobs in Russia" while 27 per cent say it is not. Smaller numbers (43%) say trade is good for the job security of Russian workers (32% say it is bad). Russians tend to think international trade harms the environment, with 44 per cent saying it is bad and just 25 per cent saying it is good (31% do not answer).

Ukraine

Kiev International Institute of Sociology, September 2006

Ukrainians believe globalization and international trade are generally positive for their country, though they are less sure that it protects jobs. Fifty-five per cent say that globalization is "mostly good" for their country, and just 11 per cent feel it is "mostly bad," though one-third (34%) are unsure or do not answer. However, large majorities believe that international trade is good for the Ukrainian economy (78%) and Ukrainian companies (69%). More modest majorities think trade promotes individual well being: Two-thirds (66%) say that it is good for "consumers like you" and a modest majority (53%) agrees that it is good for "your own standard of living." Two-thirds (66%) believe it is good for creating jobs in the Ukraine (14% bad) but only half (50%) think it is positive for "job security for Ukrainian workers," with 16 per cent saying it is bad (34% do not answer). More than four out of five respondents (85%) believe countries signing trade agreements should maintain "minimum standards for working conditions." Ukrainians tend to see international trade as good for the environment (40%) though one in four (25%) say it is bad and more than a third (36%) do not reply. An overwhelming majority (88%) says environmental protections should be included in trade agreements. Forty per cent of Ukrainians say their country should comply with adverse World Trade Organization rulings "as a general rule" but 29 per cent say it depends and 12 per cent say it should not (19% do not answer).

6

Does Globalization Cause Inequity among Rich and Poor Nations?

M Stephen Lucas

Free movement of goods and services, capital, people and technology, helps both developed and developing nations in varied ways. International trade allows each nation to maximize the benefits of its input factors where it has a comparative advantage. Control of these resources must be dispersed to individuals so that they are empowered to make decisions that will improve their economic condition.

Introduction

Globalization and international trade have been around for millennia. Over the most part of the past century, nations have increased the amount of trade that crosses international borders. As trade agreements are made between countries, one nation's resources become available to another nation's citizens. The resources in each country are limited and scarce. The differences and availability of the proportions of each nation's input factors of production is the catalyst for trade (Pugel, 2004). These factors include land, labor, capital, and enterprise.

Source: Global Economics, March 2007 (www.mises.org). © Ludwig Von Mises Institute. Reprinted with permission.

Land is the real estate that is comprised within the country's border. It contains the natural resources that are limited in nature, such as oil, gold, silver, coal, etc. It also includes resources that can be grown on the land such as timber and agricultural products, which are limited by the size of the land that is available to grow such products and technology.

Labor includes the skill sets of a nation's people and is limited by the population size. Labor can be divided into skilled and unskilled. In some countries, it may be typical to work a 40-hour week; in others thirty-five may be more of the average. The larger the population size, the more a country can produce and consume. The health of the citizens can also become a variable to the labor input factor.

Capital is the money invested into a business. As countries accumulate wealth from the profits of the land and labor, it is reinvested in facilities, inventories, machinery and technology, which help maximize the profits from land, as physical capital, and labor, as skilled workers.

Each nation sets policy to manage its resources to maximize the benefits of trade for its people. Governments decide the policies not only concerning trade with other nations, but also the degree to which the state is involved. The state must meet demand in the marketplace by also setting policy for production of goods and services within its own borders and the ease at which individual ownership of goods and services. Neoclassical economists have added enterprise as a fourth factor of production. It is the risk-taking, organization and the innovativeness of the entrepreneur who puts the factors together to create a product that is greater than the sum of its parts (Ruby, 2005). By reducing the amount of time and costs it takes for business start-ups, governments can help entrepreneurs.

International trade is more than the movement of goods and services across international borders. Globalization can be defined as the process of an increased relationship between national economies through international trade, foreign direct investments by multinational firms, and international financial investments (Pugel, 2004). As trade increases between nations, the allocation of these resources will redistribute goods and pricing in a process to find equilibrium in the marketplace. During this process, countries can experience transitional pains, such as, unemployment, lower prices for natural resources, and lower standard of living. Other countries can experience an increased demand for employment, inflation, and an increased standard of living. There will be gains and losses perceived for some input factors from the redistribution of wealth. Some people blame these inequities on globalization. It is their argument that poor countries are taken advantage of by the wealthier nations. At the other end of the spectrum, others will claim that globalization is the cure for poverty. The goal of this paper is to examine the impact of trade on rich and poor nations and determine if globalization is to blame for the international inequality of wealth.

International Inequality

Inequality must be defined and be able to be measured so that comparisons can be made between rich and poor countries. Once the causes are determined, the effects of globalization can be evaluated and be measured. The World Bank defines inequality as the disparity of income and standard of living among nations and their citizens (Birdsall, 2002). To compare inequality among nations, incomes and living standards of their citizens should be reviewed. The World Bank has determined that people living on $1 per day in developing countries and people living on $2 per day in medium economies are considered poor (Infoplease, 2005). In contrast to the $1-$2 per day standard, in the United States, Japan, Europe or other developed nations, a person trying to live on less than $1,000 per year is unimaginable because the cost of living is many times this amount. The US Census Bureau defines poverty for a single, elderly person (over age 65) earning less than $25 a day as poor (US Census, 2005). Younger workers and/or people living in multiple person families have a higher threshold than $25 a day before they are considered poor.

The income gap that exists between rich and poor countries has become substantial. Although great strides have been made in improving income for poor nations, many regions of the world have 25% or more of their population living off less than $1 per day (World Bank, 2005). Some people think that with the poor people having limited earning capacity, they also have limited access to the world's wealth. In 2003, the richest fifth of the world's population received 85% of the total world income, while the poorest fifth received just 1.4% of the global income (Infoplease, 2005). When the GDP is compared between the richest and poorest nations over the past century, a wider income gap can be seen growing. Between 1900 and 2000, the richest quarter of the world's population saw its per capita GDP increase nearly six-fold during the century, while the poorest quarter experienced less than a three-fold increase (IMF, 2005). Income inequality has increased and has continued widening.

Income alone is not the only indicator to measure the wealth of a country's citizens. Besides income, there are quality of life characteristics that should also be considered. Sri Lanka has a low income, but has impressive social indicators such as life expectancy is the same as in developed nations, high literacy rates, low mortality rates and a declining population growth rate; results of a social welfare system put in place during the 1940s (IMF, 2005; Sri Lanka, 2005). Cuba is another such example where living conditions have improved, yet the incomes of the people have stagnated. Cuba has had limited trading opportunities with a US boycott in place and the cessation of Soviet support to the island-nation; yet its healthcare and education draw praise from the World Bank (Newsbatch, 2005). There are social benefits that a government can provide that will improve the quality of life and can be measured.

Poverty is measured by several different organizations, but many are similar to the UN measure for poverty. The UN's Human Poverty Index is a measurement of poverty that factors in illiteracy, malnutrition among children, early death, poor health care, poor access to safe water, vulnerability to famine or flooding, lack of sanitation, exposure to disease, a diet poor in nutrients, and the absence of education (Infoplease, 2005). These factors are as much the signs of poverty as material deprivation. The UN considers nations that share in these characteristics to be in poverty. Countries with these conditions under control can limit the exposure that their people have to poverty.

The World Bank has 14 key indicators (Appendix 1) that measure poverty within a country. They are subdivided into four sections: growth and poverty reduction, governance and investment climate, infrastructure for development, and human development. A connection (Appendix 1) has been established that for each percentage point of economic growth, the average number of households existing on $1 per day decreases by 2% (World Bank, 2005). Several factors can drive economic growth, including increases in education, life expectancy and economic policies – such as openness to trade.

The World Bank's measurement of poverty from the number of persons living on a dollar per day has decreased over the past decades, which would lead one to believe that poverty has decreased. However, when adjusted for inflation, the findings are that the income gap has widened and is well below the income levels of the leading industrialized countries in 1870; but the social conditions of today's poor countries far exceed the social conditions of the leading industrialized countries of 1870 (IMF, 2005). Incomes have risen for poor countries modestly, yet their social conditions have improved considerably due to increased aid packages. Richer nations have made advances in medical research and have given aid to poor countries for vaccines and expensive drugs that can improve the quality and length of life for the citizens in the poor country.

Inequality among rich and poor nations exists in terms of income and living conditions. Rich nations have tried to address this issue by distributing aid packages aimed at specific needs of each poor country. These aid packages ranged from literacy programs to food handouts and health programs. Poor nations need more than aid packages; they need economic conditions that can sustain growth.

Trade Verses Aid

Wealthy nations have not always been rich. They have needed to have years of a stable government and the ability to accumulate wealth. Establishing a fair and equitable system of distributing economic and political power creates stable governments. These nations have been able to develop relationships with trading partners beyond their own borders by lowering trade barriers and having a government seen as non-corrupt.

Wealthy nations have invested in infrastructure such as proper disposal of sewage, education for its children, healthcare, transportation systems, early immunization against childhood disease, and efficient drainage systems. When the society invests in these types of programs and infrastructure, all the citizens that live in the country reap the benefits. The nations where people live longer and healthier contribute more labor hours to the production of goods on a per person basis. As a nation is able to increase its productivity, it is able to trade with other nations. A nation's wealth is not limited by what it is able to produce domestically when that nation engages in trade beyond its own borders.

Nations that pursue international trade are able to increase their growth rate. During the 20th century nearly all nations encountered unparalleled economic growth as global per capita GDP increased almost five-fold with the strongest expansion in the second half of the century, a period of rapid growth accompanied by increase in trade (IMF, 2005). International trade has enabled economies to recover more quickly after war, natural disaster, and economic crisis. The developing countries of China, India and Mexico, which represent about 3 billion people, have adopted policies enabling their citizens to take advantage of globalization and their economies are catching up with rich ones (Manzella, 2002). Many economists predict that China's economy will surpass the United States' in terms of GDP in a few decades (Johnson, 2005). International trade has had a beneficial impact on these countries due to their policy changes and willingness to open their society.

Nations that do not participate in international trade hinder their own growth. After World War I, the countries around the globe became very protectionists and began putting high tariffs on goods from abroad. This is argued by many economists to have been the reason for high unemployment during the global depression of the 1930s, with such legislation like the Smoot-Hawley Tariff Act that raised tariffs to historical highs (Newsbatch, 2005). Even today there are countries that do not want to allow trade with other nations. The incomes of the least globalized countries, including Iran, Pakistan and North Korea, have declined or remained static over the past several decades (Manzella, 2002). Countries that do not open up their society to international trade choose to limit their growth potential.

Examination of the per capita income between rich and poor countries verifies that poor nations have other factors working against them. Poverty in the developing African nations is not the result of slow growth since the per capita incomes of poor nations grew since 1960 as fast as, and perhaps faster than the per capita incomes of rich countries; it is the result of ineffective government spending such as the Kenyan International Airport, which is barely used (Becker, 2005). Aid is part of the problem that keeps corrupt politicians in power and keeps real economic development from happening.

In an interview with an African economist, James Shikwati discussing the best approach by Western nations to help the developing nations of Africa, as cited by Thielke (2005):

Huge bureaucracies are financed (with the aid money), corruption and complacency are promoted, Africans are taught to be beggars and not to be independent. In addition, development aid weakens the local markets everywhere and dampens the spirit of entrepreneurship that we so desperately need. As absurd as it may sound: Development aid is one of the reasons for Africa's problems. If the West were to cancel these payments, normal Africans wouldn't even notice. Only the functionaries would be hard hit. Which is why they maintain that the world would stop turning without this development aid.

Foreign aid to poor countries should be able to help the government develop the infrastructure and institutions to eventually become self-sufficient. Rich nations have been giving considerable amounts of aid, including low-interest rate loans to developing nations for the last half of the 20th century, yet many of these nations are still poor. This is done through direct foreign aid from a donor country and through international organizations like the World Bank. In many of these poor countries, the economic system is comparable to pre-capitalist conditions where the goods and services they produce are very limited in scope.

Even if a country chooses to accept aid to improve the conditions of its people, the people may not be able to benefit due to corrupt leadership and institutions. Many developing nations have corrupt leaders that do not invest in the social services or infrastructure needed for its people. They are more concerned with staying in power and tend to reward people that will help them stay in power. The developing nations suffer from poverty not because of high debt burdens, but because inefficient governments redistribute the existing economic pie to privileged political elites rather than trying to make the pie grow larger through sound economic policies (Easterly, 2001). In their attempt to gain economic stability, they are in a constant search for more resources to generate wealth. African tribes war against one another to scramble for land. President Yoweri Museveni of Uganda, has continued to spend money on questionable military adventures in the Democratic Republic of the Congo; and other governments like Angola, Ethiopia, and Rwanda have also preferred a military route rather than engaging in economic trade with their neighbors (Easterly, 2001). These corrupt governments spend large amounts of their budgets on their military and pet projects that do not serve the people well. Another example is the government of North Korea that has spent its resources developing nuclear weapons while its people are starving. When government money is spent on the military and war, it is not spent on providing education, clean water, medicine, or the basic amenities that allow a country's people to move out of extreme poverty.

Many of the nations that receive aid packages are dictatorships and do not always spend the money where it will do the most good for the people. The World Bank financed the dictatorial socialist regime of Robert Mugabe in Zimbabwe until 2000, when the bank refused to give him any more money until he stopped his murdering rampage (Bovard, May 2003). There are countless examples of dictatorships misusing funds to support their own agenda without moving forward their own people out of poverty. Cited by Bovard, 2003, William Easterly, former senior World Bank economist, discussed the failure of foreign aid, "When governments' incentives are for political patronage rather than development, aid supports incompetent but politically connected schoolteachers, builds schools without textbooks, and roads that attract crooked contractors but little maintenance." When donor nations see misuse of funds they become less likely to support poor nations and their governments. Scandinavian countries have recognized that corrupt governments are part of the problem and have started denying them aid (Lambsdorff, 1999). Financial aid packages are given with good intentions by the donors that the aid will be used to help the people that need it. Instead the people that need it are oppressed and do not have the political means to change their own situation. Once the people can have more control over their own political future, their economic future can improve.

Without trade, foreign aid is the alternative of choice to help the people move out of poverty. Yet many of the people continue to live in poverty year after year due to inefficient governments and distribution of resources. Transparency International, a nongovernmental organization dedicated to stop corruption in governments, reported that nine out of ten developing nations are corrupt and inefficient (Lambsdorff, 2005). Even when aid is given, these nations are so corrupt that very little of the aid makes it to the people that it is suppose to help.

Without aid, people will depose inefficient governments and collect the political willpower to engage their problems and search for long-term solutions. Aid allows inept and corrupt governments to stay in power. A unilateral transfer payment in the form of aid is not a long-term solution. For a solution to become permanent, governments must be stable and be perceived as non-corrupt and willing to spend on the proper infrastructure and encourage trade.

Culture Clash

Not everyone believes international trade can benefit the poor, developing countries. People who are not in favor of expanding international trade and desire preservation of local culture and customs are referred to as anti-globalists. They are an assortment of several different groups with different issues; all motivated toward a common cause: to stop global trade (Wikipedia, 2005). They believe many trade agreements and multinational corporations can undermine the environment, labor rights, national sovereignty, and the third world.

The 20th century has seen international trade and the income gap between rich and poor nations increase. Some anti-globalists perceive that international trade and the widening of the income gap between rich and poor countries to be correlated. The *World Economic Outlook* studied 42 countries for which data was available for the entire 20th century and reached the conclusion that output per capita has risen but that the distribution of income among countries has become more unequal than at the begin ing of the century (IMF, 2005). This conclusion has erroneously accused rich countries of getting richer by exploiting poorer countries.

Inequity does exist, but it is not because rich countries are taking advantage of poor countries. However, multinational corporations are taking advantage of market forces and introducing it to developing nations as a peaceful means to promote economic growth. Each nation uses its most abundant resources to a comparative advantage. This is true with land and the products it can produce; true when too much money is available to invest in businesses; and, true when there is too much labor. Developing countries are labor abundant. When labor is abundant, there is a higher ratio of labor to other factors for the poor country than there are for its trading partners (Pugel, 2004). These market forces allow an efficient distribution of resources.

Population growth in poor nations is high and the people have little education, as it does not take much education to work on a farm. Cited by Birdsall, 2002, Dr. Wade, a professor of political economics at the London School of Economics, blames this rising inequality on differing rates of population growth between rich and poor countries and the pressures of technological change. Many of these poor countries still have an agrarian economy. Since the people cannot afford technology, like tractors to work the land or irrigation systems to increase productivity, human capital is employed. It is more advantageous for a family to have more children, so they can help work the farm. Many of the children will get sick and some die, due to lack of proper healthcare. In some countries like India, there is a growing industrialized sector. As these countries' economies become industrialized, the population, who is uneducated in everything but farming, begin to move to the cities as unskilled laborers if they are lucky enough to find work. Unfortunately, most people who move to the city will become part of the growing unemployed. These developing countries are abundant with unskilled labor due to high population growth and lack of education, especially among women, that make the country a source for inexpensive, unskilled labor in exchange for jobs. Its large population is a resource that makes another nation want to trade with it.

Many of these developing countries do not have continuing growth as part of their culture, which leads to the continuation of the stagnate economic conditions. Economic growth needs to be examined to verify or disprove the widening inequity gap because poor nations are being exploited by rich nations. Economic growth is defined as the increase in the value of goods and services produced by an economy and can be measured as the percent rate of increase in real gross domestic product (Wikipedia, 2005). There are two types of economic growth a nation can undergo to move itself out of poverty: intensive and extensive. Intensive growth is due to an increase in the quality of a nation's factors of production, usually due to a change in technology or international trade; where as, extensive growth is growth due to an increase in the quantity of a nation's factors of production, usually increased by acquiring land via war and colonialism. Technology means change to a society, and many pre-capitalist societies were based on tradition and certainty, and change was uncertain, therefore discouraged (Berri, 2004). In order for pre-capitalist economies to grow they had to increase their factors of production. Land was limited and technology did not exist to yield more crops. Lack of technology also limited capital accumulation. Population increases labor, but still limited by the same technologies and quality, per-capita growth does not increase. Therefore in the absence of trade, economic growth in pre-capitalist societies is zero (Berri, 2004). Capitalist nations have been able to increase technology and embrace change to become the wealthier nations on the globe.

Many of these non-capitalists countries are still considered developing nations. Antiglobalists regard the extension of international markets and financial interests as the cause of increasing global inequality (and poverty) and declining levels of human welfare (Birdsall, 2002). The population of these poor countries is plentiful and willing to work at cheap wages, as they are labor abundant. Their own government is eager to oblige the multinational corporation and in many cases, such as in Nigeria, the environmental laws are more relaxed than in their home countries. However, if the wages were not low or environmental regulation required more expensive technology to be employed, the corporation might choose to stay in their home country or choose to build in another country. The developing country's government needs the multinational corporation to provide investment and jobs for the people. Without these jobs, the government would spend money that it doesn't have to care for the people, still increasing its debt burden.

India is a good example of how efficient government policies open up a society to trade to improve the economic condition. Since its independence in 1947, India has been given more aid than any other nation. Yet for 40 years it had been grouped among the world's poorest countries and had a very slow growth rate. Around 1990, recessions in donor nations threatened foreign aid to India. Dr. Manmohan Singh, a reform-minded economist, was brought in as finance minister. India implemented many of his basic economic reforms, which included decreasing very high tariffs and quotas, substantially reducing regulation of private domestic investments, encouraging foreign direct investment, and privatizing many government sectors. India's rate of economic growth increased, due to these reforms, to more than 6% per year, without increased foreign aid (Becker, 2005). India changed its policy without getting increased aid and was able to increase its growth rate and begin to alleviate poverty conditions in its country. Aid had handicapped economic growth for India. Only when India was able to participate in trade with other nations was it able to break its cycle of dependence on foreign aid.

Governments in developing countries have convinced their people that the aid and limits to international trade is necessary for their continued development. These governments have limited their own growth by imposing tariffs and quotas on imports and claiming that international trade has kept their own countries from developing stable economies.

Many of the poor nations are forced to agree to economic reform before they are allowed to receive aid, and additionally, many of these nations are reluctant to accept foreign aid because they believe it will have a negative impact on their cultural identity. These economic reforms are seen as to favor the rich nations by allowing them more access to the poor nation's resources. The World Bank and International Monetary Fund (IMF) have lending policies that compel poor countries to adopt economic policy reforms, which are perceived to benefit only their wealthy trading partners and leave the emerging economy with an overwhelming debt burden (Newsbatch, 2005). Poor countries think international trade will destroy their culture and lifestyle. Many of these poor nations believe that if they participate in globalization, their culture will change and they will lose part of their identity (Tomlinson, 2003). Modern technology has actually led to the opposite being true. Globalization does not destroy local civilization and customs, but proliferates individual culture by using modern communication like the Internet and television satellite, so that a culture is not limited by location (Tomlinson, 2003). A person in his home country will go about his routine without giving any thought to their identity; however, when he travels to another country for employment or vacation, like the Mexican laborer in the US, they become more aware of their national identity. Globalization as a destroyer of cultural identity is a misconception that encourages poor countries to remain in the same cycle of poverty.

Poor nations remain in the same cycle of poverty because of their culture is not growth-oriented, has high population growth, low-level of education and a distrust of wealthier nations placing conditions on their economic aid. By accepting economic policy reforms, many nations feel they no longer have control over their nation's economic affairs. Developing nations have a distrust of rich nations, which prevents them from taking advantage of market forces that will allow them to move toward peaceful economic growth.

Trade Liberalization

Trade allows people to make individual decisions concerning their own wellbeing. This requires a different approach to the traditional beliefs that the governments are best qualified to distribute goods to its people. In the 1980s, the *laissez-faire* capitalist policies of Ronald Reagan and Margaret Thatcher broke down trade barriers and business regulations as privatization and trade liberalization was seen as a more favorable method to distribute benefits and resources to the public, resulting in a more weakened public sector (Wikipedia, 2005). Many anti-globalists would like to see governments take a more active role in this distribution process. As multinational corporations control more resources and the means to distribute them, they have more power when negotiating trading terms with poor countries.

The poorest of the least-developed countries' problem is not that they are being impoverished by globalization, but that they are in danger of being largely excluded from it. Of the impoverished countries, 0.4% of these countries had declining trade with international partners in 1997, down by half from 1980. Their access to foreign private investment remains negligible (PREM, 2000). These nations have limited the outside world's access to their nation, and in doing so, have limited their own growth.

There are four aspects of globalization that should help poorer countries become more self-sufficient. These include trade, capital movements, movements of people, spread of knowledge and technology (IMF, 2000). Trade allows individuals to exchange labor, goods, land and technology and is more efficient at putting these items into more peoples control rather than trying to control these from a single point like the government or aid organizations. In developing countries, as a whole, trade has increased from 19% in 1971 to 29% in 1999, but not all countries have benefited equally. Countries in Southeast Asia, China and India are on track to becoming economic powerhouses as they export primarily manufactured goods and have opened their society to allow international trade. Then there are others, mainly in Africa, who primarily exports raw materials and food, and trade has not fared as well (IMF, 2000). The agricultural subsidies of the rich countries inundate their markets with artificially low-cost agricultural products, as a result ruining domestic agricultural industries (Newsbatch, 2005). Further observation has also shown that African countries are more dictatorial and aid packages have remained prevalent.

Capital movements are the movement of financial assets across international borders. Since the 1980s, trade has opened up, allowing business investment to replace foreign aid as the single most important category to help transition developing economies to market economies. The World Bank (Appendix) shows the net private flows to developing nations are at higher levels than net official flow consistently from 1992 through 2002, the period of the observed data. Not only did net private flows to developing nations outpace official net flows, they did so by a significant amount. By the end of the 1990s, private investment exceeded net official assistance by seven times (World Bank, 2004). Private investment is investment that is made by private companies to developing countries that does not require direct repayments from the country itself. The government does not control private investment; but the government does benefit indirectly. Multinational corporations build factories and hire workers, and usually pay them above local wages, yet below the wages of their home country. Local governments can then collect more revenue from the increased tax base from the workers and the industry.

Workers will move to where the jobs are located. This means that unskilled workers will move to where more unskilled labor is required; or skilled workers moving to where more skilled labor is required. Wages communicate the demand for the labor that is required by each country. Most migration is between developing nations, but some migration does occur between developed nations and developing nations and in this process, skills can be transferred (IMF, 2000). If an unskilled, labor abundant nation wants to develop a more skilled workforce; they should want to engage in trade with a country that is more abundant in skilled labor. Nations that participate in trade will have higher wages than those who do not. There is a direct relationship (Appendix) between the openness to trade and per capita income. In a more open society, companies compete against other companies, and provide better opportunities for qualified individuals, offering higher wages for the required labor. The poor nation will also benefit when workers go abroad and can earn higher wages in another country and send money back home, which will also pump money into the economy of the poor nation.

Technology is spread by business investment as new equipment and technology are installed in the developing nations. Knowledge is also shared regarding production methods, management techniques, export markets and economic policies. These are available at low cost, and it represents highly valuable resources for the developing countries (IMF, 2005). Technology is expensive and is developed by richer nations and then put in poorer nations for production. The poorer nation can benefit from the expensive technology as a rich nation generates the new technology, a multinational corporation invests in the production, and the unskilled labor of the poor country will have jobs that pay a better wage.

Nations that embrace these policies will benefit from trade with international markets. Countries, whose economies have flourished, have learned to let their people be responsible for their own economic welfare. These governments have privatized many of their industries allowing them movement in and out of countries as they search for economic benefits. In doing so, these companies are able to share capital, people and technology that can benefit both countries without engaging in direct unilateral gift exchanges, in the form of aid.

Conclusion

This paper has demonstrated that inequality exists and that it is widening. When the rich nations get richer other factors are at work such as more efficient use of resources, which need stable, open governments and the infrastructure for improved social conditions. Many poor nations fail because the state fails, or with a large population growth rate, have difficulties managing the allocation of their resources. Rich nations have implemented policies and a capitalist approach to distribution of goods and services that propagates long-term growth. Not all nations are endowed with an equal proportion of factor inputs; inequality will exist. By opening up trade, nations can share their factors more equitably and the total global pool of wealth will increase.

For most of the 20th century, rich nations gave aid to poor nations only to see it squandered. The people of the country must have the political will and capability to select leaders that choose a path of economic growth instead of cultural stagnation. Many of these countries are poor and have an unequal distribution within the country itself due to corrupt government leaders that view international aid as a source of personal income.

Several of the poorer nations do not want to open up to international trade due to fear of loosing their own identity, when in fact they are loosing an opportunity for its people to move out of poverty. Many of the poorer nations have an agrarian economy that is labor intensive, without technology. They are changing over to an industrial economy that is not as labor intensive. During this transition, they will provide cheap labor markets for multinational corporations, and wages for these people will increase.

Globalization, when there is free movement of goods and services, capital, people and technology, helps poorer nations. International trade allows each nation to maximize the benefits of its input factors where it has a comparative advantage. Control of these resources must be dispersed to individuals so that they are empowered to make decisions that will improve their economic condition.

(M Stephen Lucas is associated with Ludwig Von Mises Institute.)

Bibliography

Becker, Gary. (July 11, 2005). *Becker-Posner-blog.com*. Retrieved October 18, 2005 from *http://www.becker-posner-blog.com/archives/2005/07/aid_to_africa_w.html*

Berri, David J. (May 24, 2004). Power point slides 2: Historical economic growth. *The development of the American economy*. California state university – Bakersfield. Retrieved from October 18, 2005 from *http://www.csub.edu/%7Edberri/ECON304pp2.ppt#15*.

Birdsall, Nancy. (2002). *That silly inequality debate*. Brookings institute. Retrieved from September 22, 2005 from *http://www.globalpolicy.org/globaliz/econ/2002/05silly.html*

Bovard, James. (May 2003). "America's hypocritical, counterproductive foreign aid". *The future of freedom foundation*. Retrieved from September 22, 2005 from *http://www.fff.org/freedom/fd0205e.asp*.

Easterly, William. (November/December 2001). "Think again: debt relief. foreign policy". The magazine of *global politics, economic, and ideas*. Retrieved from September 24, 2005 from *http://plato.acadiau.ca/COURSES/POLS/Grieve/Debt%20relief%20easterly.html*

IMF staff (April 2000), "Globalization: threat or opportunity? International monetary fund". Retrieved from October 15, 2005 from *http://www.imf.org/external/np/exr/ib/2000/041200.htm#III*

Information please database. "2005 Pearson education, inc". Retrieved from September 22, 2005 from *http://www.infoplease.com/ipa/A0908762.html*

Johnson, Chalmers. (March 19, 2005) "The real 'China threat'". *Asian times*. Retrieved October 15, 2005 from *http://www.freerepublic.com/focus/f-news/1367758/posts*

Lambsdorff, Dr. Johann Graf (November 1999). Corruption in empirical research – a review. *Transparency International* (TI). Retrieved September 22, 2005 from *http://www.transparency.org/working_papers/lambsdorff/lambsdorff_eresearch.html*

Manzella, John. (September 1, 2002) Globalization's effects. *A world connected.* Retrieved September 22, 2005 from *http://www.aworldconnected.org/article.php/231.html.*

Mauro, Paulo. (February 1997). *Why worry about corruption?* International monetary fund. Retrieved September 22, 2005 from *http://www.imf.org/external/pubs/ft/issues6/index.html*

Newsbatch.com (September, 2005). Globalization, free trade, and foreign aid. Retrieved October 26, 2005 from *http://www.newsbatch.com/globalization.html*

PREM economic policy group and development economics group. April 2000. Retrieved September 22, 2005 from *http://web.archive.org/web/20010208181115/www.worldbank.org/html/extdr/pb/globalization/paper1.html*

Pugel, Thomas A. (2004). *International economics.* Twelfth edition. McGraw Hill. (p 5, 62, 69)

Ruby, Douglas A. (2005). *www.digitaleconomist.com,* Updated: 09/02/2005. Retrieved September 18, 2005 from *http://www.digitaleconomist.com/prod_4010.html*

Thielke, Thilo. (July 4, 2005). "For God's sake, please stop the aid!" Der spiegel. Retrieved September 22, 2005 from *http://service.spiegel.de/cache/international/spiegel/0,1518,363663,00.html*

Tomlinson, John (2003). "Globalization and cultural identity". (p. 269, 271) Retrieved September 22, 2005 *http://www.polity.co.uk/global/pdf/GTReader2eTomlinson.pdf*

US census bureau (2005). Retrieved September 22, 2005 from *http://www.census.gov/hhes/www/poverty/threshld/thresh04.html*

Wikipedia (2005). "Anti-globalization". Retrieved September 18, 2005 from *http://en.wikipedia.org/wiki/Anti-globalization*

World bank staff (2004). "Globalization: foreign investment and foreign aid". World bank. Retrieved October 15, 2005 from *http://www.worldbank.org/depweb/english/beyond/beyondco/beg_13.pdf#search='planned%20market%20economies%20transition%20foreign%20aid'*

APPENDIX

1. Increase in economic growth results in poverty reduction.

   (http://ddpext. worldbank.org/ext/GMIS/gdmis.do?siteId=1&goalId=1&menuId=LNAV01LST1)

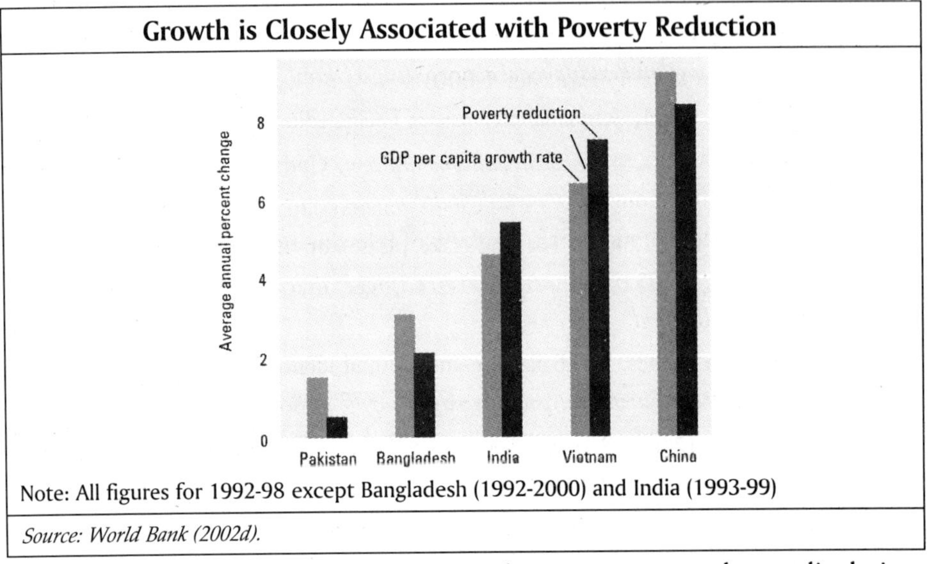

Note: All figures for 1992-98 except Bangladesh (1992-2000) and India (1993-99)

Source: World Bank (2002d).

2. The 14 selected country outcome indicators are grouped accordingly into four categories, with the first two mainly reflecting the first pillar, and the rest reflecting the second pillar:

Growth and poverty reduction

1. GDP per capita (constant 2000 US$)
2. Population below $1 a day (%)

Governance and investment climate

1. Public financial management (number of HIPC benchmarks met)
2. Cost required for business start-up (% of GNI per capita)
3. Time required for business start-up (days)

Infrastructure for development

1. Access to an improved water source (% of population)
2. Fixed line and mobile phone subscribers (per 1,000 people)
3. Access to an all-season road (% of rural population)
4. Household electrification rate (% of households)

Human development

1. Under 5 mortality rate (per 1,000)
2. Prevalence of HIV, female (% ages 15-24)*
3. Births attended by skilled health staff (% of total)
4. Primary completion rate, total (% of relevant age group)
5. Ratio of girls to boys in primary and secondary education (%)

* Due to changes made by WHO/UNAIDS in reporting the original indicator Prevalence of HIV, female (% ages 15-24), an alternative indicator Prevalence of HIV, total (% of population aged 15-49) is used here to monitor progress made in HIV/AIDS. *(http://ddp-ext.worldbank.org/ext/GMIS/gdmis.do?siteId=1&menuId=LNAV01)*

3. As a developing economy opens up to trade, per capita incomes rise.

   http://www1.worldbank.org/economicpolicy/globalization/documents/AssessingGlobaliz ationP2.pdf

Trade Rise Incomes...

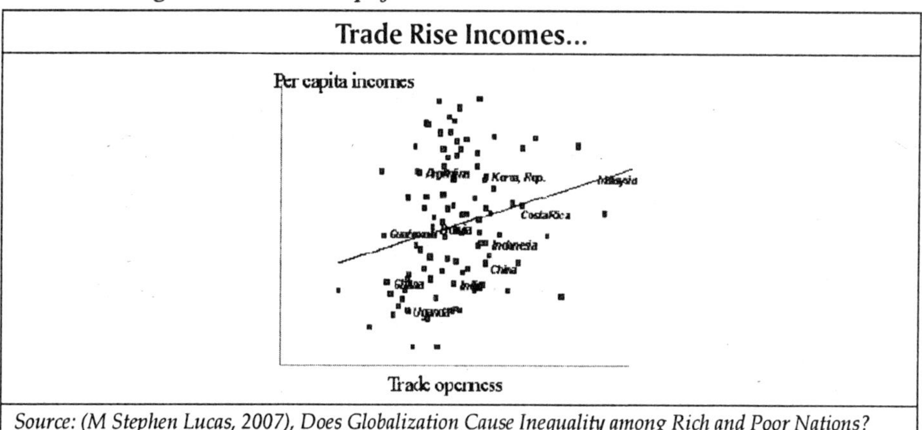

Source: (M Stephen Lucas, 2007), Does Globalization Cause Inequality among Rich and Poor Nations?

4. The spread between net official flows and net private flows to developing countries 1992-2002.

(http://www.worldbank.org/depweb/english/beyond/beyondco/beg_13.pdf#search='planned%20market%20economies%20transition%20foreign%20aid')

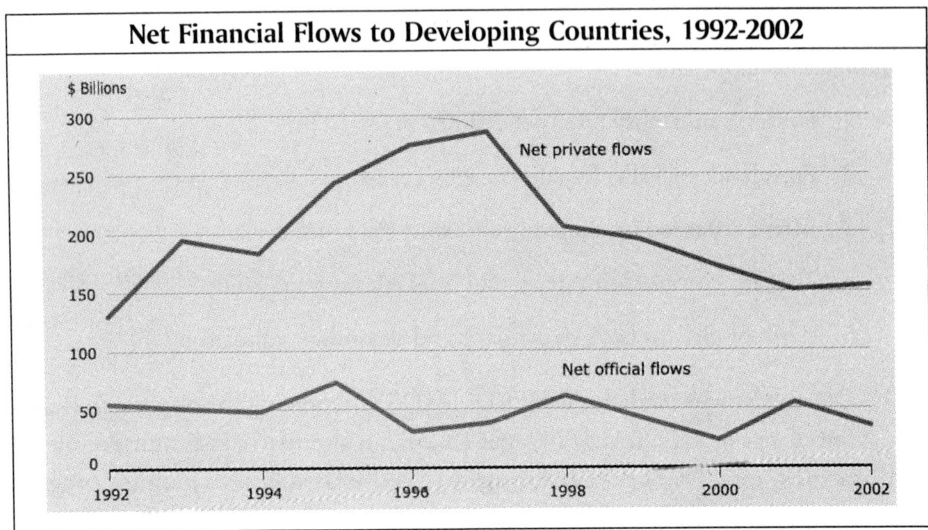

Net Financial Flows to Developing Countries, 1992-2002

7

Trade and Inequality
The Role of Economists

Dean Baker

The role of economists in trade debates is especially pernicious because there is no area of economics in which economists have been less honest about what their models show. They have consistently exaggerated the benefits that are predicted by standard trade models. At the same time they have ignored or downplayed the distributional consequences. In doing so, they consistently deride those who raise questions about the path of recent trade policy for failing to accept fundamental realities of the modern world.

Economists have come to play an enormously important role in public policy debates. The use of their expertise to effectively act as priests, telling the less informed public what the impact of their various policy proposals will be on the economy's future performance. Economists often tell the public that its preferred policy path will not have the intended effect, and may actually lead to outcomes that are the opposite of what is intended.

Source: Real-world economics Review, Issue No. 45, March 2008 (www.paecon.net). *© Dean Baker. Reprinted with permission.* *This talk was presented at the "Inequality, Democracy and the Economy" plenary session of the Association for Social Economics in New Orleans, Louisiana, January 3, 2008.*

Since economists, or at least the mainstream of the economics profession, are accorded enormous respect by the major media outlets, any politician who challenges the prognostications from this group is likely to be ridiculed in the media. This ridicule is generally sufficient to derail the career of any politician who does not already possess an independent and determined base of support and/or a vast amount of wealth that she can use to sustain her political career.

As a result of their ability to influence the media, economists can be incredibly important in steering public policy, often in directions that may not be supported by most of the country. Trade policy provides an excellent example of a case in which the mainstream of economics profession has been adamant in pushing economic policies that clearly do not have the support of the bulk of the public.

The role of economists in trade debates is especially pernicious because there is no area of economics in which economists have been less honest about what their models show. They have consistently exaggerated the benefits that are predicted by standard trade models. At the same time they have ignored or downplayed the distributional consequences. In doing so, they consistently deride those who raise questions about the path of recent trade policy for failing to accept fundamental realitics of the modern world.

Before laying out this case more fully, it is important to note that I am not raising any questions on the trade models themselves. There are important assumptions of these models that may be viewed as unrealistic. Most importantly, trade models generally assume full employment. If this assumption is relaxed, then it is far less clear that the elimination of trade barriers will necessarily lead to gains for the country as a whole.

The standard story of gains from trade is that fully utilized resources will be used more efficiently in the absence of barriers to trade. However, if one of the main outcomes is that a substantial number of workers end up unemployed as result of the being exposed to international competition, then the lost output due to higher unemployment can swamp any efficiency gains from reducing trade barriers.

While it is standard for economists to assume that periods of unemployment due inadequate demand are rare occurrences that can be safely assumed away for purposes of analyses, it is certainly hard to accept that this has been the case in the recent past. Alan Greenspan, along with many other economists, viewed the economy as suffering from a world-wide glut of savings in the years following the collapse of the stock bubble. Insofar as this description of the economy was accurate (and arguably still is), the economy's main problem is a failure to fully utilize its resources, not a failure to direct them to their most efficient uses. In this context, the removal of trade barriers may quite plausibly have lead to less employment and less output, even if the employed workers were more efficiently distributed.

However, for purposes of this discussion, I will ignore the possibility that unemployment may in fact, often be a problem and that trade may be a factor contributing to higher unemployment. Instead, I want to focus on three issues that follow directly from the standard trade models in which all the assumptions are chosen to support the gains from trade conclusion:

1) Trade does create winners and losers, and given current patterns of trade, the winners are likely to be owners of capital and highly educated workers, with the rest of the population ending up as losers.

2) It is possible to redistribute from the winners to the losers. However, the taxes necessary to pay for any redistributions are themselves distortionary. It is not possible to determine a priori whether the distortions created by taxes to finance redistribution are more or less distortionary than the trade barriers that were eliminated.

3) There are trade barriers that have the effect of protecting workers in the most highly paid professions, such as doctors, lawyers, and accountants. There are large potential economic gains from eliminating these barriers. Removing these barriers would both increase economic efficiency and reduce inequality.

I will discuss each of these items in turn.

The Winners and Losers from Trade: Does the Redistribution ever take place?

The basic story of the gains from trade story is that removing trade barriers leads to a change in the relative prices of traded goods. This leads to a change in the price of factor inputs. The price of the relatively scarce factor in each country is supposed to fall, while the price of the relatively plentiful factor rises[1]. In the context of the United States removing barriers to trade with developing countries, the expected outcome would be a decline in the relative price of less-educated labor (the relatively scarce factor in the United States), and in increase in the relative price of more educated labor. In other words, we should expect to see an increase in wage inequality as the direct result of the trade agreements that have been pursued over the last two decades, not an accidental outcome. The gains from trade and the increase in inequality are part of the same process of a change in relative prices.

Whether or not less-educated workers end up as absolute losers in this story depends on the relative size of the two predicted effects from removing trade barriers. If the efficiency gains from removing barriers are large enough, then it is possible that less-educated workers end up as absolute gainers, even if inequality increases. The actual history of the last quarter century suggests that this is not the case. The growth of wage inequality since 1979 has meant that most workers have seen almost no real wage growth over this period. In the years from 1979 to 2005, the median hourly wage has risen by just 9 per cent. The wages of workers at the 30th have risen by just 3.5 per cent and they have fallen by 2.3 per cent for worker sat the 10th percentile. Even workers at the 70th per centile have seen real growth of just 10.4 per cent over this period. In other words, the vast majority of the workforce have seen only minimal gains in real wages over a period in which net productivity has risen by more than 40 per cent[2].

The rise in wage inequality over the last quarter century is not really in dispute, nor is the stagnation of wages for most of the workforce. The only real question is the extent to which the growth in inequality can be attributed to increased trade. There has been extensive research on this topic, which has produced a wide range of estimates. At the high-end, Cline (1997) estimated that trade and immigration together explained 40 per cent of the growth in wage inequality over the last quarter century[3].

1 This is main implication of the Stolper-Samuelson theorem.

2 The wage data are taken from Mishel, Bernstein, and Allegretto, 2007, Table 3.4). The net productivity figure is a "usable productivity" measure that is based on a net output measure and a CPI deflator for output. This measure allows for real wage growth to be directly compared to productivity growth. This measure is explained in Baker (2007). It is worth noting that then on-wage share of compensation increased by 8 percentage points from 1980 to 2006. This rise in non-wage compensation (mostly due to employer paid healthcare benefits) explains part of the gap between productivity growth and real wage growth.

3 This was the finding in Cline (1997) in an analysis that only covered the years through from 1973 to 1993 found that 39 per cent of the rise in inequality over this period could be explained by trade and immigration flows. Since the trade share of GDP has increased by more than one-fourth since the end point of this study and immigration flows have increased by at least 20 per cent, the impact of trade on inequality predicted by this methodology would be considerably larger today.

Krugman (1995) used a simple computable general equilibrium model to conclude that trade accounted for 10 per cent of the increase in inequality over this period, coming in near the lower end of the range of estimates. Based on the increase in trade with developing countries in the last decade, Bivens (2006) uses the same methodology to conclude that trade would explain 14 per cent of the change in relative wages over the period since 1980.

Such changes in relative wages imply substantial reductions in incomes for most workers. For example, if trade and immigration can explain 40 per cent of the 20 percentage point gap between the growth in usable productivity and the growth in wages for the typical worker, then it implies a reduction in compensation of $2,900 a year for a full-time worker earning the median wage[4]. Even the 14 per cent figure implied by Bivens update of Krugman's calculation, implies a loss of more than $1000 per year for a typical worker. While the additional growth attributable to trade may partially offset these losses, most of the workforce is likely to end up as serious losers from trade.

This point is important because most discussion of trade policy only treats the workers who directly lose jobs because of trade as the losers from increased trade. The policies proposed to redistribute to the losers from trade involve retraining or in some other way compensating the workers who can directly trace their job loss to trade. This group typically numbers in the low hundreds of thousands, as opposed to the tens of millions of workers who can realistically claim to have suffered wage declines due to trade. For the most part, the trade adjustment assistance received by these workers has not made them whole in the sense of leaving them as well off as they were before they lost their jobs. However, even the most generous trade adjustment assistance to displaced workers does nothing for the tens of millions of workers who suffer wage reductions as a result of trade.

It is certainly possible to imagine political scenarios in which various forms of trade adjustment assistance will be substantially expanded so that those who lose their jobs as a result of trade are not as negatively affected as is the case presently. It is not possible to imagine any measures that will offset the losses to the larger group of

[4] This calculation assumes a wage of $15.00 an hour (Mishel, Bernstein, and Allegretto, 2007, Table 3.4), non-wage compensation that is equal to 20 per cent of wage compensation and a 2000 hour work-year.

workers who suffer wage reductions. They are expected to simply endure this reduction in living standards as a necessary sacrifice for a larger economic agenda.

Economists have been especially notably for their silence on this issue. With very few exceptions they have eagerly embraced the trade agenda of recent administrations. They have been quick to denounce opponents of this agenda as "protectionists" who should not be allowed in polite circles. Yet, they rarely acknowledge the unavoidable implication of trade theory – that a large segment of the US workforce will have to endure lower living standards as a result of the current course of trade liberalization. Apparently, economists believe that these people have an obligation to sacrifice in the interests of economic efficiency.

Economic Efficiency and Redistribution

Most of the supporters of the current trade agenda, and especially the more liberal supporters of this agenda, do make a point of advocating redistribution from winners to losers, so that in principle at least everyone can gain from trade. As noted, this redistribution usually takes the form of retraining or readjustment assistance for workers who can demonstrate that they directly lost their jobs due to trade. Although, it has never really appeared as a serious proposition in political debate, in principle it would be possible to tax away enough of the gains from the winners to compensate all the people who lose from trade.

Before addressing efficiency questions at stake in this proposition, it is worth pointing out the different order of magnitude of the necessary transfers compared to those being discussed in national political debates presently. Most forms of trade readjustment assistance are relatively small items in the federal budget. For example, the 2008 appropriation for trade adjustment assistance is less than \$200 million, approximately 0.006 per cent of the federal budget[5].

By contrast, suppose that trade had the effect of lowering the wages of the bottom 70 per cent of the wage distribution by an average of 2.0 per cent, a relatively conservative estimate of the impact of trade on inequality. In this case, the amount of money that would have to redistributed from higher income people to low wage

[5] The cost of the training component of trade adjustment assistance can be found at the Department of Labor's website *http://www.doleta.gov/tradeact/docs/2008AllocationTable.pdf*

workers would be close to $50 billion annually, or 1.6 per cent of the federal budget. This would be a qualitatively larger sum to raise in taxes, which perhaps explains the reason that no politician has championed this effort to date.

There is a second more fundamental point that needs to be addressed in assessing such large redistributions from the standpoint of trade policy. The argument for trade liberalization depends primarily on the claim that it increases economic efficiency. However, any revenue that is raised to pay for compensation from winners to losers will require taxes. These taxes will themselves be distortionary. While it is easy to say that the distortions that result from the taxes necessary to fund a $200 million job retraining program will not create enough distortions to offset the gains from trade liberalization, it is far from obvious that this is true if it's necessary to raise $50 billion to redistribute to the losers from trade.

Trade modelers often evade this issue of distortionary domestic taxes by assuming that the tax revenue lost from trade liberalization will be made up by a lump sum tax. A lump sum tax has two interesting properties. First, it does not create any economic distortions. A lump sum tax effectively just sucks up money from the economy without affecting anyone's behavior, therefore it does not create distortions. The other interesting feature of lump sum taxes is that they do not actually exist in the world. In the real world we have to raise revenue by doing things like taxing income, sales, or property. These taxes all do lead to economic distortions, unlike lump sum taxes.

As a practical matter then, an efficiency-minded economist would want to compare the efficiency gains from reducing tariffs, or other obstructions to trade, with the efficiency losses associated with whatever taxes might be raised, both to offset lost tariff revenue and also to compensate the losers from trade. To do this sort of analysis you have assume that real world taxes will be used to raise the necessary revenue.

Of course once this step is made, it is far from obvious that reducing trade barriers will always increase efficiency. In some cases, import tariffs can be a relatively efficient form of taxation. This is especially likely to be the case in developing countries without well developed tax administrations. Taxing goods when they enter through ports or main border crossing is likely to be far easier than imposing income taxes or even sales taxes.

In the case of a wealthy country like the United States, income taxes or sales taxes are likely to be less distortionary than tariffs as a source of revenue, however if there is going to be compensation paid to the losers from trade, then it is necessary to raise such taxes by considerably more than is necessary to just replace lost tariff revenue[6]. In this case, it is far from obvious, and certainly not obvious *a priori* that trade liberalization coupled with an effective program for compensating losers is a net efficiency gain. In this scenario, one source of inefficiency is eliminated – the barrier(s) to trade – but another source of inefficiency had been added, the tax needed to compensate losers and possibly also to replace lost tariff revenues.

The story looks even worse from the standpoint of trade liberalization when we consider the fact that any redistribution program will incur administrative costs, which could be substantial, and that no adjustment program will be ever be perfectly targeted. To cover these additional costs, it will be necessary to raise more than one dollar in tax revenue for each dollar paid in compensation to the losers from trade. The question that economists, who are committed to compensating losers, must then ask is whether the efficiency gains from eliminating a set of trade barriers are greater than the efficiency costs associated with a tax increase that is large enough to both compensate losers, and cover the costs associated with a program directed to these losers.

Without having examined any data on this question, I would be skeptical that the answer would in general be yes. Economists usually do not think that most government programs are very efficient, and they often have some cause for this view. If we envision adjustment assistance programs that are one or two orders of magnitude larger than the existing programs and the tax revenue needed to pay for such programs, it seems quite plausible that the distortions that result from the necessary tax increases are considerably larger than the gains from trade liberalization. But, this is really the topic that proponents of the current trade agenda should be investigating. There is no basis for determining the answer to this question based on existing research.

[6] If the liberalization involved the elimination of non-tariff barriers such as quotas or other obstacles to imports, then the revenue needs are somewhat lower.

Professional Protectionism: The Barriers to Trade in Highly Paid Professional Services

While economists can be criticized for failing to be forthcoming about the fact that most of the workforce likely ends up losing from current trade policies, and that the distortions created by policies designed to compensate losers may be larger than the efficiency gains from trade liberalization, these are not the worst sins of the economics profession when it comes to trade policy. The biggest failing of the economists concerns what they have kept off the table, specifically the large array of legal and practical barriers that protect workers in highly paid professions (e.g., doctors, lawyers, economists) from competition with their counterparts in the developing world.

The standard view among economists seems to be that there is already free trade in these professions and that the people who hold these highly paid positions in the United States just happen to be the best in their specialties, true winners in global competition. It is easy to show that this view is nonsense.

There are a wide range of barriers that prevent professionals in the developing world from working in the United States. The most important of these restrictions is the rule that applies to employers seeking foreign workers, which requires that they first attempt to find a United States citizen or green cardholder, before they seek out a non-citizen for the job. They must also claim that they are offering the prevailing wage for the job in question.

While this restriction may be poorly enforced, the fact that the law exists on the books is likely to prevent the emergence of Wal-Mart hospitals, Wal-Mart law firms, or Wal-Mart universities that explicitly seek to hire professionals from the developing world, and pay them wages that are much lower than the standard in the United States. These Wal-Mart institutions could then charge much lower prices than existing hospitals, law firms, and universities and thereby gain enormous market share. Eventually, the existing institutions would also have to cut the wages they paid for professionals in order to stay in business. This would lead to lower wages in the highest paid professions, but also lower costs for medical care, legal services, and education.

In this scenario, we would see the same sorts of gains from trade that economists love to tout, except that it would lead to greater equality rather than greater inequality.

(We can have retraining programs for the doctors, lawyers, and economists who lose their jobs due to trade.) Yet, virtually no economists ever discuss this sort of vision when they push an agenda for liberalized trade.

To convince themselves that they and their professional friends and relatives really are just the hardworking and/or lucky winners in global competition, economists tend to embrace the "Mexican avocado theory of international trade (MATIT)." According to the MATIT, there are no barriers to trade in agricultural products in the United States because it is possible to buy an avocado grown in Mexico in most grocery stores. The MATIT as applied to the highly paid professions leads to the conclusion that there are no barriers to foreign professionals working in the United States because their doctor was born in India or the economist in the next office was born in China. Using the MATIT, economists have little difficulty concluding that the United States has free trade in highly paid professional services because they personally can identify one or more foreign born professionals working in the United States.

Of course this is not serious analysis. Intelligent and highly motivated professionals from the developing world can overcome the barriers that are intended to limit entry, but this fact hardly proves that such barriers do not exist. Economists would openly ridicule the application of the MATIT to any other sector of the economy, but somehow they find it compelling when discussing trade in highly paid professional services.

The ability of economists to overlook barriers to trade in highly paid professional services is truly astounding. In 1997 there was an effort by the major doctors' associations to restrict the number of foreign doctors who were entering the country. They complained that the large number of foreign doctors entering the country was depressing their wages. (Note, the doctors did not claim that the foreign doctors lacked adequate training and were threatening the public's health. The argument was about wages, not safety.) On the other side, people argued that foreign doctors were working in underserved areas in the inner cities and countryside where US born doctors did not want to work.

There were no prominent economists involved in this debate making the obvious economic argument, that foreign doctors are depressing the wages of US born doctors, and this is good. Lower wages for doctors, means lower health care costs, which will increase the money that consumers have available for other spending and lead to more economic growth. The model is exactly the same whether the X axis is labelled "steel" or "physicians' services."

The result of this debate was that tighter rules were imposed on foreign doctors entering the country and the number of medical residency spots available to foreign trained doctors was cut back substantially. In other words, the doctors were able to get the protection they wanted. Furthermore, they were able to get this protection without economists, or the newspaper pundits who defer to economists, calling them knuckle-scraping The Neanderthals.

In fact, this episode seems to have gone virtually unnoticed by trade economists, in spite of the large sums of money at stake. The country spends around $160 billion a year paying physician salaries. By contrast, it spends around $70 billion a year on steel. While most trade economists probably do not even know about the restrictions imposed on the entry of foreign physicians in 1997, all of them could probably explain the basic outlines of President Bush's tariffs on imported steel from 2002. The latter were explicitly time limited and peaked at 30 per cent for a small category of items. By contrast, US physicians earn almost twice as much as their counterparts in other wealthy countries (net of malpractice insurance). The gap between physicians' salaries in the US and their pay in the developing world is even larger. Clearly the economic costs of restrictions on foreign physicians dwarf the costs of the steel tariffs, but only the latter concerned trade economists.

The idea of free trade in professional services is remarkably foreign to free trade advocates. They have difficulty even understanding what it means. The basic point is very simple. We carry through the exact same sort of process that we did with NAFTA. In the case of NAFTA, US manufacturers were asked to identify the obstacles that prevented them from setting up manufacturing operations in Mexico. The trade agreement was then designed to remove these obstacles. This meant ensuring the security of investments in Mexico, protecting them against nationalization, excessive taxation, or restrictions on the repatriation of profits. On the US side the deal was constructed to prevent the possibility of barriers to imports from Mexico, not only in the form of tariffs or quotas, but also in the form of product or safety regulations that could obstruct imports.

If we believed in free trade in professional services our trade negotiators would sit down with hospitals, law firms, universities, and other employers of highly paid professionals and determine the obstacles that prevent them from hiring large numbers of professionals from the developing world. At the top of this list would be immigration restrictions that sharply limit the quantity of highly paid professionals who can enter the country and that also require that foreign professionals be paid comparable wages to US professionals. If Wal-Mart can pay less than the domestic price for Chinese made shoes and toys, thereby depressing the wages of manufacturing workers in the United States, then hospital and universities should be able to do the same in hiring physicians and professors.

It is also important that the licensing standards be made fully transparent. It would also be useful to allow for students to be tested in their home countries (by US certified testers of course). This will allow smart kids in India, China, Mexico, and elsewhere to train in their home country to meet the requirements necessary to be a doctor, lawyer, architect, or some other professional in the United States. If a student in the developing world passes the appropriate test and gets licensed, then they should have the same opportunity to work in the United States as student who was educated in New York or Los Angeles. This would be free trade in professional services[7]. Just as it is cheaper to produce shoes and toys in the developing world than in the United States, it is also cheaper to educate doctors and lawyers in the developing world. In the absence of the obstacles to trade in highly paid professional services, most professionals in the United States would be educated in the developing world.

It is worth noting that it is possible to ensure that developing countries are not harmed by this brain drain. It would be a relatively simple matter to impose a tax associated with the issuance of a work permit that would be repatriated to the country of origin to finance the education of more professionals. Since a large percentage of the most highly paid workers are in licensed professions, there is little basis for concern that these workers will work off the books to evade taxation. By the nature of their work, they have to be openly available and visible to the public. For this reason, highly paid professionals will be far less likely to work off the books than custodians, dishwashers, or other workers in relatively low-paying jobs.

7 It is worth mentioning that the flows of professionals need not have much impact on the overall rate of immigration. They are around 4 million workers in these highly paid professions. If an increased inflow of foreign professionals increased this number by 50 per cent over the next decade, this would imply an inflow of 200,000 professionals annually. This is approximately one-sixth of the current rate of immigration.

If the upward redistribution of the last quarter century is to be reversed, increased international competition for the most highly paid professionals will almost certainly have to be part of the picture. Since the upward redistribution over this period went primarily to these high-end workers, rather than corporate profits, reversing this upward shift in income will require bringing down the relative wage of these workers.

In principle, the pay of high-end workers can be reduced by having the pay of less-educated workers increase, which would then be passed on in the form of higher inflation. If the wages of higher paid workers is then prevented from keeping pace with inflation, then their real wage will have fallen. However, this process could require a lengthy period of higher inflation, which could in turn lead the Fed to raise interest rates to slow the economy and reduce inflation. Even in this case, there is no guarantee in this story that the wages of high-end workers are held in check[8].

In short, the surest route to reversing the upward redistribution of income over the last quarter century would be by embracing "free-trade." This free-trade would be about subjecting our most highly educated workers to direct competition with counterparts in the developing world. This free trade offers the promise of both increasing efficiency and equality.

Conclusion

To sum up, economists have been extraordinarily dishonest in their interventions in public debates over trade policy. They have not been straightforward on the implications of standard trade models.

First, they have acted to conceal the fact that a substantial group of workers, quite likely a majority of the workforce, can be expected to be losers from the recent path of trade liberalization. This is not an accidental outcome; it is literally the mechanism through which the economy experiences gains from trade. The vast majority of these workers will not actually lose their jobs as a direct result of trade. Rather they will receive lower wages in the same jobs. If no compensation is paid from winners to losers, then a large segment of the work force can be expected to be losers from the current trade agenda.

[8] Increases in unemployment disproportionately affect the wages of less educated workers (Baker and Bernstein, 2004).

The second key point that has been largely concealed from public debate is that the gains from trade liberalization in a regime where the losers are compensated cannot be assumed. To cover lost tariff revenue and raise revenue to pay compensation to losers, it is necessary to raise other taxes. These taxes are by definition distortionary, and it is quite possible that the distortions created by these taxes are larger than the efficiency gains from reducing trade barriers. Since any compensation program will necessarily be imperfectly targeted, and incur administrative costs in addition to the compensation paid out, it is quite likely that the taxes necessary to pay for such a program will exceed the efficiency gains from trade liberalization.

Finally, economists have been very willing to ignore the trade barriers that protect the wages of highly educated professionals. For the most part, obstacles to trade in highly paid professional services do not even get discussed in the context of trade debates, even though the potential gains from reducing barriers in this area are likely to swamp the gains from removing the remaining barriers in merchandise trade. In this case, the effect of trade liberalization would be equalizing, since it would push down the wages of the most highly paid workers.

The views of economists have carried enormous weight in trade debates. Those who have opposed the trade agendas of recent administrations have routinely been denounced as reactionary and ignorant by the media and other supposedly neutral experts. Such charges have been based on misperceptions of economic theory and its implications. Economists have been too willing to allow these misperceptions to persist and often helped to foster them.

Unfortunately, the role that economists have played in debates over trade policy is typical of their role in public policy debates. The mainstream of the profession has taken positions that tend to support the existing economic and political power structure and effectively used its claim to expertise to deprive the public of the opportunity to freely debate policy options. In addition to trade, some of the other important areas in which this usurpation has occurred include Social Security, the relationship between Europe's welfare state and European unemployment, and the conduct of monetary policy. In these, and many other areas of public policy, the mainstream of the economics profession has sought to pronounce judgments that are not supported by their own theory and/or evidence, and thereby helped to impose certain policies on the larger public. It will be a huge step forward for democracy when economists no longer have this sort of power.

(Dean Baker is Co-Director at the Center for Economic and Policy Research in Washington DC.)

References

Baker, D. (2007). "The Productivity to Paycheck Gap: What the Data Show," Washington, D.C.: Center for Economic and Policy Research *http://www.cepr.net/documents/publications/growth_failure_04_2007.pdf*

Bernstein, J. and D. Baker, (2004). *The Benefits of Full Employment.* Washington, D.C.: Economic Policy Institute.

Bivens, L. (2007). "Globalization and American Wages: Today and Tomorrow," Washington, D.C.: Economic Policy Institute *[http://www.epi.org/content.cfm/bp196].*

Cline, William. 1997. Trade and Income Distribution. Washington, D.C.: Institute for International Economics.

Krugman, P. (1995). "Growing World Trade: Causes and Consequences," Brookings Papers on Economic Activity, V. I. Washington, D.C.: Brookings Institute.

Mishel, L., J. Bernstein, and S. Allegretto, (2007). *The State of Working America, 2006-2007.* Ithaca, NY: Cornell University Press.

8

Globalization and Its Impact on Labor*

Robert C Feenstra

The spread of free trade does not come without challenges, which take several forms. There is a potential impact of globalization and free trade on wages, productivity of firms and workers in the participating countries.

1. Introduction

Last month we witnessed the enlargement of the European Union to include two new members, Romania and Bulgaria, in addition to the ten countries added in 2004. The European Union is without doubt the greatest example of the spread of free trade in the world today, and to an economist, that is what globalization is all about. But the spread of free trade does not come without challenges, which take several forms. First, there is the potential impact of trade on wages, which is an issue of ongoing concern in Europe. Outsourcing, or offshoring, continues to receive a good deal of attention in the United States, too. This aspect of trade was discussed at a conference sponsored by the US Federal Reserve Bank, held last summer in Jackson Hole. In addition, this past September the Federal Reserve Bank held a meeting in Washington, DC, to discuss the implications of outsourcing for the US economy. which I attended. I will draw on these meetings to describe the impact of outsourcing on the economy in general, and workers in particular.

* Global Economy Lecture, 2007, Vienna Institute for International Economic Studies.

Source: www.wiiw.ac.at © Robert C Feenstra. Reprinted with permission.

Second, there is the question of how free trade affects the productivity of firms. As productivity improves, we expect those gains to be reflected in lower prices, and therefore higher real wages, so this second question also relates to the impact of globalization on workers. There is less research on the impact of free trade on productivity than on wages themselves, but there are some very recent studies that we can draw on in this regard.

Third, there is the issue of labor mobility between countries, such as from new EU members to the rest of Europe. Migration is also an issue in North America, especially the migration from Mexico to the United States. In 2005, there were close to 12 million Mexicans living in the United States, which is more than 10 per cent of the population of Mexico. It is no surprise, then, that immigration is a frequent topic of debate. I will draw on the latest research to describe the effects of immigration on US wages.

I take the ongoing enlargement of the European Union, with both its benefits and its challenges, as the motivation for my talk today; but by necessity, I will focus on the area of the world I know more about – North America. It has now been over 10 years since Canada, Mexico and the United States signed the North American Free Trade Agreement (NAFTA), in 1994, allowing for free trade between the three countries. But Canada and the United States had signed an agreement five years before that, in 1989, allowing for free trade between themselves. And of course, both of these agreements carried on a process of integration of the North American market that had started some years before. So as I look at what the impact of free trade in North America has been, I will start a decade before the Canada-US agreement, giving us more than 25 years to see the effects of economic integration on that continent.

2. Outsourcing and Wages

Let me begin with outsourcing and its impact on wages in the United States. In Figure 1, I use data from the manufacturing sector to measure the wages of "non-production" relative to "production" workers. As their name suggests, non-production workers are involved in service activities, while production workers are involved in the manufacture and assembly of goods. These two categories can also be called "non-manual" versus "manual", or "white collar" versus "blue collar." Generally, non-production workers require more education, and so we will treat these workers as skilled, while production workers are less-skilled.

Figure 1: Relative Wage of Non-Production/Production Workers, US Manufacturing

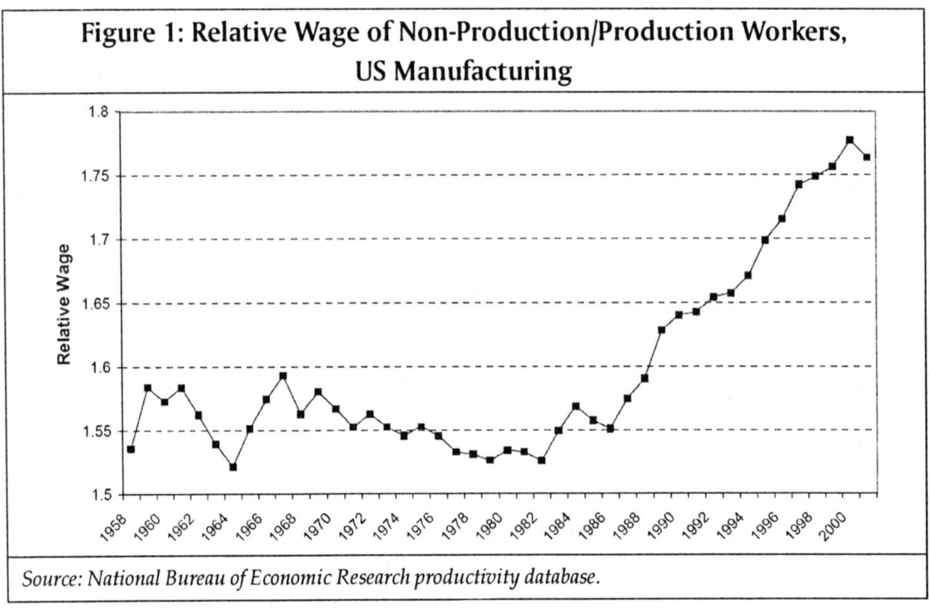

Source: National Bureau of Economic Research productivity database.

We see that relative earnings moved erratically from the late 1950s to the late 1960s, and from that point until the early 1980s, relative wages were on a downward trend. It is generally accepted that the relative wage fell during this period because of an increase in the supply of college graduates, skilled workers who moved into non-production jobs. Starting in in the early 1980s, however, this trend reversed itself and the relative wage of non-production workers increased steadily to 2000 (with a slight dip in 2001).

It should be noted that this increase in the relative wage of non-production workers also occurred in Mexico. In Figure 2, I show the relative wage of non-production labor in Mexico. We can see that the relative wage of non-production workers fell from the mid-1960s until the mid- 1980s, then rose until the mid-1990s. The fall in the relative wage during the early years is similar to the pattern in the US, and probably occurred due to an increased supply of skilled labor. More important, the rise in the relative wage of non-production workers from mid-1980 to mid-1990 is also similar to what happened in the United States, and I will argue that it is no coincidence that relative wages moved in the *same* direction in both countries.

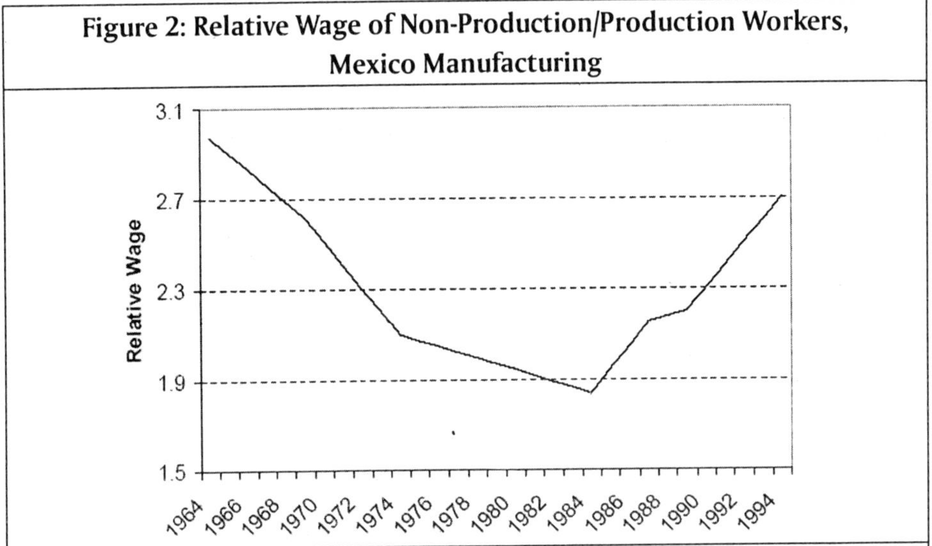

Figure 2: Relative Wage of Non-Production/Production Workers, Mexico Manufacturing

Sources: Robert C Feenstra and Gordon H. Hanson, "Foreign Direct Investment and Relative Wages: Evidence from Mexico's Maquiladoras," Journal of International Economics, 4, May 1997, 371-393; and Raymond Robertson, "Relative Prices and Wage Inequality: Evidence from Mexico," Journal of International Economics, 64, December 2004, 387-409.

Evidence from the 1980s

Going back to the United States, while there was an increase in the relative wage during the 1980s, there was *also* an increase in the relative employment of non-production (or skilled) workers. This pattern is shown in Figure 3, where I plot the relative wage of non-production workers and their relative employment in US manufacturing, during the 1980s. The annual earnings of non-production relative to production workers increased steadily during this period, as did the ratio of non-production to production workers employed in US manufacturing. The only way that this pattern can be consistent with a demand and supply diagram is if the relative demand curve for skilled labor shifted to the right, as illustrated. This led to an increase in the relative wage for skilled labor, and an increase in its relative employment.

What factors can explain this shift in demand towards more-skilled workers? Two factors are most often cited. First, the increased use of computers and other high-technology equipment, which needs skilled workers to operate it; and second, the outsourcing of the less-skilled jobs to other countries. Surprisingly, many economist feel that the first explanation – skill-biased technological change – is the dominant reasons for the shift in labor demand toward more-skilled workers. That explanation

Figure 3: Relative Wage and Employment of Non-Production/Production Workers, 1979-1990

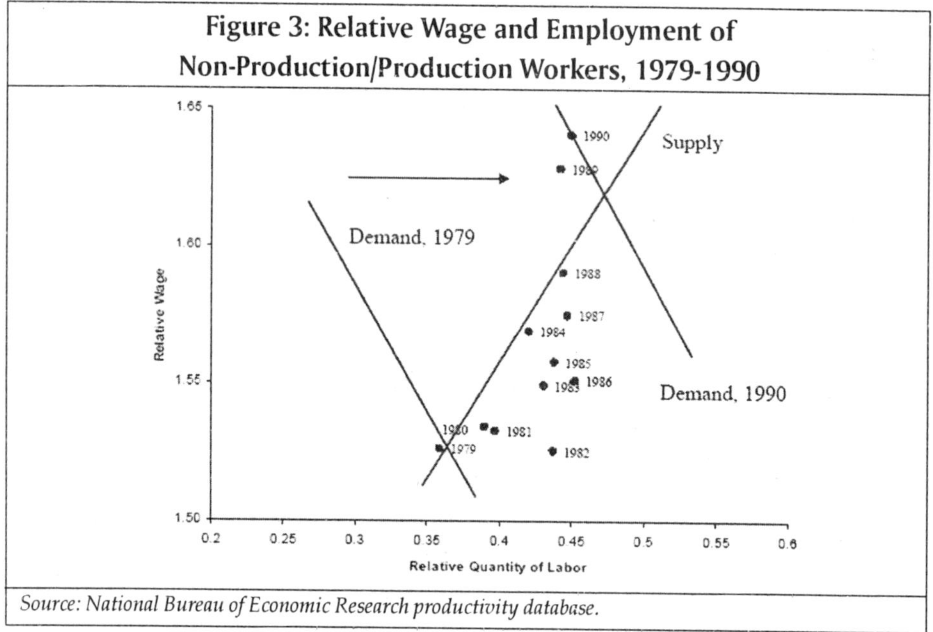

Source: National Bureau of Economic Research productivity database.

is favored, for example by the eminent economist Jagdish Bhagwati. Writing in the *Financial Times* in January 4, 2007 (p. 11), he states that:

> *The culprit is not globalization but labour-saving technical change that puts pressure on the wages of the unskilled. Technical change prompts continual economies in the use of unskilled labour. Much empirical argumentation and evidence exists on this.*

For the empirical evidence, Bhagwati cites Paul Krugman of Princeton University and myself, as well as the labor economists George Borjas and Larry Katz of Harvard.

Before reviewing that empirical evidence, it is worth asking why Bhagwati, as well as many other scholars, have been skeptical that the falling relative wages of less-skilled workers has been caused by outsourcing[1]. One reason for this skepticism is that the *same* pattern of wages changes – favoring more-skilled workers – also occurred in Mexico, as we have seen, and other developing countries and industrial countries (Feenstra and Hanson, 2003). Traditional theories of international trade, such as the Heckscher-Ohlin model, usually predict that wages will move in opposite directions in different

1 See Bhagwati and Kosters (1994) and Bhagwati (2004), especially Chapter 10, which will be re-published with a new Afterword (November 25, 2006). Early writers on the trade and wages issue include Berman, Bound, and Griliches (1994) and Lawrence and Slaughter (1993) both of which argue that trade is not the main cause of the change in wages.

countries due to trade, not in the same direction. For example, the Factor Price Equalization theorem states that wages will move towards equality across countries, meaning that labor should earn more in poor countries but less in rich countries, due to trade. That logic does not seem to be consistent with the fact that skilled workers earned relatively more in rich and poor countries alike during 1980s and 1990s. So can we really reconcile this global pattern of wage changes with international trade?

I think that we can reconcile the wage changes with international trade, but not with the Heckscher-Ohlin model or other traditional theories of international trade. Instead, we need to adopt a new paradigm, which emphasizes how tasks or activities can be sent across borders, as with outsourcing. In this new paradigm, it is fairly easy to predict that more-skilled workers will gain in all countries due to increased outsourcing. Let me take a moment to explain how this prediction is obtained, and then return to review the empirical evidence.

Model of Outsourcing

To understand how outsourcing will increase the relative demand for skilled labor, we need to use the "value chain" of a firm, which includes all the activities involved in the production of a good or service, from Research and Development (R&D) to assembly to marketing and after-sales service. For the purpose of modeling outsourcing, rather than arranging activities in the order they are actually performed, we instead arrange them in increasing ratio of skilled/unskilled labor used in each activity, as shown in Figure 4.

Figure 4: Outsourcing on the Value-Chain

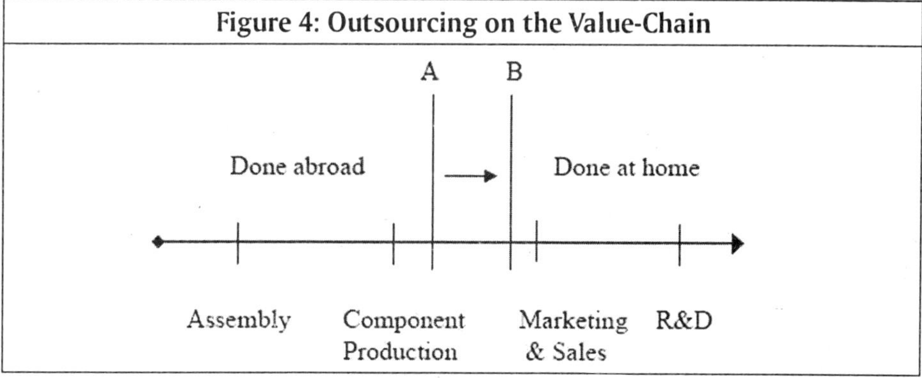

Assembly uses the least amount of skilled labor relative to unskilled labor, followed by component production, then marketing and sales, and finally R&D. A firm that is outsourcing to a country with *lower* relative wages for unskilled labor will want to send those activities using the most unskilled labor. So activities to the left of the line A will be sent offshore to the foreign country, while activities to the right of the line A will be performed at home.

Now suppose that the home firm wishes to offshore more activities. The reason for this could be a trade agreement with the foreign country, leading to reduced tariffs; or improvement in the infrastructure in the foreign country, leading to reduced costs there; or an increase in costs at home. When deciding what extra activities to offshore, the firm will look to those activities that were just on the borderline of being outsourced before, i.e., those activities just to the right of the line A, which used to be profitably performed at home but now are shifted abroad. The borderline between the activities performed at home and abroad therefore shifts from the line A to the line B.

What is the impact of this increase in outsourcing on the relative demand for skilled labor? Notice that the activities no longer performed at home (i.e., those in-between A and B) are *less* skill-intensive than the activities still done there (those to the right of B). This means that the range of activities now done at home are more skilled-labor intensive, on average, than the set of activities formerly done at home. For this reason, the relative demand for skilled labor at home increases, as occurred in the United States during the 1980s. That increase in demand will increase the relative wage for skilled labor.

What about in the foreign country? The activities that are newly sent offshore (those in-between A and B) are *more* skill-intensive than the activities that were initially outsourced to the foreign country (those to the left of A). That means that the range of activities now done abroad is more skilled labor-intensive, on average, than the set of activities formerly done there. For this reason, the relative demand for skilled labor in the foreign country *also* increases. With this increase in the relative demand for skilled labor, the relative wage of skilled labor also increases in the foreign country. That outcome occurred in Mexico during the 1980s, just like that in the United States, exactly as predicted from the model of outsourcing!

Trade Versus Technology

The key result from our model of outsourcing is that a shift of activities from one country to the other can increase the relative demand for skilled labor in *both* countries, as has actually occurred in a number of industrial and developing countries. However, the same result can occur from skill-biased technological change, such as the increased use of computers, which can increase the relative demand for skilled labor across countries. So it then becomes an empirical question as to which explanation is more important: outsourcing, or the increased use of computers leading to skill-biased technological change. To address this question, let me summarize the results from one of my own empirical studies, joint with Gordon Hanson (Feenstra and Hanson, 1999).

In this study for the United States, our goal was to explain the increase in the share of total wage payments going to non-production (skilled) labor in US manufacturing industries during the 1980s, as well as the increase in the relative wage of non-production labor over the same period. The study considers two possible explanations for the change in wages: outsourcing, and the use of high-tech equipment such as computers. High-technology equipment can itself be measured in two ways: either as a fraction of the total capital stock installed in eachindustry; or as a fraction of new investment in capital that is devoted to computers and other high-tech devices. The results are shown in Table 1.

Table 1: Increase in the Relative Wage of Non-Production Labor in US Manufacturing, 1979-1990

	Percent of Total Increase Explained by each Factor	
	Outsourcing	**High-Technology Equipment**
Part A: Share of wage payments going to non-production workers		
Measurement of high-tech equipment:		
As a share of the capital stock	20 – 23%	8 – 12%
As a share of capital flow (i.e., new investment)	13%	37%
Part B: Relative wage of non-production/ production workers		
Measurement of high-tech equipment:		
As a share of the capital stock	21 – 27%	29 – 32%
As a share of capital flow (i.e., new investment)	12%	99%

Source: Robert C Feenstra and Gordon H. Hanson, "The Impact of Outsourcing and High-Technology Capital on Wages: Estimates for the US, 1979-1990," Quarterly Journal of Economics, August 1999, 114(3), 907-940.

Using the first measure of high-tech equipment (that is, as a fraction of the capital stock), around 20% of the increase in the share of wage payments going the non-production workers was explained by outsourcing, and about 10% of that increase was explained by the growing use of high-tech capital. Thus, using the first measure of high-tech equipment, it appears that outsourcing was more important than high-tech capital in explaining the change in relative demand for skilled workers. The results are different, however, when the second measure of high-tech equipment (as a fraction of new investment) is used. In that case, outsourcing explains only 13% of the increase in the non-production share of wages, whereas high-tech investment explains 37% of that increase. So we see that both outsourcing and high-tech equipment are important explanations for the increase in the relative share of skilled labor in the US, but which one is *most* important depends on how we measure high-tech equipment.

Moving on to the increase in the *relative wage* of non-production workers, using the first measure of high-tech equipment (as a fraction of the capital stock), about 25% of the increase in the relative wage of non-production workers was explained by outsourcing, and 30% of that increase was explained by the growing use of high-tech capital. Using the other measure of hightech equipment (as a fraction of new investment), the large spending on high-tech equipment in new investment can explain *nearly all* (99%) of the increased relative wage for non-production workers, leaving little room for outsourcing to play much of a role. These results are lopsided enough that we might be skeptical of using new investment to measure high-tech equipment and therefore prefer the results using the capital stocks.

I mention these last results because using high-tech equipment as a fraction of new investment is often used by labor economists (such as Larry Katz and David Autor, 1999), which explains why they find very little scope for outsourcing to be important in their regressions. Those views might be changing, however. Interviewed for an article in the *New York Times* just a few weeks ago, David Autor said that[2]:

> *The consensus until recently was that trade was not a major cause of the earnings inequality in this country ... That consensus is now being revisited.*

[2] Louis Uchitell, "To Mend the Flaws in Trade," *The New York Times*, January 30, 2007, pp. C1-C7.

3. Outsourcing and Productivity

Summing up, both outsourcing and high-tech equipment are important explanations for the shift in demand towards non-production workers in US manufacturing, though the relative contributions of the two measures are very sensitive to how we measure high-tech equipment. But the results I have reported so far are only part of the story, since I have focused on explaining either the share of wage payments going to non-production workers, or the relative wage of non-production workers. Instead, we could ask about the *real wages* of non-production and production workers.

Regardless of how outsourcing affects the relative wages, it is entirely possible that the real wages of all workers will improve. The reason for this improvement is that outsourcing leads to a productivity increase for firms, which will lower the prices for final goods. It is certainly possible that the drop in prices exceeds the fall in the wage of either type of worker, so that real wages improve. That possibility is shown in the model of Feenstra and Hanson (1996), which uses the value-chain of a firm.

The same result occurs more strongly in the recent model of Gene Grossman and Esteban Rossi-Hansberg (2006), where the real wage of less-skilled workers is *guaranteed* to rise due to the productivity-enhancing effect of outsourcing. The model of Grossman and Rossi-Hansberg (2006) generated substantial attention when it was presented at the meeting of the Federal Reserve Bank in Jackson Hole last summer, meriting a write-up in *The Economist* magazine at the time and again last month. Let me quote from that article[3]:

> *Offshoring makes firms more productive. The tasks that are best kept close to home remain onshore; other tasks can be taken care of in cheaper places abroad. Everyone benefits from this gain in productivity, including workers who have fewer tasks to perform.*

Evidence for the United States

The real wages of production workers in US manufacturing are shown in Figure 5, and tell a mixed story. From the mid-1980s to the mid-1990s, real wages of production workers fell. Fortunately, they recovered in the latter part of the 1990s, so that by

3 *The Economist*, Economics Focus, "The Great Unbundling: Does Economics Need a New theory of Offshoring?," January 18, 2007.

2000 real wages exceeded their level in earlier years. They have continued to rise, but with a slight dip in 2004.

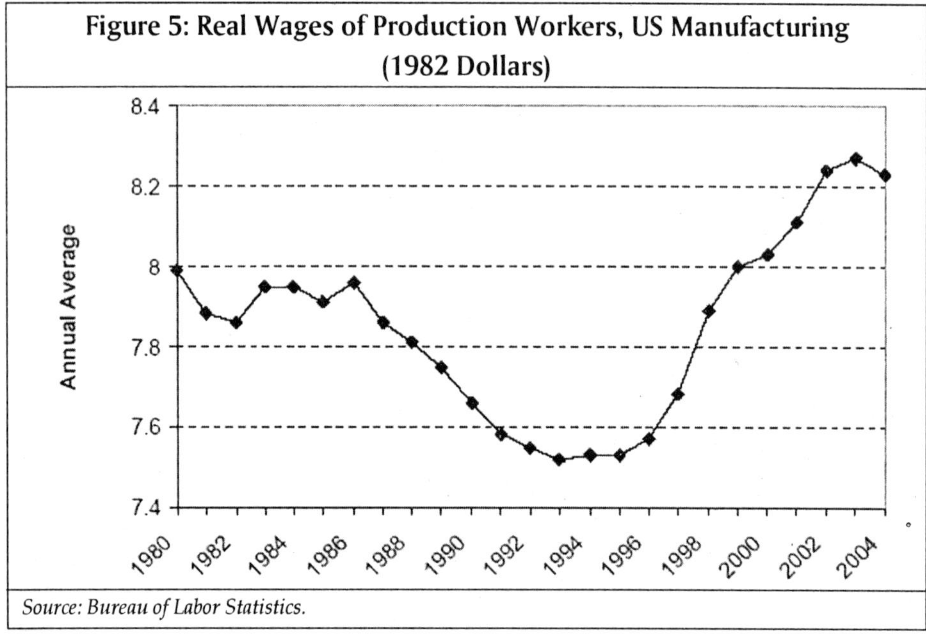

Figure 5: Real Wages of Production Workers, US Manufacturing (1982 Dollars)

Source: Bureau of Labor Statistics.

Table 2: Real Wage of Non-Production and Production Labor in US Manufacturing, 1979-1990

	Percent of Total Increase Explained by each Factor	
	Outsourcing	**High-Technology Equipment**
Part A: Real wage of non-production workers *Measurement of high-tech equipment:* As a share of the capital stock	1.1 – 1.8%	2.7 – 2.8%
Part B: Real wage of production workers *Measurement of high-tech equipment:* As a share of the capital stock	0%	0 – 0.3%

Source: Robert C Feenstra and Gordon H. Hanson, "The Impact of Outsourcing and High-Technology Capital on Wages: Estimates for the US, 1979-1990," Quarterly Journal of Economics, August 1999, 114(3), 907-940. Takes the annual percentage changes recorded in Table V and multiplies them by 11 years.

To see the impact of outsourcing on real wages, let us return to my earlier study with Gordon Hanson (1999). Let me focus on the most reliable case where high-tech capital is measured as a share of the capital stock. In Table 2, I record our estimates of the impact of outsourcing during the 1980s on real wages of non-production and production workers. For non-production workers, we estimate that their real wages rose between 1 and 2% due to outsourcing over the entire 11 year period, and closer to 3% due to the increased use of hightechnology capital. For production workers, we cannot identify any significant impact of outsourcing on their real wage, and a very slight positive impact of the increased use of high-tech capital. So for both types of labor, there is no evidence that real wages are negatively impacted at all due to outsourcing in the 1980s. These are the results that Jagdish Bhagwati refers to in his writings.

Outsourcing in the 1990s and Services

Let me turn now to briefly consider the evidence in the United States for the 1990s. The picture for the 1980s is well-known and launched dozens of research studies, but it is surprising that the picture for the 1990s is not yet familiar. For the meeting at the Federal Reserve Bank in Washington. D.C. last fall, I constructed the picture from the 1990s, as shown in Figure 6. We see that for the 1990s, there continued to be an increase in the relative wage of non-production labor in US manufacturing, but in addition, there was a *decrease* in the relative employment of these workers. This figure attracted substantial attention at the meeting because it is so different from what we saw during the 1980s.[4] What could be the reason for the *fall* in the relative employment of non-production workers?

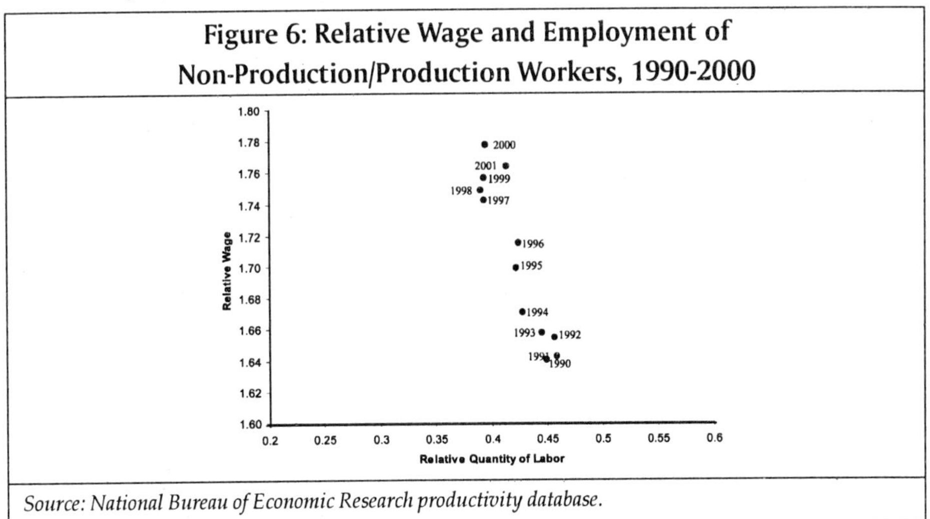

Figure 6: Relative Wage and Employment of Non-Production/Production Workers, 1990-2000

Source: National Bureau of Economic Research productivity database.

4 After I showed this figure, a senior economist at the Federal Reserve Bank, Carol Corrado, used unpublished data to compute what happened to the relative wage of nonproduction workers after 2000. From 200-2004, the relative wage of nonproduction workers *fell*, and therefore reversed much of its increase during the 1990s.

I believe that the most likely explanation is that the fall in relative employment is due to the outsourcing of service tasks from US manufacturing. To the extent that the back-office jobs being outsourced from manufacturing use the lower-paid non-production workers, then the offshoring of those jobs could very well *raise the average* wage among non-production workers. At the same time, sending these activities overseas will also lower the relative employment of non-production workers. So I interpret the pattern shown in Figure 6 as suggestive evidence for the offshoring of service activities within manufacturing.

Once again, however, there is no need for a change in the *relative wage* of non-production labor to be associated with any decline in *real wages*. The real wage of production workers can rise, or at least not fall, provided that the service outsourcing leads to a sufficiently large increase in productivity. Fortunately, it appears that outsourcing has indeed has a significant impact on productivity in US manufacturing during 1990s, and let me summarize those results (Amiti and Wei, 2005, 2006).

In addition to measuring the outsourcing of material inputs, as we did in the earlier case study, let us also evaluate the outsourcing of service inputs. In the United States, the amount of imported service inputs is small but growing. Measured as a share of total inputs purchased, imported services were 0.2% in 1992 (i.e., two-tenths of one per cent of total inputs), and grew to 0.3% in 2000 (i.e., three-tenths of one per cent), which is an increase of 50%, as shown in Table 3. The fact that imported services are small does not prevent them from being important for productivity. Over the same period, the imports of material inputs increased from 12 to 17% of total inputs used in manufacturing, also an increase of about 50%. In addition to service and materials outsourcing, I will also consider the contribution of high-technology equipment, such as computers, to productivity. High-technology equipment is measured as a share of the capital stock, which was the preferred method from the earlier study, and not as a share of new investment.

In Table 4, I show the impact of service outsourcing, materials outsourcing and hightechnology equipment on manufacturing productivity, which is measured by value-added per worker. During the 1990s, service outsourcing explains more than 10% of the total increase in productivity. Despite the small amount of service imports, it explains a significant portion of productivity growth. In addition, the outsourcing of material inputs explains another 5% or so of the increase in productivity, and likewise for the increased use of high-tech capital in manufacturing. Adding together these contributions, we see that these three factors explain as much as one-quarter of productivity growth. Since productivity rose by about 4% per year in manufacturing, we conclude that outsourcing together with the increased use of high-tech equipment can explain as much as one percentage point of productivity growth per year, which is certainly important.

Table 3: Offshoring Intensity 1992-2000

Year	Share of Imported Material Inputs %	Share of Imported Service Inputs %
1992	11.7	0.18
1993	12.7	0.18
1994	13.4	0.20
1995	14.2	0.20
1996	14.3	0.21
1997	14.6	0.23
1998	14.9	0.24
1999	15.6	0.29
2000	17.3	0.29

Source: Mary Amiti and Shang-Jin Wei, "Service Offshoring, Productivity, and Employment: Evidence from the United States," IMF Working Paper 05/238, International Monetary Fund, Washington, D.C.

Table 4: Impact of Outsourcing on Productivity in US Manufacturing, 1992-2000

Percent of Total Increase in Productivity Explained by each Factor:		
Service Outsourcing	Materials Outsourcing	High-Technology Equipment
11 – 13%	3 – 6%	4 – 7%

Sources: Mary Amiti and Shang-Jin Wei, 2005, "Service Offshoring, Productivity, and Employment: Evidence from the United States," IMF Working Paper 05/238, International Monetary Fund, Washington, DC; 2006, "Service Offshoring and Productivity: Evidence from the United States," NBER Working Paper no. 11926.

4. Productivity and Wages in NAFTA

So much for the United States. Let me now turn elsewhere in North America to see the linkages between trade, productivity and wages. I will begin with Mexico.

Evidence for Mexico

We saw earlier that the relative wage of non-production workers rose in Mexico, just like in the United States. But that evidence only went to 1994, when NAFTA began. We are more interested in what has happened to productivity and wages after NAFTA, as shown in Figure 7. There I show the growth in labor productivity for two types of manufacturing firms: first, the *maquiladora* plants in panel (a), which are close to the border and produce almost exclusively for export to the US; and second, all other manufacturing plants in Mexico in panel (b)[5]. The *maquiladora* plants should be most affected by NAFTA. In each diagram, I show what happened to productivity, to real wages and to real income.

Figure 7: Labor Productivity and Wages in Mexico

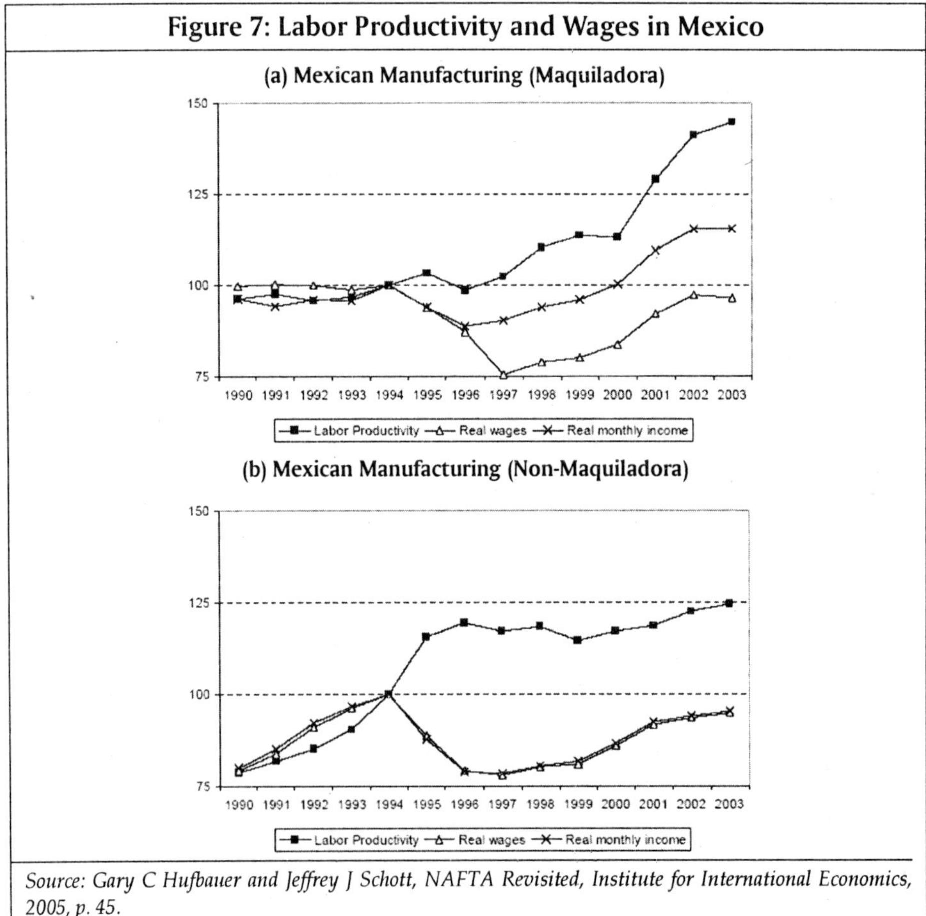

Source: Gary C Hufbauer and Jeffrey J Schott, NAFTA Revisited, Institute for International Economics, 2005, p. 45.

5 These figures are drawn from data reported in Hufbauer and Schott, 2005, Table 1.9, p. 45.

For the *maquiladora* plants, in panel (a), productivity rose by a cumulative amount of 45% in the decade after NAFTA, or about 4% per year. In contrast, for the non-*maquiladora* plants, in panel (b), productivity rose overall by 25% over the decade, or about 2.5% per year. The difference between these two numbers is an estimate of NAFTA's impact on the productivity of the *maquiladora* plants over and above what occurred in the rest of Mexico. This is a substantial boost in productivity due to trade, though as we can see from the figure, much of the growth came in the later years.

The question we are interested in is whether the gains in productivity were shared with workers through increases in their real wage. In the first years after NAFTA was formed, there was a fall of over 20% in real wages in either the *maquiladora* or non-*maquiladora* sectors, despite the rise in productivity. This fall in real wages is due to a financial crisis in Mexico that led to a large devaluation of the peso. It would be incorrect to attribute the peso crisis to Mexico's joining NAFTA, despite the fact that though they both occurred in 1994.

The *maquiladora* sector, located beside the US border, was most susceptible to the peso devaluation and did not experience much of a gain in productivity during those first few years after NAFTA, due to the increased cost of inputs imported from the US Workers in both the *maquiladora* and non-*maquiladora* sectors had to pay higher prices for imported goods, too, which are reflected in higher Mexican consumer prices. So the decline in real wages for both workers is similar. This decline was short-lived, however, and real wages in both sectors began to rise again in 1998. By 2003, real wages in both sectors had risen to nearly equal their value when NAFTA began. This means that workers in Mexico did not gain or lose due to NAFTA on average: the productivity gains were not shared with workers, which is a disappointing finding, but real wages at least recovered from the effects of the peso crisis.

The picture is somewhat better if instead of real wages we instead look at real monthly income, which includes other forms of compensation to workers besides their wages. The income data will more fully reflect non-production workers who earn salaries rather than wages. In the non-*maquiladora* sector, shown in panel (b), the data on real wages and real monthly income move together closely. But in the *maquiladora* sector, in panel (a), real monthly incomes were indeed higher in 2003 than in 1994, indicating some gains for workers in the manufacturing plants most affected by NAFTA. This conclusion is reinforced by other evidence from Mexico, which shows that higher-income workers fared better than unskilled workers in the *maquiladora* sector and also better than workers in the rest of Mexico (Hanson, 2007). From this evidence, the higher-income workers in the *maquiladora* sector, and only those workers, are the principal gainers due to NAFTA.

Evidence for Canada

Next, let me turn to the impact of free trade with the United States on productivity and wages in Canada. There were studies by the Economic Council of Canada dating back to the 1960s that predicted substantial gains from free trade with the US, as Canadian firms would expand their scale of operations and lower costs. A set of simulations performed by the Canadian economist Richard Harris (1984a,b) in the mid-1980s were very influential in convincing Canadian policy makers to proceed with the free trade agreement with the US in 1989. Enough time has passed since then to look back and see what the outcome has been.

A recent study for Canada, by Daniel Trefler (2004), does just that. Trefler uses firmlevel data during the decades before and after the Canada-US free trade agreement, and is interested in the impact of the agreement on the selection and productivity of firms. He obtains a number of clear results[6]. First, Canadian industries that had relied most on tariffs saw their employment fall by 12% due to the elimination of tariffs. In manufacturing overall, the trade agreement reduced employment by 5%. Second, these job losses were a short-term effect, and over a 10 year period, employment in Canadian manufacturing did not drop. While low-productivity plants shut down, high-productivity Canadian manufacturers expanded into the United States. Third, the trade agreement set off a productivity boom. Formerly sheltered Canadian companies began to compete with, and compare themselves to, more efficient American businesses. Some went under, but others significantly improved operations. In the formerly sheltered industries most affected by the tariff cuts, labor productivity jumped 15% per cent, or an annual rate of 1.9%, at least half from closing inefficient plants.

To summarize, Trefler finds overwhelming evidence that the Canada-US free trade agreement resulted in the self-selection of Canadian firms, with only the more

6 These results are drawn from an interview of Trefler by Virginia Postrel, "Economic Scene," *The New York Times*, January 27, 2005, p. C2, posted on the home page for Daniel Trefler at the University of Toronto.

productive firms surviving. Productivity in Canadian manufacturing overall rose 6 per cent. This productivity gain translates directly into higher wages or lower prices, and is a gain from trade for workers. Trefler's estimates of the gains are the highest we have seen from any country study, and probably higher than would occur in the US, simply because trade is a much higher fraction of GDP for Canada. But we could expect some of the European countries to show productivity gains of the same magnitude as Canada, provided that the labor market institutions are flexible enough to allow for the entry and exit of firms on the same scale as occurred in Canada.

5. Other Sources of Gains from Trade

Before moving to my last topic, which is immigration in North America, let me pause and ask whether there are any other sources of gains for workers that I have not yet considered. In fact, there are. Beside increasing the productivity of firms, free trade can be expected to expand the variety of goods available to consumers, leading to gains for that reason. This source of gain due to product variety has been well known in theory for several decade, but it is only very recently that we have been able to estimate such gains. To explain why it has been difficult to estimate these gains, let me go back to the simulation models for Canada-US free trade by Richard Harris (1984a,b).

Harris based his model on the idea that firms have economies of scale, but in the small Canadian market, firms would be unable to expand their output to realize these economies. That is why free trade with the United States is so attractive from the Canadian standpoint: it allows for an expansion of firms' scale and a fall in costs, which is just another way of saying that productivity rises. Harris based his estimates of economies of scale on engineering studies, and was able to predict substantial gains for Canada due to free trade, as Trefler confirmed.

But Harris was reluctant to build into his model another common assumption: that firms produce differentiated products. The reason, I believe, is that Harris realized that the calculated gains from trade would be very sensitive to the extent of differentiation across products, i.e., on the elasticity of substitution. If the elasticity of substitution is high, then products easily substitute for each other, and consumers do not gain much from having new varieties available. A high elasticity of substitution may describe T-shirts for example, where we probably don't care too much whether our T-shirts comes from China, India, Vietnam, or wherever.

But as soon as we leave such basic items of clothing, and go to higher-fashion items, then the product sold by one company is probably quite different from the product sold by another. Consumers gains by having more choices available when they shop for fashion items, or electronics, or nearly anything else. So the elasticity of substitution between these items is lower, which indicates that consumers benefit more from having greater variety available.

Harris was reluctant to build product differentiation into his simulation model for Canada because he did not know what value to use for the elasticity of substitution in each industry. For technical reasons (as described in Feenstra, 2006), the estimates for the elasticity that were available in the 1980s were quite poor. Often the elasticities were too low, which would result in exaggerated estimates of the consumer benefits from product variety. Harris realized this potential for bias in his simulation results, so whereas he always made use of economies of scale, he added product differentiation only a secondary feature to the simulation models.

But now two decades later, we do have the statistical technique we need to estimate the elasticity of substitution between varieties of each and every product. This statistical technique comes from Feenstra (1994), which deals with the empirical methods needed to analyze the gains from trade due to expanding product variety. I applied that statistical technique to just half a dozen products, obtaining estimates of the elasticity of substitution for each. Now more than ten years later, our computing power has increased by several orders of magnitude, and the same technique been applied to over 30,000 products in recent work by Christian Broda and David Weinstein (2006), for the United States. They treat imports coming from new supplying countries as new product varieties. By combining the data on imports from new supplying countries with estimates of the elasticity of substitution, Broda and Weinstein come away with an estimate of the gains from trade for the US due to the expansion of import varieties, which amounts to 2.6 per cent of GDP in 2001.

Economists sometimes get very excited over small numbers, but 2.6 per cent of GDP is actually a very large number. It indicates the *ongoing annual gains* from having the import varieties available from new supplying countries. I would expect that a number of the same or greater magnitude would apply to the gains to the European Union from having new import varieties available, and there could quite possibly be even larger gains from internal-EU trade. Those estimates for Europe have not yet been made, but I hope that they will.

Evidence for Europe

While estimates of the gains from product variety are not available for Europe, there are a number of studies looking at a closely related topic, which is the impact of unification of the European market on the *prices* charged by firms. Simulations done in the late 1980s by Alasdair Smith and Tony Venables (1988, 1991) predicted large gains to the 1992 Single Market reforms in Europe, allowing for greater unification of the market. Smith and Venables expected that firms would be forced to equalize their selling prices across markets. In other words, rather than treating Europe as a collection of segmented markets, where firms could choose their prices in each country separately, Europe would instead become a unified market where firms could not price-discriminate. As price-discrimination is eliminated, then the average prices are expected to fall, providing benefits to consumers.

Given the 15 years since the Single Market reforms of 1992, and the much shorter period since the adoption of the Euro in 2002, we can ask whether the prediction of unified and lower prices within Europe has been realized. Some positive results are starting to appear. A recent paper by Harald Badinger (2006) uses sectoral data from 1981 to 1999 and finds solid evidence of markup reductions in manufacturing and construction, but not in services. The service industry that we are all perhaps most familiar with is restaurants, where it is widely believed that prices increased following the adoption of the Euro. But a new paper by Hobijn, Ravenna and Tombalotti (2006) argues that this increase can be understood as making up for unusually small price changes prior to the adoption of the Euro, and in fact, the real puzzle is why such price increases were not more widespread. So I conclude that there is some evidence in favor of falling markups in Europe, but not in all sectors.

Clearly, Europe is the ideal testing ground to look for the positive impact of trade on productivity, as well. We can hope that further empirical research will add to the results that we have already, demonstrating the gains from a unified market in Europe.

6. Immigration to the United States

Let me turn now to my final topic, the question of how migration within North America affects wages. Migration within the European Union is of major concern, of course, as Romania and Bulgaria have joined, along with the 10 central and eastern European countries in 2004. Established members of the EU are understandably concerned with the pressure on wages and employment that might result from immigration from countries with much lower wages. We have an analogy within North America with the large inflow of immigrants to the United States from Mexico and other developing countries. How has this wave of immigration over the past twenty-five years affected US wages?

The idea that immigrants lead to downward pressure on local wages has *not* been realized to the extent that was feared the United States. There are two offsetting effects which limit the need for local wages to adjust. First, there can be an expansion of industries employing the immigrants, thereby allowing these workers to be absorbed without a fall in wages. Second, it turns out that the immigrants coming into the United States are at different education levels – either less-educated or more-educated – than the majority of the US population. That also limits the fall in wages due to competition between workers, and in fact, allows for some complementary effects of immigrants on local wages.

Mariel Boat Lift

To see these effects at work, let me begin with an isolated example from the United States that has been studied in depth. Known as the Mariel Boat Lift, this case occurred in 1980 when, for political reasons, a wave of refugees were allowed to leave the port of Mariel, Cuba and sail to Miami, Florida. From May to September of that year, about 125,000 refugees arrived in Miami, and increased that city's overall population by 7%. Not surprisingly, the refugees were less skilled than the other workers in Miami. What is surprising, however, is that this influx of low-skilled immigrants does not appear to have pulled down the wages of other less-skilled workers in Miami (Card, 1990). The wages for low-skilled workers in Miami pretty much followed national trends over this period, despite the large inflow of workers from Cuba. This finding contradicts the prediction that the inflow of low-skilled workers should bid down wages, and calls for an explanation.

One explanation comes from a careful study of what happened to the output of various industries in Miami during this time period (Lewis, 2004). It turns out that certain labor-intensive industries in Miami, such as apparel, declined by less than we would have predicted from national trends. In other words, the industries using less-skilled workers intensively, like apparel, expanded relative to the national trend to absorb more of the Cuban workers. As some industries expand relative to their trend, it is logical to expect other industries to contract, which also occurred in Miami. A group of skill-intensive industries (including motor vehicles, electronic equipment, and aircraft) fell more rapidly in Miami after 1980. This finding illustrates that there was a change in the industry mix in Miami, towards those industries using less-skilled labor and away from those using more-skilled labor, which allowed the city to absorb the Cuban refugees without a decline in wages.

This example from Miami could perhaps be useful as we think about the immigration from the new EU members to other European countries. Britain was one of the European Union countries that opened its jobs to all nationals from the 10 countries joining in 2004, and as a result, 400,000 immigrants came in. That pressure has led Britain to limit the number of migrants permitted from Bulgaria and Romania, at least for now. The inflow of 400,000 migrants to Britain is slightly more than 5% of the population of London, which is less than the percentage inflow into Miami due to the Mariel boat-lift. As economists of the future look back on the experience of Britain due to this inflow, as well as other European countries, I submit that one crucial factor will be the extent to which industries can expand and contract, as needed, to absorb the inflow of immigrants. With sufficiently flexibility in industry output and employment, we should not expect that wages need to adjust to bear the burden of the labor inflows.

Mexican Migration to the United States

Let us shift from the isolated case of Cuban refuges in Miami to the overall inflow of immigrants to the United States. In 1980, the percentage of foreign-born persons in the US population was 6%, and since that time, the percentage has doubled to 13% in 2005. A sizable percentage of these immigrants are from Mexico.

As shown by my colleague Giovanni Peri, the combination of legal and illegal immigrants in the US creates a "U-shaped" pattern between the number of immigrants and their educational level, illustrated in Figure 8. Among those workers in the US with only less than 8 years of education, about 70% were foreign born, and for those with 8-11 years of education, slightly more than 20% were foreign born. These two categories of high-school dropouts include many illegal immigrants and attract much attention in the US debate over immigration, even though they make up only 10% of US workers.

Figure 8: Share of Foreign-Born in US Workforce, 2004

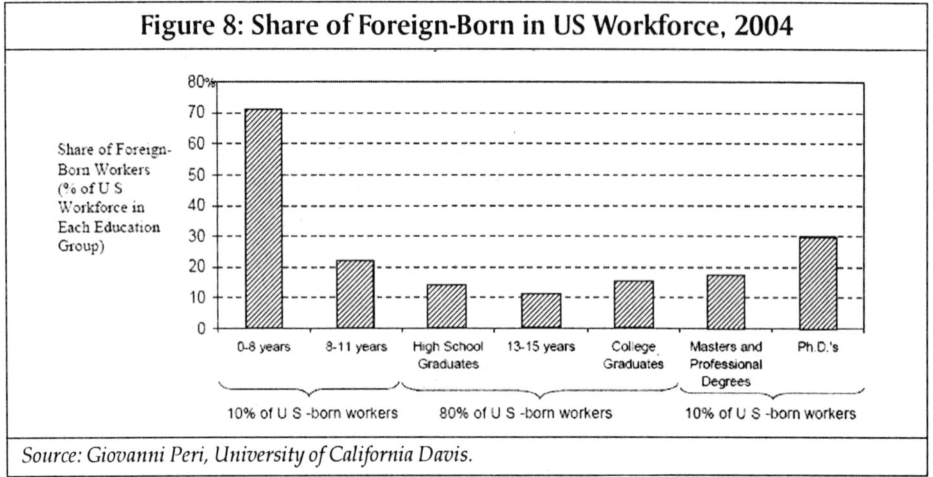

Source: Giovanni Peri, University of California Davis.

At the other end of the spectrum, another 10% of US workers have Masters degrees or Ph.D.'s, and in these categories the foreign born make up about 15-30% of the US workforce. In the middle educational levels, consisting of high school and college graduates and comprising 80% of the US labor force, foreign-born workers have much smaller shares. Figure 8 shows that immigrants into the United States compete primarily with workers at the lowest and highest ends of the educational levels, and much less with the majority of US-born workers with middlelevels of education.

Because of this pattern of immigration in the United States, the impact on wages is felt primarily at the lowest and highest educational levels, as shown in Table 5. Part A reports the estimated impact of immigration over 1990-2004 on the wages of various workers, distinguished by their educational level. The first row summarizes the estimates from a model where capital and land are kept fixed within all industries, which is the approach taken by George Borjas of Harvard University. In that case, immigration leads to a fall in wages of 9% for high-school dropouts and 5% for college graduates. But the impact on the wages of the majority of US workers (those with mid-levels of education) is much less: high-school graduates had wages reduced by 2.4%, and individuals with less than four years of college had wages reduced by less than 1%. The negative impact of immigration on wages is thus fairly modest for these workers.

Furthermore, the impact on wages is offset further when we recognize that capital can move between industries in the long run. Under this approach, we allow capital to grow in each industry to accommodate the inflow of immigrants, keeping fixed the rate of return on capital (Ottaviano and Peri, 2006). In the second row of Table 5, we see that total US immigration has a negative impact on only the lowest and highest-education workers, and a *positive* impact on the other workers (due to the growth in capital). So there is actually a complementary effect of immigration on the wage of US workers in the middle of the educational spectrum. The average US wage now rises by 0.3% due to immigration (combined with capital growth), rather than falling. In part B, I focus on the illegal immigration to the US, rather than total immigration, again keeping the real return to capital fixed. In this case, only the wages of the lowest-educated persons are negatively affected. All other workers gain from illegal immigration. We conclude that immigration has not had the negative impact on wages in the United States than what might be expected, and in fact, the growth in capital that is facilitated by the inflow of labor leads to an increase in the real wages for many workers.

Table 5: Immigration and Wages in the US

	Percentage Change in the Wage of Workers with Educational Level				
	Less than 12 years	**12 years**	**13-15 years**	**16 years or more**	**Overall average**
Part A: Effect of Total Immigration, 1990-2004					
Method:					
Capital and land fixed	–9.0%	–2.4%	–0.8%	–5.0%	–3.2%
Real return to capital fixed	–4.4	1.0	2.2	–0.2	0.3
Part B: Effect of Illegal Immigration, 1990-2004					
Method:					
Real return to capital fixed	–7.9	0.8	0.8	0.8	0.1

Source: Gianmarco I.P. Ottaviano and Giovanni Peri, "Rethinking gains from Immigration: Theory and evidence from the US" University of California Davis, January 2006.

7. Conclusion

To summarize my talk today, a comparison that is often made when thinking about the unification of markets within the European Union is to the 50 states within the United States, which of course have unrestricted movements of goods and labor. But with the entry of countries at quite different levels of development into the European Union, let me suggest that a better comparison is between the EU with the North

American market as a whole. While there are many differences between NAFTA and the EU, both regions now share a wide range of income and productivity levels across countries, that create both new opportunities for trade, as with outsourcing, but also challenges, as with immigration.

There is substantial evidence for North America that free trade has led to higher levels of productivity and real wages. That is especially true for Canada and the United State. So far, Mexico has not shared in productivity gains in manufacturing to the same extent as those with its neighbors to the north. So this is subject for ongoing investigation. At the same time, the chief concern when Mexico joined NAFTA was with the potential competitive effects in agriculture, and especially on corn, which is a staple crop for the rural poor in Mexico. Fortunately, it appears that competition from US exports of corn has had a much more modest effect than was expected (McMillan, Zwane and Ashraf, 2007). There are several reasons for this outcome. First, the poorest farmers are not sellers of corn, but instead consume it themselves while buying the extra that they need. So these farmers benefited from cheaper prices for corn imported from the United States. Second, the Mexican government was able to use subsidies to offset the reduction in income for other corn farmers. Surprisingly, the total production of corn in Mexico has actually risen after NAFTA instead of falling.

Even with these modest improvements in the agricultural sector in Mexico, the pressure for immigration to the United States remains very high. But there is little evidence to support the fear that such immigration leads to falling wages in the United States. On the contrary, once we recognize that industries can adjust their outputs and capital stocks, it turns out that immigration has a complementary effect on wages for many American workers. I hope that future generations of economists looking at the European Union will likewise find that the immigration has played a positive role, provided for higher incomes not only for the immigrants, but also for their new host countries. I congratulate the European Union on its continuing ability to absorb new members, thereby sharing the gains from trade with an ever widening group. It is a splendid example to the rest of the world of the benefits of free trade, as well as the willingness to work through the challenges involved.

(Robert C Feenstra, University of California, Davis and NBER).

References

Amiti, Mary and Shang-Jin Wei, (2005),"Service Offshoring, Productivity, and Employment: Evidence from the United States," IMF Working Paper 05/238.

Amiti, Mary and Shang-Jin Wei, (2006), "Service Offshoring and Productivity: Evidence from the United States," National Bureau of Economic Research working paper no. 11926.

Badinger, Harald, (2006), "Has the EU's Single Market Programme fostered competition? Testing for a decrease in markup ratios in EU industries," *Oxford Bulletin of Economics and Statistics*, forthcoming.

Berman, Eli, John Bound, and Zvi Griliches, (1994), "Changes in the Demand for Skilled Labor within US Manufacturing: Evidence from the Annual Survey of Manufactures", *Quarterly Journal of Economics,* 104, 367-398.

Bhagwati, Jagdish, (2004), *In Defense of Globalization,* Oxford University Press.

Bhagwati, Jagdish and Marvin H. Kosters, (eds.,) (1994), *Trade and Wages,* The AEI Press.

Broda, Christian and David E. Weinstein, (2006), "Globalization and the Gains from Variety," *Quarterly Journal of Economics,* May, 121(2), 541-585.

Card, David, (1990), "The Impact of the Mariel Boatlift on the Miami Labor Market," *Industrial Labor Relations Review,* Vol. 43, No. 2, January, p. 245-257.

Feenstra, Robert C., (1994), "New Product Varieties and the Measurement of International Prices," *American Economic Review*, 84(1), March, 157-177.

Feenstra, Robert C., (2006), "New Evidence on the Gains from Trade," *Review of World Economics/Weltwirtschaftliches Archiv,* December.

Feenstra, Robert C. and Gordon H. Hanson, (1996), "Foreign Investment, Outsourcing and Relative Wages," in R.C. Feenstra, G.M. Grossman and D.A. Irwin, eds., *The Political Economy of Trade Policy: Papers in Honor of Jagdish Bhagwati,* MIT Press, 89-127.

Feenstra, Robert C. and Gordon H. Hanson, (1999), "The Impact of Outsourcing and High-Technology Capital on Wages: Estimates for the US, 1979-1990," *Quarterly Journal of Economics,* August, 114(3), 907-940.

Feenstra, Robert C. and Gordon H. Hanson, (2003), "Global Production Sharing and Rising Inequality: A Survey of Trade and Wages," in Kwan Choi and James Harrigan, eds., *Handbook of International Trade,* Basil Blackwell, 2003, 146-187.

Grossman, Gene and Esteban Rossi-Hansberg, (2006), "Trading Tasks: A Simple Model of Outsourcing," National Bureau of Economic Research working paper no. 12721.

Hanson, Gordon H., (2007), "Globalization, Labor Income and Poverty in Mexico," in Ann Harrison, ed., *Globalization and Poverty*, University of Chicago Press, forthcoming.

Harris, Richard, (1984a), "Applied General Equilibrium Analysis of Small Open Economies with Scale Economies and Imperfect Competition," *American Economic Review*, 74(5), December, 1016-32.

Harris, Richard, (1984b), *Trade, Industrial Policy, and Canadian Manufacturing*. Toronto: Ontario Economic Council.

Hobijn, Bart, Federico Ravenna and Andrea Tombalotti, (2006), "Menu Costs at Work: Restaurant Prices and the Introduction of the Euro," *Quarterly Journal of Economics*, 121(3), August, 1103-1131.

Hufbauer, Gary C. and Jeffrey J. Schott, (2005), *NAFTA Revisited: Achievements and Challenges*, Institute for International Economics.

Katz, Lawrence F. and David Autor, (1999), "Changes in the Wage Structure and Earnings Inequality," in Orley Ashenfelter and David Card, eds., *Handbook of Labor Economics, Vol. 3A*, Amsterdam: Elsevier Science, 1463-1555.

Lawrence, Robert Z., and Matthew Slaughter, (1993), "International Trade and American Wages in the 1980s: Giant Sucking Sound or Small Hiccup?" *Brookings Papers on Economic Activity: Microeconomics*, 161-226.

Lewis, Ethan, 2004, "How did the Miami Labor Market Absorb the Mariel Immigrants?", Working Paper 04-3, Federal Reserve Bank of Philadelphia.

McMillan, Margaret, Alix Peterson Zwane, and Nava Ashraf, (2007), "My Policies or Yours: Does OECD Support for Agriculture Increase Poverty in Developing Countries?" in Ann Harrison, ed., *Globalization and Poverty*, University of Chicago Press, forthcoming.

Ottaviano, Gianmarco I.P. and Giovanni Peri, (2006), "Rethinking Gains from Immigration: Theory and Evidence from the US" University of California Davis.

Smith, Alasdair and Anthony J. Venables, 1988, "Completing the Internal Market in the European Community: Some Industry Simulations," *European Economic Review*, 32, 1501-1525.

Smith, Alasdair and Anthony J. Venables, (1991), "Economic Integration and Market Access," *European Economic Review, Papers and Proceedings*, 35, 388-395.

Trefler, Daniel, (2004), "The Long and Short of the Canada-US Free Trade Agreement," *American Economic Review*, 94(4), September, 870-895.

9

Economic Effects of Globalisation

Lessons from Trade Models*

Cristina Manteu

The theoretical models surveyed predict that globalisation is welfare improving for the countries involved in the long run. Welfare improving means that countries gain with globalisation in terms of the income of the average inhabitant. These welfare gains may arise from reallocating factors to their most productive use across industries, from providing consumers access to a broader range of product varieties than is available domestically and from aggregate industry productivity increases due to self-selection of the most efficient firms.

1. Introduction

Globalisation is a general term used to designate the growing process of international economic integration, covering the significant rise in trade of goods and services and increasing cross-border factor mobility. Globalisation is not a recent phenomenon

* The analyses, opinions and findings of this article represent the views of the author, they are not necessarily those of the Banco de Portugal.

Source: Economic Bulletin, Volume 14, Number 1, Page No # 71-90, Spring 2008 (www.bprotugal.pt) © Banco de Portugal, Departmento de Estudos EconÃ³micos. Reprinted with permission.

but intensified as of the early 1990s. In 1990-2005, the average growth of world trade of goods and services increased and continued to exceed world output growth. Trade openness has thus increased significantly both in advanced economies and in major emerging market economies (Chart 1). Financial openness also gained ground in these two groups of countries as of the early 1990s reflecting, to a large extent, the strong increase in world flows of foreign direct investment.

Chart 1: Trade and Financial Openness

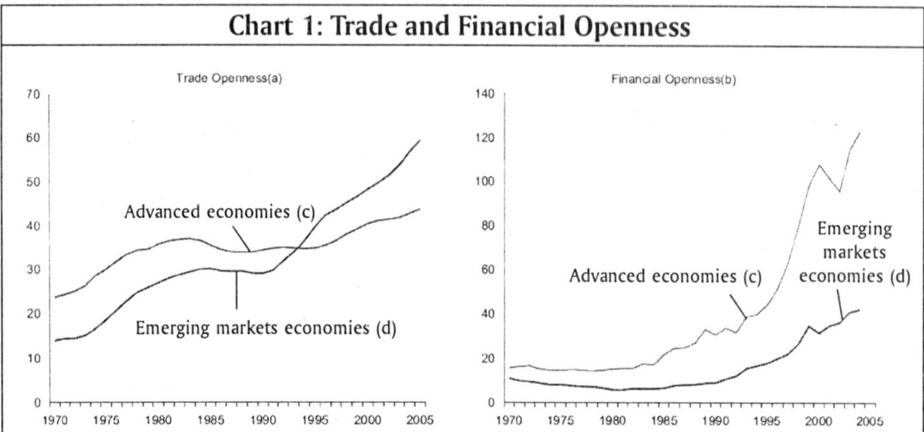

Notes: (a) Measured as the sum of exports and imports in percent of GDP (five-year moving average). (b) Measured as the sum of the stocks of external assets and liabilities of foreign direct investment and portfolio investment in percent of GDP. (c) Australia, Austria, Belgium, Canada, Denmark, Finland, France, Germany, Greece, Iceland, Ireland, Italy, Japan, Luxembourg, the Netherlands, Norway, Portugal, Spain, Sweden, Switzerland, the United Kingdom, and the United States. (d) Argentina, Brazil, Chile, China, Colombia, Czech Republic, Dominican Republic, Ecuador, Egypt, Hungary, India, Indonesia, Korea, Malaysia, Mexico, Peru, the Philippines, Poland, Romania, Russia, South Africa, Thailand, Turkey, and Venezuela.

Source: IMF World Economic Outlook (April 2006).

The increased pace of the globalisation process reflects a number of factors. First, it is the result of further advances in the liberalisation of world trade and capital movements and was made possible by technological progress that implied a significant decrease in transport, communication and co-ordination costs. Second, the acceleration in globalisation reflects the growing openness of developing and emerging market economies – in many cases in the wake of political and economic reforms – with special emphasis on large economies such as China and India and countries of Central and Eastern Europe. The group of developing and emerging market economies has been experiencing strong increases in both activity and international trade flows, which is mirrored in its rising economic relevance at global level. Finally, the emergence of these new economies with abundant labor supplies and the decrease in transport, communication and co-ordination costs has reinforced the trend towards the reorganisation of productive processes on a global basis with a view to reducing costs. In particular, the most recent period has seen an increase in transfers of industrial activities and business services from most advanced economies to countries with lower production costs. This transfer consists in contracting part of the productive process with foreign suppliers, covering the production of parts, components or semi-finished products, as well as services. Evidence of this growing geographical fragmentation of productive processes is given by the rising volume of trade of intermediate goods and business services as well as in the increase in foreign direct investment flows.

The rapid change of the global environment implied by these forces is expected to have a broad impact on both advanced and emerging market economies. Some of the questions that are frequently raised and which are at the basis of the policy debate include whether globalisation is welfare improving for the economies involved, how will potential benefits and costs materialize (and through which channels), how specialization patterns might be affected, how it might impact on the distribution of income within an economy and what can be done to facilitate adjustment.

The debate on the impact of globalisation is not always guided by sound economic theory (or based on systematic empirical evidence). However, international trade theory in particular should be able to provide well-informed answers to many of the questions raised. In this context, the aim of this article is to present a selective and non-analytical survey of the effects of globalisation for advanced economies that emerge from trade models. It can be seen mainly as a contribution to improve the quality of the globalisation debate. In reviewing the considerable research that trade economists have undertaken, we overlook some issues (e.g., imbalanced trade, as the models reviewed typically assume trade balance equilibrium[1]). Short term adjustment costs associated to the trade induced changes in specialization are also not a feature of the models surveyed. Changes in specialization require restructuring, i.e., economies must be able to move resources to alternative uses, which the models assume to take

1 For a recent reference incorporating imbalances into a quantitative model of trade flows, see Dekle, Eaton and Kortum (2007).

place instantaneously[2]. As the title of the article suggests, we also leave aside the issues raised by financial globalisation. Our main focus is on assessing the impact of the globalisation of trade, giving special emphasis to the consequences of integrating large labor abundant economies in the world trade system and of the growing international fragmentation of production. We are particularly interested on the effects of these developments on the welfare and income distribution of advanced economies.

The remainder of the article is organised as follows. In section 2, the expected impact of globalisation is analysed in the framework of textbook trade models, which include the Ricardian single factor model, the Hechscher-Ohlin-Samuelson two-factor model and the new trade models incorporating scale economies and monopolistic competition developed in the 80's. The focus of section 3 is on the findings of the more recent trade literature, namely the so-called "new new" trade models incorporating firm heterogeneity. Section 4 reviews the implications of models developed to account for a distinguished feature of the present globalisation process: the growing international fragmentation of production. Section 5 discusses some issues raised by globalisation regarding economic policy, in particular, for a small open economy. Section 6 summarizes the main findings.

2. Textbook Trade Models

According to international trade theory, countries engage in trade for two reasons: to take advantage of their differences and to benefit from economies of scale in production and product differentiation. In the first type of models, trade arises because countries can benefit from their differences by specializing in the production of goods that they are relatively efficient at producing, that is, in which they have a comparative advantage. The Ricardian model emphasizes technological (productivity) differences as the source of comparative advantage; the Heckscher-Ohlin-Samuelson model focuses on differences in factor endowments. The resulting trade is of the inter-industry kind, that is, trade in which a country's exports and imports come from different industries. In the second type of models, a combination of scale economies and consumer preferences for variety leads each country to specialize in

2 The models assume, for example, that all workers were employed before trade liberalisation and that following liberalisation all workers are automatically redeployed to other sectors or firms. However, in the real world, the transition will certainly take time and entail welfare losses associated to temporary unemployment due to wage rigidity or to costs incurred through job search, re-location and re-training. While transitory unemployment is not a fundamental argument against globalisation, it provides support to policy initiatives enhancing labor market flexibility and adaptability that may contribute to a rapid and efficient resource reallocation in the economy.

the production of only some varieties. The resulting trade is intra-industry, that is, it consists of two-way trade in similar products or varieties (countries' exports and imports are in the same industry). Both patterns of trade are present in the undergoing globalisation process. However, comparative advantage trade models appear more pertinent to evaluate the impact of the growing integration in the world trade system of emerging market economies which differ considerably from more advanced economies in terms of relative productivities and/or availability of factors of production.

2.1 Ricardo Model

The Ricardo model is the simplest trade model that can be used to answer the question of how advanced economies may benefit from increasing trade with low cost emerging market economies. First, it is important to note that large differences in wage rates between advanced and emerging market economies largely reflect differences in labor productivity. That is, wages in China and India are low because productivity there is also low[3]. Second, these wages and productivities are national averages. There is considerable variation across the various sectors/industries of the economies. These differences across sector productivities and across countries are precisely what gives rise to international trade according to comparative advantage and associated benefits.

In its simplest form, the Ricardo model assumes two countries, two goods and only one factor of production (usually labor), which is immobile between countries. Goods are produced at constant returns to scale and there is perfect competition. The main concept of Ricardo's model is comparative advantage. The principle of comparative advantage is just a matter of relative efficiency and it states that all countries can gain if each tends to specialize in the production of goods that they are relatively more efficient at producing. Even if one country has higher productivity in all sectors *vis-à-vis* another country – that is, the country has an absolute advantage in producing everything – it can be shown that the two countries can trade to their mutual advantage. The high productivity country specializes in producing goods where its advantage is relatively greater and the less productive country specializes in producing goods where its

[3] See Golub (1998) for evidence that international differences in unit labor costs are much smaller than differences in wages rates because large disparities in wages mostly reflect equally large differences in productivity.

production disadvantage is relatively smaller. In other words, each economy should specialize in the sector in which it has comparative advantage[4].

Trade specialization according to comparative advantage allows both countries' living standards to increase because the resulting world pattern of production is more efficient than if each country produced only for its own market. From trading according to comparative advantage, the residents in each country can import foreign goods at a lower relative price and export the home-produced goods at a higher relative price, creating an unambiguous increase in real income.

Given the simplicity of the Ricardian model it may be tempting to say that its implications may not be useful to describe the real world. However, the laws of comparative advantage have been shown to be valid in more general models (Deardorff (1980, 2005b)).

Another question that can be answered in the context of the Ricardo model is how the free trade equilibrium changes when the technological productivities available to one of the trading partners are altered. The question is pertinent given that some emerging market economies have been experiencing rapid productivity growth. The issue was raised in a paper by Samuelson (2004), which made the comparison between free trade and free trade with a trading partner experiencing technical progress in one sector. This author showed that the results were not clear cut. Rises in productivity due to technical change abroad may represent a benefit for both countries, but it can also benefit only one country while making the other worse off by reducing the potential gains from trade[5].

Consider the case in which one of the countries (the advanced economy) has an absolute advantage in the production of both goods and the other (the emerging market economy) experiences an increase in productivity in one of its sectors. The advanced economy will gain if the increase in productivity occurs in the production of the good in which the emerging market economy had a comparative advantage

4 More formally, assuming that production requires only labor in fixed amounts per unit of output (let a_{GC} be the amount of labor needed to produce one unit of good G in country C), then country A has a comparative advantage in producing good 1 if it can produce it with less labor relative to good 2, compared to country B. That is, $\frac{a_{1A}}{a_{1B}} < \frac{a_{2A}}{a_{2B}}$ Comparative advantage involves a double comparison, across both goods and countries. Hence, it is impossible by definition for a country to have a comparative disadvantage in every good.

5 Gomory and Baumol (2004) report similar findings in the context of a Ricardian model with scale economies.

(and which the advanced economy was already importing). The rationale is that the advanced economy was entirely dependent upon foreign supply of that good in the initial trading equilibrium, so that the improvement in foreign technology encourages more production, which must improve the terms of trade for the advanced economy. Increased income in the emerging market economy may also lead to greater demand for the advanced economy exportable good. The emerging market country suffers a loss in its terms of trade. If such a relative price change is sufficiently large so as to offset the initial favourable effects of the increase in the country's productive capacity, a reduction in its welfare levels may occur. This is the case of immiserizing growth[6] for the emerging market economy, although most would argue that both economies would benefit from such a productivity increase.

If the productivity improvement in the emerging market economy occurs in the good in which it had not so far a comparative advantage, the advanced economy might end losing but there is also the possibility that it gains[7]. In the example presented in Samuelson (2004), the productivity increase was assumed to be of a magnitude that eroded the economies' entire comparative advantage – that is, countries became identical in terms of relative productivities – so that there was no longer a reason to trade. In that case, the advanced economy was made worse off by growth in the emerging market economy because it loses the gains from international trade and its welfare is the same as in autarky. The emerging market economy is better off in this no trade position than it was in initial autarky, since it now has the benefit of its higher productivity. Although the case is theoretically interesting – it can be seen as a worst case scenario – one should not overstate its practical relevance in a world where international trade is growing at rates exceeding output growth rates. Moreover, it can be shown that productivity improvements abroad in the good the advanced economy initially exports may result in an actual gain for its residents if the alteration in productivities leads to a reversion of comparative advantage between the two countries (i.e., the advanced economy becomes an exporter of the good it previously imported). In sum, when faced with a productivity advance in the emerging market economy, the return to autarky would always imply a welfare loss for the advanced economy *vis-à-vis* the new free trade equilibrium, except in the extreme case considered by Samuelson, in which the two would be equivalent.

---

6 Bhagwati (1958) was the first to use the term immiserizing growth to designate growth that worsens the terms of trade sufficiently so that the country's real income falls.

7 Ruffin and Jones (2007) detail the conditions for the different outcomes, when analysing the international transfer of technology in a Ricardian model.

The discussion above serves to highlight that the terms of trade are highly relevant in assessing the welfare effects of globalisation. Note, however, that this indicator is also influenced by factors which may not relate directly to globalisation[8]. The evidence in Chart 2 seems to suggest that the intensification of globalisation and the rapid productivity growth experienced by emerging market economies have not been associated with a deterioration of advanced economies terms of trade. In fact, the terms of trade of this group of countries did not show major changes in the recent period, although this may hide some variation across economies. In particular, Chart 3 shows that while the terms of trade have remained virtually stable in the US, they have showed a slight decrease in the euro area. Japan did experience a more significant loss of terms of trade in the same period. A worsening of terms of trade was also observed in emerging market economies in Asia.

The questions that the Ricardian model can not be used to answer are the ones relating to the distribution of the gains from globalisation within the countries. Ricardo's is a representative agent model of the economy where everyone is the same, so that free trade must be welfare improving for all parties.

Chart 2: Terms of Trade in Goods and Services

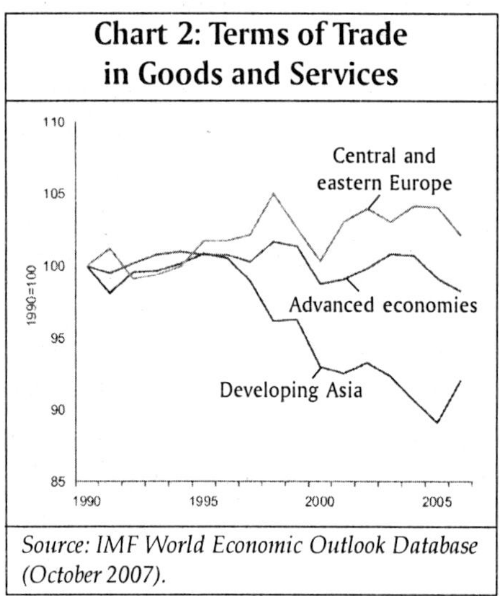

Source: IMF World Economic Outlook Database (October 2007).

Chart 3: Terms of Trade in Goods and Services

Sources: IMF World Economic Outlook Database (October 2007) and Thompson Datastream.

8 In recent years, there has been a rise in international prices of raw materials such as oil and metals, which may be indirectly associated to the intensification of globalisation. The increase in global production linked to globalisation implies an increase in the demand for raw materials which, given an inelastic supply, is likely to induce a rise in their relative price.

2.2 Heckscher-Ohlin-Samuelson Model

To think about potential issues concerning the distribution of the gains from globalisation within countries, the Heckscher-Ohlin-Samuelson (henceforth H-O-S) model is the one commonly used. This model explains why there may be winners and losers from globalisation within countries and exactly who they might be. The H-O-S model links specialisation and trade to differences between countries in the availability of factors of production such as capital and labor. Specifically, comparative advantage in this model results from differences in relative factor endowments across countries and differences in relative factor intensities across industries.

The H-O-S model in its original formulation considered two goods, two countries and two factors (labor and capital). The assumptions of the model consider identical countries except for relative factor endowments (that is, same preferences and technology). Both countries produce both goods and the production of both goods uses both factors, which move freely between sectors but not between countries. This model generates some important propositions.

The first is the Heckscher-Ohlin theorem that states that each country will specialize in and export the good whose production is relatively intensive in the factor in which the country is relatively more abundant. For illustrative purposes, let us assume that the advanced economy is capital-abundant and the emerging market economy is labor-abundant (abundance being defined in terms of the capital/labor ratio). Consider that the two goods are machinery and textiles, whose production is capital and labor intensive respectively (intensity depending on the ratio of capital to labor used in production). In the absence of trade, the relative price of machinery would be lower in the advanced economy than in the emerging market economy. Trade leads to a convergence of relative prices: the relative price of the machinery will rise in the advanced economy and decrease in the emerging market economy. In the advanced economy, that rise in the relative price of machinery will lead to an increase in the production of machinery and a decline in relative consumption, so that the advanced economy becomes an exporter of machinery and importer of textiles. The inverse takes place in the emerging market economy.

The second proposition emerging from the H-O-S model is the Stolper-Samuelson theorem that shows who wins and who loses when a country opens up to trade.

It states that when the relative price of a good falls, the real return to the factor used intensively in its production will fall. Thus, the answer is that the relatively abundant factor gains and the relatively scarce factor loses. If capital is the relatively abundant factor in the advanced economy, an opening of trade will lead the return on capital in that economy to rise more than proportionately compared to the price of either good, whereas the return on labor will fall relative to the price of either good. This is a very important result widely cited in the debate on globalisation and income inequality. Changes in relative prices in the H-O-S model have quite large effects on income distribution: a change in relative goods prices changes the distribution of income in a way that benefits the owners of one factor of production while harming the owners of the other.

Finally, the factor price equalization theorem postulates that international trade will bring the returns to factors closer together across countries, implying complete equalization in certain circumstances. The intuition is that trade in final goods essentially substitutes for movement of factors between countries to equalize differences in relative factor returns.

Although the results from the simple 2x2x2 H-O-S model are not easily generalised to models with higher dimensionality (more factors or more goods) or less strict assumptions, it can be shown that they may remain valid in a weaker form (Jones and Neary (1984))[9].

The available evidence tends to confirm the idea that capital/labor ratios are much lower in emerging market economies than in advanced economies (Chart 4)[10]. In addition, workers with high skill levels (using as a proxy those which attained tertiary education) have a larger weight in the labor force of advanced economies than on some of those emerging market economies (Chart 5). This evidence, and the Heckscher-Ohlin theorem, give support to the view that advanced economies will tend to have a comparative advantage in the production of capital and some skilled-labor intensive goods, whereas the comparative advantage of emerging market

9 Demonstrating that the H-O-S model holds empirically has been a difficult task (see Krugman and Obstfeld (2000) for an overview). Note, in particular, that complete factor price equalization is not evident in the data, which may reflect the fact that the some crucial assumptions needed to establish this result are not observed in the real world.

10 There are several problems involved in the measurement of factor endowments, in particular of capital stocks. While using alternative data sources and methodologies may result in figures differing from the ones presented in Chart 4, the qualitative assessment does not change.

Chart 4: Physical Capital/ Labor Ratios

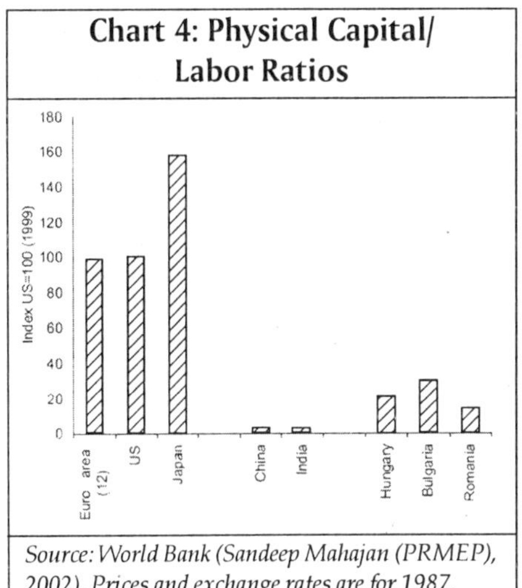

Source: World Bank (Sandeep Mahajan (PRMEP), 2002). Prices and exchange rates are for 1987.

Chart 5: Labor Force with Tertiary Education[a]

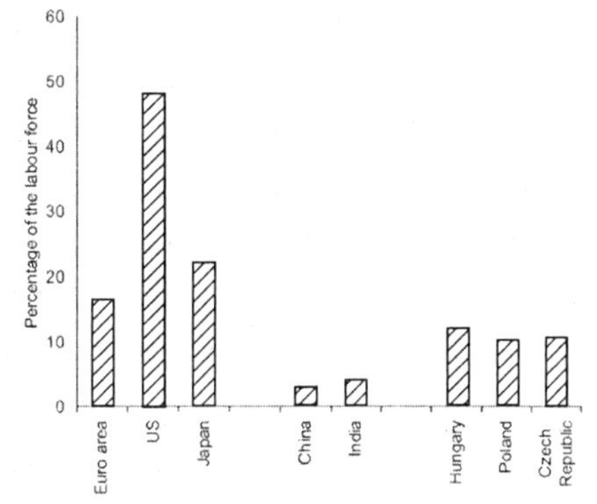

Percentage of the labour force: Euro area, US, Japan, China, India, Hungary, Poland, Czech Republic

Note: [a] Percentage of the labor force aged 15 and over that attained tertiary education in 2000.

Source: Barro, R. and J. Lee (2000), International Data on Educational Attainment: Updates and Implications.

economies is more likely to lie in the production of low-skilled labor-intensive goods. This may seem obvious, but as remarked by Rogoff (2005), "(...) even today, it is amazing how many people seem convinced that China (which, with 1.3 billion people, is clearly a labor rich country) is going to export everything to everybody as free trade opens up".

The Stolper-Samuelson theorem remains the central theoretical result guiding the understanding of the distributional effects of trade between countries with different factor endowments. According to this theorem, the increasing integration of labor abundant economies in the world economy is expected to put downward pressure on the returns to labor in advanced economies (in which it is the relative scarce factor). This implies that the share of national income received by labor – the labor share, which can be expressed as the ratio of labor compensation per worker to average worker productivity – in those economies should fall as trade flows with emerging market economies increases and the associated specialization progresses. The data shows that there has been a decline in the labor share since the early 1980s across the advanced economies (see Chart 6). Nonetheless, this evolution may reflect other factors besides globalisation.

The period under review was also characterized by significant changes in technology and labor market policies. Technological progress, especially in information and communication sectors, is expected to stimulate capital accumulation and to favour demand for skilled-labor over unskilled labor. Therefore, globalisation and capital augmenting technological change are expected to have analogous impacts on compensation and the labor share. The labor share may also be indirectly affected by labor market policies, as these may help or hinder the adjustment of the economy to globalisation and technological progress. Because of the complex ways in which these factors interact, it is empirically difficult to isolate their effects.

Chart 6: Labor Income Shares in Advanced Economies[a]

Notes: [a] Income share of labor estimates the share of labor compensation of employees and "nonemployees" in value added. [b] Advanced economies include Australia, Austria, Canada, Belgium, Denmark, Finland, France, Germany, Ireland, Italy, Japan, Netherlands, Norway, Portugal, Spain, Sweden, United Kinddom, United States; weighted using series on GDP in US dollars. [c] Europe includes Austria, Belgium, Denmark, Finland, France, Germany, Ireland, Italy, Netherlands, Norway, Portugal, Spain, Sweden

Source: IMF World Economic Outlook (April 2007).

Empirical work carried out by the IMF (2007) show that technological progress and, to a lesser extent, globalisation have contributed to the decrease in the labor share in advanced economies, whereas changes in labor market policies have generally had a smaller but positive impact on the labor share. These results are broadly consistent with findings reported in other recent studies (International Labor Office and the World Trade Organization (2007), Guscina (2007), Jaumotte and Tytell (2007), Ellis and Smith (2007))[11].

2.3 New Trade Models of Increasing Returns and Monopolistic Competition

Trade does not have to be the result of comparative advantage. Reciprocally beneficial trade can arise as a result of economies of scale and product differentiation. Increasing returns to scale make it advantageous for firms in each economy to specialize in producing only a limited range of differentiated products (or varieties), which enables a more efficient

11 There is also an extensive empirical literature linking wage inequality between skilled and unskilled workers to globalisation and technological progress, in particular for the US economy (see Slaughter (1998) for a survey). Most of these studies conclude that skill-biased technological change was a more important cause of wage inequality than international trade.

production. The countries then trade with each other in order to be able to consume the full range of products. This will be two-way trade within industries (that is, horizontal intra-industry trade), because firms in the two economies produce differentiated goods.

The new trade models introduced scale economies, product differentiation and utility functions including preference for variety and replaced the assumption of perfect competition on product markets with the one of monopolistic competition[12]. The seminal articles on this class of models were by Helpman (1981) and Krugman (1979, 1980, 1981). These models were to a large extent designed to explain why similar countries trade so much and why so much of their trade is intra-industry (as opposed to inter-industry trade driven by comparative advantage). For that reason, these models may be less pertinent to evaluate the impact of the current wave of globalisation which is characterized by particularly fast growth of trade flows between economies differing in their resources and production technologies. However, the process of convergence of per capita income of emerging market economies will likely be accompanied by a movement towards greater similarity of capital-labor ratios, skill levels, technology, etc., *vis-à-vis* advanced economies. This implies that trade between these groups of countries will gradually shift from inter-industry to intra-industry type and that the findings of the new trade models may acquire growing relevance.

How does the existence of intra-industry trade driven by scale economies and product differentiation change the conclusions reached in the previous sections concerning the effects of trade on the welfare and income distribution for advanced economies?

First, intra-industry trade produces supplementary gains, in addition to those arising from trade based on comparative advantage. By engaging in intra-industry trade, a country can at the same time reduce the number of goods it produces and increase the variety of goods available to domestic consumers. By producing fewer varieties, the country can produce each at larger scale, with higher productivity and

---

12 We will only refer to trade models of economies of scale internal to the firm (that is, the firm's average costs fall as its own output rises), which imply an imperfect competition market structure. External economies of scale, which occur when the unit cost depends instead on the size of the industry, can also be a cause of international trade. However, trade based on external economies of scale has more ambiguous effects on national welfare compared to trade based on internal economies of scale. For a general introduction to both types of models, see chapter 6 of Krugman and Obstfeld (2000).

lower costs (pro-competitive and scale effects). At the same time, consumers benefit from increased choice of differentiated products (variety effect)[13].

Second, the previous section's analysis of the distribution of the gains from trade demonstrated that trade would not benefit everyone, that is, trade in the H-O-S model induces changes in the income distribution within a country that are always enough to insure that the real income of the scarce factors of production diminishes. If, however, intra-industry trade is the dominant kind of trade, the extra gains from increased choice and scale economies are expected to outweigh any income-distribution effects and everyone may actually gain from trade (Krugman (1981)).

Hence, the impact of trade with emerging market economies on the income distribution of advanced economies depends on the determinants of that trade. If horizontal intra-industry trade gains increasing weight *vis-à-vis* inter-industry trade in the exchanges between these two groups of countries, the benefits from trade will tend to be more evenly shared among factors of production than would be the case if only the second type of trade was present.

3. "New New" Trade Models with Firm Heterogeneity

The trade models surveyed in the previous sections have in common the fact that they treat the sector as the unit of analysis, ignoring differences among firms belonging to the same sector. However, recent empirical evidence shows that differences among firms are crucial to understanding several stylized facts of world trade. For example, most firms do not export at all while exporting firms tend to export only a small fraction of their total sales and tend to be larger and more productive than other firms in the same industry[14]. Hence, the "new new" trade theory emerged, incorporating firm-level heterogeneity to account for some of these firm-level empirics (see Bernard, Eaton, Jensen and Kortum (2003) and Melitz (2003) for early theoretical papers in this literature; Bernard, Jensen, Redding and Schott (2007) for a recent survey).

---

13 Recent empirical work measuring the gains from variety has shown that these may be considerable. Broda and Weinstein (2006) estimated that the number of imported product varieties offered to the United States' consumer has been multiplied by a factor of four over the period 1971-2001, entailing a welfare gain for the United States economy corresponding to almost 3 per cent of GDP.

14 See Tybout (2003) for a survey. Bernard, Jensen, Redding and Schott (2007) and Mayer and Ottaviano (2007) present recent reports on this empirical evidence for the United States and European firms, respectively.

These models – which currently comprise a significant share of international trade research – have shown that firms' differences have important consequences for assessing the gains from trade and globalisation and their distribution across firms and factors of production. Above all, these models have identified an additional source of welfare gain from trade: the opening up of the country to international trade produces an aggregated productivity gain, driven by reallocations of market share and resources towards the more productive firms in each industry.

We will start by briefly reporting the implications of globalisation in the Melitz (2003) model[15], which incorporates firm level productivity differences into a model of intra-industry trade. The basic setting of the model considers that firms produce horizontally differentiated varieties within the industry under conditions of monopolistic competition. There is a group of prospective firms that can enter the industry by paying a fixed entry cost, which is thereafter sunk. These potential entrants face uncertainty concerning their productivity. After paying the entry cost, it is assumed that these firms draw their productivity level from a known distribution. This productivity remains fixed thereafter, but firms face a constant exogenous probability of a bad shock in every period that forces them to leave. The existence of fixed production costs implies that firms drawing a productivity level below some lower threshold (the "zero-profit productivity cut-off") face negative profits and therefore exit the industry immediately after entering and never produce. In addition, there are fixed and variable costs of exporting. The fixed costs of exporting will typically include costs of research into product compliance, distribution networks, advertising, etc. in foreign markets and, in most part, are sunk prior to entry in the export market. This means that, of the surviving firms in an industry, only the relatively more productive will decide to export. That is, there is self-selection of the most productive firms into the export market: only those who draw a productivity level above a higher threshold (the "export productivity cut-off") find it profitable to export in equilibrium. The remaining firms will only serve the domestic market.

Melitz (2003) shows that the impact of trade liberalisation in this type of model is to induce reallocations between firms, which in turn generate both aggregate productivity and welfare gains. In the model, trade has redistributive effects within

[15] The Melitz framework is particularly amenable to analysis and leads to predictions regarding the impact of trade liberalisation similar to the ones derived from the framework developed by Bernard, Eaton, Jensen and Kortum (2003), which introduced stochastic firm productivity into a multi-country Ricardian model.

industries, which operate through the domestic factor market where firms compete. Falling trade costs affect both the decisions about export market entry and industry exit. It offers new profit opportunities for the most productive firms that were selling only to the domestic market and can now sell to foreign markets as well (therefore reducing the "export productivity cut-off"). It also induces more entry as prospective firms react to the higher potential profits associated with a good productivity draw. Thus, labor demand within the industry rises, due both to expansion by existing exporters and to new firms beginning to export. This increase in labor demand bids up factor prices and reduces the profits of non-exporters (that is, it raises the "zero-profit productivity cut-off"). The reduction in profits in the domestic market induces the least productive firms to exit the industry. As these less productive firms exit and as output and employment are shifted to more productive firms, aggregate productivity rises.

The Melitz model ignores comparative advantage by considering just one factor and industry and as such can provide only limited answers regarding the impact of globalisation. However, Bernard, Redding and Schott (2007) have remedied this by introducing firm heterogeneity in the model of inter and intra-industry trade of Helpman and Krugman (1985). Their model combines factor endowment differences across countries, factor intensity differences across industries, and heterogeneous firms within industries and is able to simultaneously generate inter-industry trade (countries are net exporters in their industries of comparative advantage), intra-industry trade (even within an industry where a country is a net importer, two-way trade happens), and selection into export markets (within both net exporting and net importing sectors, some firms export while many others do not). This model yields richer results concerning the gains from globalisation and their distribution across sectors, firms and factors of production for a given economy.

First, as in single-industry models of heterogeneous firms, trade liberalisation is followed by compositional changes within industries, which increase aggregate productivity in all industries or sectors. However, in the model of Bernard, Redding and Schott (2007) these increases are stronger in the sector where the economy has comparative advantage. The idea is that the greater export opportunities in this sector lead to a larger increase in factor demand than in the comparative disadvantage sector, which bids up the relative price of the factor used intensively in the comparative advantage sector. This leads to greater exit by low-productivity firms and thereby larger rises in average productivity in this sector compared with the comparative disadvantage sector. These differential productivity gains give rise to differences in average sector productivity that magnifies comparative advantage based on factor abundance and provides a new source of welfare gains from trade.

Second, according to the model, trade liberalisation may have an impact on the distribution of income across factors that differ from the ones derived from more traditional models. While the Stolper-Samuelson effect still operates in this model, it is augmented with an additional effect. The opening of trade increases average industry productivity in both sectors and implies a decline in consumer prices for both goods, and so an increase in the real reward of both factors. This second effect contributes to increase the real return of relatively abundant factors while mitigating, or even potentially overturning, the decline of real returns of relatively scarce factors. If the productivity effect is sufficiently large, it becomes possible for both factors of production to gain from international trade.

Finally, the model by Bernard, Redding and Schott (2007) generates a more novel result, as it shows that trade liberalisation is associated to factor reallocation both within and across industries. In particular, although trade liberalisation generates net job creation in comparative advantage sectors and net job destruction in comparative disadvantage sectors, there is simultaneous job creation and job destruction in all sectors as low productivity firms exit and high productivity firms expand. This contrasts with the findings from more traditional models, in which there would be a simple flow of factors from comparative disadvantage sectors to comparative advantage sectors.

4. Models of International Fragmentation of Production

The models surveyed in previous sections assumed for simplicity that all the tasks involved in the production of a good or service were carried out within a country. However, the recent globalisation phase is not only characterized by rapid growth of international trade but also by a remarkable change in the nature of that trade, involving the rising international fragmentation of production, also referred to as offshoring, outsourcing, trade in tasks, global production sharing, vertical disintegration of production across borders, etc. All these terms have been used to designate the relocation of components of the production of some goods and services to other countries, creating an interconnectedness of production processes across countries, with each specializing in a particular stage of the good's production sequence and trading between them the partially processed good[16]. Baldwin (2006) called it "the second unbundling" in the globalisation process: in his view, the first unbundling corresponded to the spatial separation of factories and consumers, while the second unbundling, characterizing the recent globalisation phase, spatially separates the factories and offices themselves. During the first unbundling, countries produced basically complete products that they consumed and traded with other nations. However, the tasks comprising the production of the goods had to be performed in close proximity due to high transport, communication and monitoring costs. The second unbundling results from a sharp reduction in these costs, which facilitates direct trade in tasks and generates global production networks for several goods and services.

The growing share of parts and components in world trade is an indication of the increase in the international fragmentation of manufacturing production. Jones *et al.*,, (2005) reviews empirical work documenting this trend. Yeats (1998) finds that trade in parts and components has grown much faster than trade in final goods and estimates that it could account for 30 per cent of world trade in manufactures in 1995. Recent advances in information technology have implied that trade integration has also progressed quickly in services. Amiti and Wei (2005) report that outsourcing of services has increased considerably, but remaining at relatively low levels compared with manufacturing outsourcing.

How does the possibility of dividing a productive activity into parts that can now be done in different locations alter the conclusions of the previous sections regarding the impact of globalisation? The answer is that while trade models incorporating international fragmentation of production do not change the basic message about the overall benefits of free trade, they nevertheless may change the views on the sharing of these gains among the different factors of production.

International fragmentation of production can be modelled as if it were just like trade in new goods (intermediate goods). Contributions on this line of research include, among several others, Arndt (1997), Venables (1999), Deardorff (2001, 2005a), Bagwati *et al.,* (2004) and Markusen (2005), besides Jones and Kierzkowski (1990),

16 This can be accomplished by the firm opening a subsidiary in a foreign country or by contracting with a foreign supplier under an outsourcing arrangement. A branch of trade literature has examined which organisational form is preferable in different circumstances (e.g., Grossman and Helpman (2005), Helpman (2006)).

the most common cited reference in this area[17]. This branch of literature presents a set of alternative conceptual frameworks, by adapting the trade models surveyed in section 2 to allow for the breakdown of the production process of a good into sub-processes that can be undertaken in different locations. The main conclusion from these studies is that outsourcing/offshoring leads to the usual gains from trade with the standard caveats applicable to conventional trade. The idea is that breaking down the integrated production process into separate stages opens up new possibilities for exploiting gains from specialization and trade[18]. The main caveat results from the possibility of an adverse movement in the terms of trade, specifically that the beneficial impact of the introduction of outsourcing may give rise to sufficiently strong adverse terms of trade effect that offsets the former. Regarding income-distribution effects, this literature does not offer general conclusions as the impact of offshoring on factor rewards depends upon many variables. In some cases, the scarce factor is made worse off by the possibility of offshoring, but it is also possible to find situations in which all factors are better off after the change. While this line of research has produced interesting insights, it can be viewed as a collection of special cases: the results depend heavily on the assumptions and it is not possible to draw general principles from the analysis.

Hence, Grossman and Rossi-Hansberg (2006a,b) have alternatively proposed a more general model of offshoring, which they boldly called a new paradigm. They developed a model of trade in tasks – defined as the individual steps involved in the production process – as compared to the usual approach of modelling just trade in goods. In their model, the production process in each sector – one exportable and one import competing – involves a continuum of tasks to be performed by each of the factors of production (unskilled labor, skilled labor or others, like capital). As in the H-O-S model, it is assumed that the two goods differ in their factor intensities and that the country exports the good that makes intensive use of its relatively abundant factor.

The tasks can be performed abroad or domestically. Offshoring tasks might entail savings in factor costs but also imply costs. Some tasks are moved abroad more easily than others. The cost of offshoring a task may reflect how much routine it incorporates,

17 See Baldwin and Robert-Nicoud (2007) for a brief survey of these works.

18 Offshoring some parcels of production allows Ricardo's logic of trade according to comparative advantage to be applied separately to each of those individual parcels of production.

how important it is that the task be delivered personally, how difficult it is to transmit or transport the output of the activity, etc. While the model recognises these differences, it assumes that the costs of offshoring the various tasks are exogenous.

The model can be used to study the impact of task trade or offshoring on factor prices. In the papers, these factor prices are the wages of skilled and unskilled labor, as it is assumed that the relevant tasks are performed by these two types of labor but the results could be re-interpreted in terms of the returns to labor and capital. It is also assumed that when there is a reduction in the cost of offshoring tasks requiring a given skill level, this reduction is proportional across both sectors of the economy. This insures that when, for example, unskilled labor-intensive tasks are offshored then they are offshored by the two sectors. The model allows decomposing the effect on wages of this cost reduction for offshoring tasks into three components.

The first is the relative price effect. Improved possibilities for offshoring some tasks provide different incentives for the two sectors to expand, which changes the composition of output. If the offshoring country is a large one, this would create imbalances in world markets at the initial prices and so the relative price of goods will have to adjust. This change in relative prices has implications for factor returns that are familiar from the H-O-S model (Stolper-Samuelson theorem).

The second is the labor supply effect. The increasing offshoring of some tasks imply that the demand for workers performing those tasks at home is reduced, which, other things constant, imply that their wage would have to fall to maintain full employment[19].

Finally, the authors identify a productivity effect that benefits the factor performing the kind of tasks that are moving offshore. This effect seems to have been largely unnoticed in the previous literature. When the tasks performed by a certain type of labor can be transferred abroad, the firms that use this type of labor intensively in their production processes are the ones that gain the most in cost savings[20].

19 This effect did not appear in the H-O-S model with incomplete specialization of section 2.2 (in that model, factor growth can be accommodated by a change in the composition of output in each country, without any impact on factor prices). However, in other trading environments, in which the number of the country's factors of production exceeded the number of tradable goods that it produces, factor prices do respond to factor supplies.

20 Firms' costs fall for two reasons. First, firms choose to offshore new tasks that were previously performed at home. Second, firms save on inframarginal tasks that were already performed abroad before the drop in the cost of offshoring. This second effect is the most important. The idea is that the information and technology revolution changes the ability to perform entire ranges of tasks.

Thus, these firms experience the greatest increase in profitability which induces them to expand relative to firms that use intensively other types of labor. Expansion of these firms leads to a net increase in demand for the type of labor which was used in the offshored tasks. Thus, the real wage for that type of labor rises, other things constant. Grossman and Rossi-Hansberg derived the name for the effect by drawing an analogy between falling costs of offshoring tasks and factor-augmenting technological progress: both reduce the cost of using a factor and the amount of local factor needed to produce a given amount of output, both benefit firms that use the factor intensively, both create incentives for these firms to expand and the expansion of these firms can lead to a net increase in demand for factor whose productivity has increased.

The authors show how the productivity effect can prevail over the other two effects in well-known trade environments. When this happens, reductions in the costs associated to offshoring imply an actual rise in the real wages of the domestic workers that have skill levels similar to those used in performing the tasks that are being offshored. Thus, in contrast to the distributional conflict that results from reductions in the cost of trading goods in traditional trade frameworks like the H-O-S model, reductions in the cost of trading tasks may generate gains for all domestic factors[21].

In the framework developed by Grossman and Rossi-Hansberg, adjustments to globalisation occur at the task rather than the sector level, that is, the tasks chosen to be offshored may be undertaken in a wide range of sectors (e.g. data-entry tasks in all sectors). The model also highlights that not all tasks requiring a given skill level can be transferred abroad, i.e., there is a weak relationship between the tasks being offshored and the level of labor skill required to perform them[22].

5. A Small Open Economy: Some Policy Issues

The results from the models surveyed in the previous sections apply directly to a small open economy, such as Portugal. The models show that, in the long run,

21 Grossman and Rossi-Hansberg report some rough evidence that productivity gains associated to offshoring of tasks performed by low skilled-labor have contributed to sustain wages for that type of workers in the United States. However, the available empirical evidence on the productivity effects of offshoring is mixed (see Olsen (2006)).

22 Blinder (2006) empirically documents this less than perfect relationship by referring to the cases of typing services (a low-skill job) and security analysis (a high-skill job), both of which are examples of services already being offshored to low cost countries. In contrast, there are the cases of services of taxi drivers and airline pilots. Neither can be offshored, but the first is a job with negligible educational requirements and the second is quite the reverse. He also mentions that most physicians need not fear that their jobs will be moved offshore, while radiologists are already seeing that happen.

participating economies may gain from the intensification of the globalisation process. One source of those gains is the change of patterns of comparative advantage, which implies restructuring and reallocation of productive factors. Those changes in comparative advantage patterns may be particularly significant for countries like Portugal – with relatively low levels of human capital and technological development compared with other advanced economies – thus requiring policy actions to improve the economy's adjustment capacity.

The benefits from globalisation do not come automatically. The restructuring process associated with globalisation implies that firms must be able to reallocate resources rapidly to take advantage of new opportunities and potential income gains and to minimise adjustment costs. The velocity of the adjustment matters, as a rapid adjustment would minimize the losses from having resources locked into inefficient uses in the transition period.

In this context, globalisation may well have increased the importance of economic policy. In particular, the realisation of the full net benefits of globalisation requires the establishment of a suitable institutional framework that facilitates the needed changes and minimizes the adjustment costs. As referred by Rodrick (2007), there is a wide consensus supporting the idea that trade openness alone is unlikely to lead to economic growth in the absence of a wide range of complementary institutional and governance reforms.

Globalisation may require government responses on many levels to reduce the related adjustment costs. The duration of the adjustment period and the magnitude of the adverse effects on employment are linked to the flexibility of the labor market, i.e., how easily labor can move from declining to advancing sectors. Therefore, the promotion of a set of policies in the labor market to ensure flexibility is essential to facilitate a rapid resource reallocation, especially in countries such as Portugal where several rigidity factors still hamper an efficient functioning of the labor market. Initiatives aimed at improving the sectoral and occupational mobility of labor – in particular by investing in human capital, including worker retraining – are also important. These will ultimately enhance the adaptability of the economy to change, whether driven by globalisation or by other perhaps even more important factors like skill biased technology shocks. Policies and regulations promoting product market flexibility and competition also contribute to the efficient use of available productive factors, their adequate sectoral allocation and the incentive to adopt new productive processes. Finally, sustained investments in research and innovation, in particular by the private sector, are also required to take advantage of the opportunities created by the increasing integration of markets, given the ongoing changes in comparative advantages at the global level.

6. Conclusion

The theoretical models surveyed predict that globalisation is welfare improving for the countries involved in the long run. What is meant by welfare improving is that countries gain with globalisation in terms of the income of the average inhabitant. These welfare gains may arise from reallocating factors to their most productive use across industries, from providing consumers access to a broader range of product varieties than is available domestically and from aggregate industry productivity increases due to self-selection of the most efficient firms[23].

However, the benefits of globalisation are obtained by relocating resources. This restructuring is likely to be associated with distributional impacts, both in the short term, as a consequence of adjustment costs, and in the long term, as a result of permanent changes in relative factor demands (Rodrick (1998)). Therefore, globalisation implies efficiency gains but also costly dislocations and potentially distributional consequences.

Based on the more traditional trade models, e.g., the H-O-S model, the reshuffling process triggered by globalisation is expected to take place mainly across sectors. According to these models, each country would have a set of identifiable exporting sectors and import-competing sectors. Increasing trade would imply that exporting sectors would expand production and their demand for labor, while import competing sectors would reduce production and possibly lay-off workers. For advanced economies, it was expected that labor-intensive sectors would shrink, while skill and/or capital intensive sectors would expand. Jobs would therefore be destroyed in labor-intensive sectors and capital employed in those sectors would have to be re-employed. Regarding the distributional consequences of globalisation, the traditional result based on the

23 These aggregate productivity increases may also result from self-selection within firms, in a general equilibrium model of international trade with multi-product firms which are heterogeneous in both firm-specific ability and firm-product-specific expertise (Bernard, Reddding and Schott (2006)). Following trade liberalisation, there is reallocation of resources across firms (as firms with low overall productivity exit) and within firms (as surviving firms drop their marginally productive products).

Stolper-Samuelson theorem was that it would negatively affect the returns to the relatively scarce factor – labor or unskilled labor – in the advanced economies.

The more recent theoretical literature shows that the adjustment to globalisation and its impact on the income distribution may be more complex and nuanced. Regarding the adjustment processes, the recent trade models with firm heterogeneity predict that significant resource reallocation may also take place within sectors and not only between sectors. These models incorporate mechanisms according to which globalisation encourages the expansion of high-productivity firms and the closing down of less efficient firms in all sectors, that is, in both net-exporting and net-importing sectors. The recent task trade model by Grossman and Rossi-Hansberg also suggests that job destruction and creation associated to offshoring need not take place according to a well established sectoral pattern or specific skill level. Regarding the distributional effects of trade, the prediction of the Stolper-Samuelson theorem is mitigated in the more recent trade models. In the models of scale economies and product differentiation, in the "new new" trade models with firm heterogeneity and in the model of task trade, there is the possibility that globalisation may generate gains for all production factors.

Acknowledgments

The author thanks I Abreu, N Alves, J Amador, S Cabral, M Centeno, R Duarte, C Leal, L Opromolla and J Sousa for their comments and suggestions.

(Cristina Manteu, Economics and Research Department, Banco de Portugal.)

References

Amiti, M. and S. Wei (2005), "Fear of Service Outsourcing: Is It Justified?", *Economic Policy*, Vol. 20 (April), pp. 308–47.

Arndt, S. (1997), "Globalisation and the open economy", *The North American Journal of Economics and Finance*, 8 (1), pp. 71-79.

Baldwin, R. (2006), *Globalisation: the Great Unbundling(s)*, paper for the Finnish Prime Minister Office, Economic Council of Finland as part of EU Presidency.

Baldwin, R. and F. Robert-Nicoud (2007), "Offshoring: General equilibrium effects on wages, production and trade", March 2007, NBER *Working Paper* N. 12991.

Bhagwati, J. (1958), "Immiserizing Growth: A Geometrical Note", *The Review of Economic Studies*, Vol. 25, N. 3., pp. 201-205.

Bhagwati, J., A. Panagariya and T.N. Srinivasan (2004), "The Muddles over Outsourcing", *The Journal of Economic Perspectives*, Vol. 18, N. 4, Fall 2004, pp. 93-114(22).

Bernard, A., J. Eaton, J. B. Jensen and S. Kortum (2003), "Plants and Productivity in International Trade", *American Economic Review*, 93(4), pp.1268-1290.

Bernard, A., J. B. Jensen, S. Redding and P. Schott (2007), "Firms in International Trade", *Journal of Economic Perspectives*, Vol. 21, N. 3, Summer 2007, pp.105-130.

Bernard, A., S. Redding and P. Schott (2006), "Multi-product firms and trade liberalisation", NBER *Working Paper* No. 12782.

Bernard, A., S. Redding and P. Schott (2007), "Comparative Advantage and Heterogeneous Firms", *Review of Economic Studies*, 74 (1), pp. 31–66.

Blinder, A.S. (2006), "Offshoring: The Next Industrial Revolution?" *Foreign Affairs*, 85:2, pp. 113-128.

Broda, C. and D.E. Weinstein (2006), "Globalisation and the Gains from Variety", *Quarterly Journal of Economics*, May, 121(2), pp. 541-585.

Deardorff, A. (1980). "The General Validity of the Law of Comparative Advantage", *Journal of Political Economy* 88 (October), pp. 941-57.

Deardorff, A. (2001), "Fragmentation in Simple Trade Models," *North American Journal of Economics and Finance*, 12: 2, pp. 121-137.

Deardoff, A. (2005a), "A Trade Theorist's Take on Skilled-Labor Outsourcing", *International Review of Economics & Finance*, Volume 14, Issue 3, 2005, pp. 259-271.

Deardoff, A. (2005b), "How robust is comparative advantage?", *Review of International Economics*, Volume 13, Number 5, November 2005, pp. 1004-1016(13).

Dekle, R., J. Eaton and S. Kortum (2007), "Unbalanced Trade", NBER *Working Paper* No. 13035.

Ellis, L. and K. Smith (2007), "The global upward trend in the profit share", BIS *Working Papers* No. 231, July 2007.

Golub, S. (1998), "Does Trade with Low-Wage Countries Hurt American Workers?", *Federal Reserve Bank of Philadelphia Business Review* March/April 1998.

Gomory, R. and W.J. Baumol (2004), "Globalisation: Prospect, Promise and Problems", *Journal of Policy Modeling*, Vol. 26, Issue 4, June 2004, pp. 425-438.

Grossman, G. and E. Helpman (2005), "Outsourcing in a Global Economy", *Review of Economic Studies*, 72:1, pp. 135-159.

Grossman, G. and E. Rossi-Hansberg (2006a), "The Rise of Offshoring: It's Not Wine for Cloth Anymore", paper presented at Federal Reserve Bank of Kansas City symposium,

The New Economic Geography: Effects and Policy Implications, Jackson Hole, Wyoming, August 24–26. Available via the Internet: *http://www.kc.frb.org/PUBLICAT/SYMPOS/2006/PDF/Grossmanand-Rossi-Hansberg.paper.0831.pdf*

Grossman, G. and E. Rossi-Hansberg (2006b), "Trading Tasks: A Simple Theory of Offshoring", NBER *Working Paper* No. 12721.

Guscina, A. (2006), "Effects of Globalisation on Labor's Share in National Income", IMF *Working Paper* 06/294 (Washington: International Monetary Fund).

Helpman, E. (1981), "International Trade in the Presence of Product Differentiation, Economies of Scale, and Monopolistic Competition: A Chamberlin-Heckscher-Ohlin Approach", *Journal of International Economics*, 11, pp. 305-340.

Helpman, E. (2006), "Trade, FDI, and the Organization of Firms", *Journal of Economic Literature*, Vol. 44, N. 3, September 2006, pp. 589-630.

Helpman, E. and P.Krugman (1985), *Market Structure and Foreign Trade*, Brighton: Harvester Press.

International Labor Office and World Trade Organization (2007), *Trade and Employment: Challenges for Policy Research*, (Geneva: World Trade Organization).

IMF (2007), "The Globalisation of Labor", *World Economic Outlook* – April 2007, Chapter 5.

Jaumotte, F. and I. Tytell (2007), "How Has The Globalisation of Labor Affected the Labor Share in Advanced Countries?", IMF *Working Paper* 07/298 (Washington: International Monetary Fund).

Jones, R. and H. Kierzkowski (1990), "The Role of Services in Production and International Trade: A Theoretical Framework," in Ronald Jones and Anne Krueger, eds., *The Political Economy of International Trade*, Basil Blackwell, Oxford.

Jones, R., H. Kierzkowski and C. Lurong (2005), "What does the evidence tell us about fragmentation and outsourcing?", *International Review of Economics and Finance*, 14 (3), pp. 305-316.

Jones, R. and Neary, P. (1984), "The Positive Theory of International Trade" in *Handbook of International Economics*, ed. R. W. Jones and P. Kenen, Volume 1, Chapter 1, North-Holland.

Krugman, P. (1979), "Increasing Returns, Monopolistic Competition and International Trade", *Journal of International Economics* 9, pp. 469-479.

Krugman, P. (1980), "Scale Economies, product differentiation and the Pattern of Trade", *The American Economic Review*, Vol.70, N.5, pp.950-959.

Krugman, P. (1981), "Intraindustry Specialisation and the Gains from Trade", *Journal of Political Economy*, Vol.89, N.5, pp. 959-973.

Krugman, P. and M. Obstfeld (2000), *International Economics – Theory and Policy*, 5th edition, Publisher: Addison Wesley.

Markusen, J. (2005), "Modeling the Offshoring of White-Collar Services: From Comparative Advantage to the New Theories of Trade and FDI", Prepared for the Brookings Forum, *Offshoring White-Collar Work: The Issues and Implications*, May 12-13, 2005.

Mayer, T. and G. Ottaviano (2007), "The Happy Few: The Internationalisation of European Firms", *Bruegel Blueprint Series* Volume III, November 2007.

Melitz, M. (2003), "The Impact of Trade on Intra-Industry Reallocations and Aggregate Industry Productivity", *Econometrica*, 71 (6), pp. 1695-1725.

Olsen, K. (2006), "Productivity Impacts of Offshoring and Outsourcing: A Review", OECD *Science, Technology and Industry Working Paper* No. 2006/1.

Rodrick, D. (1998), "Symposium on Globalisation in Perspective: An Introduction", *The Journal of Economic Perspectives*, Vol.12, N°4. (Autumn, 1998), pp. 3-8.

Rodrick, D. (2007), "How to save globalisation from its cheerleaders", CEPR *Discussion Paper* 6494.

Rogoff, K. (2005), *Paul Samuelson's Contributions to International Economics*, Prepared for volume in honor of Paul Samuelson's 90th birthday, edited by Michael Szenberg.

Ruffin, R. and Jones, R. (2007), "International Technology Transfer: Who Gains and Who Loses?", *Review of International Economics*, Volume 15, Number 2, May 2007, 209-222.

Samuelson, P. (2004), "Where Ricardo and Mill Rebut and Confirm Arguments of Mainstream Economists Supporting Globalisation", *Journal of Economic Perspectives*, Volume 18, Number 3, summer 2004, pp. 135-146.

Slaughter, M. J. (1998), "International Trade and Labor-Market Outcomes: Results, Questions, and Policy Options", *The Economic Journal* 108, pp. 1452-1462.

Tybout, J. (2003), "Plant- and Firm-Level Evidence on the "New" Trade Theories" In *Handbook of International Trade*, (ed.) E. K. Choi and J. Harrigan, Chapter 13, Oxford: Basil Blackwell.

Venables, A.J. (1999), "Fragmentation and multinational production", *European Economic Review* 43 (1999), pp. 935-945.

Yeats, A. J. (1998), "Just How Big is Global Production Sharing?", World Bank *Policy Research Working Paper* No. 1871.

10

International Migration, Economic Development and Brain Drain

Issues and Evidence

Abhilas Kumar Pradhan

Integration of national economies with the world economy has increased the economic interdependence among nations and consequently increased global welfare. At the same time, globalization has further boosted outflow of scarce professional skills from many developing and poor nations to affluent countries. The socioeconomic implications in the long run for the developing and poor nations resulting from international migration are highly debatable. This article discusses various issues and statistical findings related to international migration. It also discusses the policy measures that are to be initiated both at the government and corporate level to keep international migration at a socially acceptable level.

Source: Global CEO, January 2008. *© The Icfai University Press. All rights reserved.* *This article also appeared in the book "Globalization, Economic Development and Brain Drain" published by the Icfai University Press.*

Brain Drain or drain of social capital may be referred to as outflow of scarce professional skills such as doctors, engineers, nurses and technical talents, etc., from poor and developing nations to developed countries. The concept of brain drain migration gained popularity in the 1960s, when a number of poor countries across the globe lost skilled manpower.[1] Over the period 1990 to 2002, international migration has exceeded more than 40 millions.[2] Currently, the migrants across the globe account for approximately 2.5% of the world population.[3] There is a burgeoning concern about the long-term socioeconomic consequences that would result from international migration of technically qualified persons from the developing countries to the rich nations. In the recent years, integration of national economies with the world economy has further expanded the scope of emigration of skilled professionals from developing countries. The positive aspect of international migration is that, the migrant workforces send remittance income to their home country and secondly, international migrations partly ease out the unemployment and underemployment problems in the labor surplus developing countries. These are the beneficial aspects of international migration.

However, these benefits are received at the expense of certain costs, both social as well as economic; whose long-term effect might have serious repercussions on the sending nation's economy. The migration mechanism may be analyzed in terms of the 'push-pull' model.[4] Push factors drive people to leave home and pull factors attract migrants to a new location in search of better job opportunities and different lifestyle. The major driving forces that stimulate international migration are the high real wage differentials and the low cost of migration. The net social and economic effects on both the sending and receiving countries resulting from international migration are still questionable. In this backdrop, the article discusses some issues and evidence related to international migration.

Costs and Benefits in the Sending and Receiving Countries

Table 1 discusses the cost and benefit aspects of the sending and receiving countries as a result of international migration.

Table 1: Costs and Benefits		
	Sending Countries	**Receiving Countries**
Costs	• Loss of skilled professionals (Brain Drain). • Loss of training investments on the emigrating professionals. • Loss of consumption and tax receipts. • Decline in morale and commitment among remaining workers.	• Recruitment costs. • Resettlement costs. • Decline in compensation and working conditions of domestic workers. • Decline in morale and commitment among domestic workers. • Reduction in tax receipts from domestic workers.
Benefits	• Remittance received from expatriates. • Improvement in skills of returnees.	• Relief of supply shortages. • Tax receipts from foreign workers. • Enhanced local competitiveness. • Efficiency Gain.
Source: www.focus-migration.de/uploads/tx_wilpubdb/PB07_Health.pdf		

How do Rich Countries Benefit

Rich nations being capital abundant and labor scarce, suffer from acute shortage of human capital. Apart from this, these economies also create millions of jobs that the domestic workers refuse to fill; whereas migrant workers would prefer those jobs up.[5] Due to rapid economic expansion and supply shortages, developed nations are in quest of potential workforce outside their national boundaries to sustain their business, economic and social activities. For a given level of skill, migrant workforce would be willing to serve at a relatively low salary, perks and working condition as compared to their counterparts in the receiving countries. The host nations also don't have to make training investments on the migrant workforce as they are already trained from the public exchequer of the developing or poor nations. Similarly, outsourcing of business and economic activities to the developing countries proves to be highly cost-effective for the developed nations. For example, German car manufacturers may produce vehicle engines and components in their home country, with assembly work being carried out in Malaysia.[6] The huge difference in per unit labor cost across countries is the major factor that has contributed to job offshoring by developed nations. Table 2 provides a comparative analysis of the hourly wage rates in the US and India across different occupational category for a given standard of services.

Table 2: Hourly Wage Rates for Selected Occupations, US and India, 2002-03

Occupation	Hourly Wage, US (in $)	Hourly Wage, India (in $)
Telephone Operator	12.57	Under 1.00
Health Record Technologist/ Medical Transcriptionist	13.17	1.50-2.00
Payroll Clerk	15.17	1.50-2.00
Legal Assistant	17.86	6.00-8.00
Accountant	23.35	6.00-15.00
Financial Researcher/Analyst	33.00-35.00	6.00-15.00

Source: www.u21global.com/PartnerAdmin

Similarly, developed nations are also benefited substantially in terms of human capital inflow. If we analyze the percentage of Indian technical persons to the total technical talents working in the US economy, the figure seems to be quite substantial. Table 3 provides the statistics on migrant talents in the US economy in various fields.

Table 3: Indian Faculty in the US Science and Engineering Fields, 1997

	Total S & E* in US	Indian origin	% of Indians to	
			Total	Foreign
Total Science and Engineering	224,707	6,876	3.1	15.3
Physical Sciences	37,020	688	1.9	9.3
Life Sciences	53,055	1,014	1.9	13.4
Math. and Comp. sciences	44,375	2,086	4.7	18.3
Social Sciences	65,509	1,491	2.3	15.5
Engineering	24,748	1,597	6.5	17.8

* S & E: Scientists and Engineers

Source: www.wider.unu.edu/publications/rps/rps2004/rp2004-062.pdf

Migration, Remittance and Economic Development

The inflows of remittance income to the developing countries make significant contribution to their national economies. Remittance income adds to the foreign exchange reserves in the developing nations, which can be used for international payment and import of critical items.[7] At the household level, remittance income has a significant impact on the standard of living as well as availing better education and healthcare facilities for the migrants' family members and other dependents, staying in the home country.[8] Apart from this, in a tight domestic labor market, out migration could have a favorable impact on the local wage rates as well.[9]

Remittance Income

Table 4 provides a list of remittance income (in $) to major remittance recipients countries in the year 2004.

Table 4: Remittance Income

Country	Remittances in 2004 (in $ bn)
India	23
Mexico	17
Philippines	8.1
China	4.6
Pakistan	4.1
Morocco	3.6
Bangladesh	3.4
Colombia	3.1
Egypt	3.0
Brazil	2.8
Lebanon	2.7
ElSalvador	2.5
Dominican Republic	2.3

Source: www.u21global.com

Brain Drain

The dark side of international migration is the loss of skilled professionals from the sending nations. If international migration is of permanent nature, it can stifle economic growth in the poor and developing countries. Table 5 provides the statistics for the level of educational attainment and migration flows in the OECD countries from different developing nations.

Determinants of International Migration

This section discusses the major determinants or the driving forces behind migration of technical talents.

High Wage Differentials between the Sending and Receiving Nations

The real wage differential between the sending and receiving countries for a given skill level is the crucial motivational factor behind the international migration. The salaries, perks, general working conditions, educational prospects for children and lifestyle in western countries are beyond comparison of what developing countries are offering for the same standard of jobs. For example, a doctor in Sri Lanka is paid Rs.45,000 and their counterpart in Australia is paid Rs.1,500,000.[10] Similarly, Philippines nurses employed in the US earn 20 times higher than what they could earn in their home country.[11] Besides the compensation part they also enjoy a relatively higher social status for certain job category as compared to the status in their home countries. The Figure (Schematic representation of migration mechanism) explains the basic migration mechanism.

Table 5: Number of Immigrants (Age 25 and Older) to the OECD by Level of Educational Attainment, 2000

Country	Total Immigrants	Educational Level		
		Primary or Less	Secondary	Tertiar
East Asia				
China, PR	722,400	148,029	185,295	389,076
Indonesia	142,450	3,910	32,347	106,283
Philippines	356,134	27,604	70,079	258,451
Eastern Europe, Central Asia				
Turkey	1,913,782	263,078	534,429	1,116,275
Latin America, Caribbean				
Brazil	176,519	16,026	64,097	96,396
Jamaica	117,119	9,483	54,647	53,069
Middle East, North Africa				
Morocco	560,658	30,706	168,179	361,773
Tunisia	142,828	10,027	41,782	91,019
Egypt	20,373	733	3,796	15,844
South Asia				
Bangladesh	44,417	3,852	12,902	27,663
India	375,283	18,471	57,199	299,613
Pakistan	85,668	6,022	22,458	57,188
Sri Lanka	64,143	1,455	16,741	45,947
Total	4,721,944	539,396	1,263,951	2,918,597

Source: www.u21global.com

Low Cost of Migration

Apart from the real wage differentials the cost of migration is also another determinant behind international migration. Rise in the per capita income levels of the developing nations, decrease in transportation (air and shipping) cost, and low cost of searching for a job (information cost) have made international migration highly feasible.

Figure: Schematic Representation of Migration Mechanism

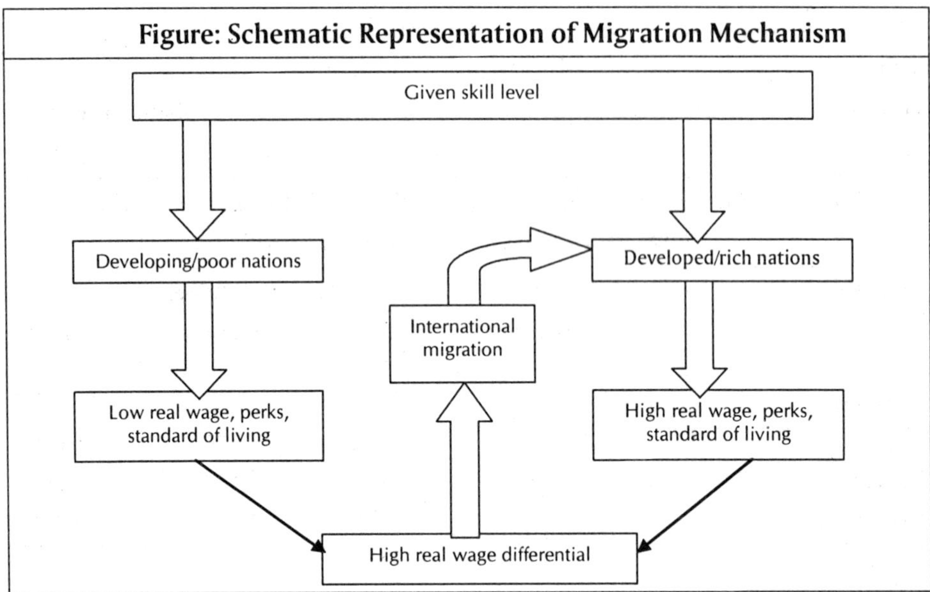

Labor Demand

Almost all developed nations have found that they need migrant labors, apart from their domestic workforce. A part of the demand arises to support the rapid economic expansion as well as to sustain business activities and the other arises from a pure economics point of view (cost-effectiveness). There are certain jobs that the domestic workers would be unwilling to take up but the migrant labors would accept the same at a relatively low salary.

Network Effects

Family, friends, relatives and ethnic/national networks provide a strong support system for migrants who help them obtain information about jobs and other relevant national characteristics of the host nation.[12]

Immigration Policy

Immigration policies in both the sending and host countries serve as a crucial factor for international migration.

Conclusion

International labor migration is an integral part of the globalization process and economic interdependence among nations. Undoubtedly, it is beneficial both for the receiving and sending countries as it helps them in the process of their economic growth and development.

For the host countries it fills the supply shortages and for the sending nations it eases out the unemployment pressure as well as serves as a potential source of finance in the form of substantial remittance income. On the flip side, concerns are growing about the damaged one to the Less Developed Countries by permanent emigration of skilled professionals or the so-called 'Brain Drain'. Therefore, suitable policy measures and adequate incentive systems must be devised to keep migration at a socially desirable level.

As a policy measure, developing nations should encourage short-term rather than permanent migration. A proper mechanism should be developed for retention of the skilled professionals as well as encouraging return migration of the technically qualified persons who are working for rich economies. The developing and the poor nations revise their existing migration policies. Not only policy initiatives are to be taken at the government level, but the corporate world has to also play a major role in curbing out migration of talents from the developing nations. With the explosive growth of various sectors in recent years, it is not a tough job to retain the technically qualified workers through a proper incentive mechanism.

Both retention and return migration of talents are possible if the salaries, perks and benefits in real terms are at par with their counterparts in the developed nations. The corporate world has the ability to meet these challenges and in the process may save the developing nations from future 'Brain Drain'.

(Abhilas Kumar Pradhan, Faculty Member, The Icfai Business School, Pune. The author can be reached at abhilas_p@ibsindia.org).

Endnotes

1 *www.queensu.ca/samp/transform/cohen1.html*

2 *www.globalization101.org/uploads/File/Migration/migrall.pdf*

3 Ibid.

4 *www.globalization101.org/uploads/File/Migration/migrall.pdf*

5 Ibid.

6 *www.u21global.com/PartnerAdmin/ViewContent?module=DOCUMENTLIBRARY&oid=157296*

7 *www.wider.unu.edu/publications/rps/rps2004/rp2004-062.pdf*

8 Ibid.

9 Ibid.

10 *www.searo.who.int/LinkFiles/Regional_Health_Forum_Volume_10_No_1_05 Migration_of_Health_Workforce.pdf.*

11 Ibid.

12 *www.ilo.org/public/english/bureau/integration/download/publicat/4_3_290_wcsdg-wp-37.pdf*

11

Globalization and American Wages
Today and Tomorrow

L Josh Bivens

A common argument in the globalization debate grants the point that trade theory argues that American workers have something to fear from global integration but minimizes the empirical relevance of globalization's costs. By now, all serious people concede that the United States has seen a sharp increase in inequality over the past 25 years.

The continuing integration of the rich United States with a far poorer global economy has provoked much anxiety among American workers. Because it is well-known that basic economic theory predicts that global integration leads to gains for all nations, this anxiety is often treated as a political puzzle. A once again fashionable explanation for this puzzle is that globalization's benefits are huge but diffuse (primarily, lower prices for imported goods), while its costs are small but concentrated (workers displaced by imports); hence, the gains are hard to see, but the losses are all too visible[1].

This Briefing Paper reexamines what conventional economics *actually* predicts about the effects of integrating the rich United States and poor global economies.

Source: EPI Briefing Paper # 196, October 10, 2007 (www.epi.org). © Economic Policy Institute. Reprinted with permission.

Contrary to popular rhetoric, there is no puzzle to be explained: conventional economic theory argues that American workers will indeed be harmed by this integration—and their anxiety is well-founded.

The paper also provides rough empirical estimates of integration's effect on American wages and inequality. Lastly, it uses some prominent forecasts about the future potential reach of service-sector offshoring to make a very rough guess as to the future wage implications of these forecasts.

The key findings indicate:

- In 2006, the impact of trade flows increased the inequality of earnings by roughly 7%, with the resulting loss to a representative household (two earners making the median wage and working the average amount of (household) hours each year) reaching more than $2,000. This amount rivals the entire annual federal income tax bill paid by this household.
- Over the next 10-20 years, *if* some prominent forecasts of the reach of service-sector offshoring hold true, and, *if* current patterns of trade roughly characterize this offshoring, *then* globalization could essentially erase all wage gains made since 1979 by workers without a four-year college degree.

What Economic Theory Actually Teaches about Globalization and Wages

When people argue that economics teaches that liberalizing trade is a "win-win" proposition, what they mean (whether they know it or not) is that trade is "win-win" between countries. The great insight of *comparative advantage*, the cornerstone of international economics, is that even when one country can produce *everything* more cheaply than its trading partners, trade still provides benefits to both nations.

An important caveat, however, notes that even as globalization raises national income, it can still reduce the incomes of *most workers*. Global integration has at least two potential impacts on American wages. First, workers employed in industries directly in competition with low-cost imports from abroad can expect to see immediate job dislocation and/or downward wage pressures. Second, as relative prices change across industries, the return to factors of production, including different kinds of labor inputs, can be expected to change as well. A simple example can capture the essential insights of this second impact (which is almost surely the less intuitive one).

Start with a couple of assumptions about the US economy. Say that the labor force of the US can be divided into *workers* (those who supply labor) and *professionals* (those who also supply additional skills, capital, and credentials). Assume further that there are just two sectors in the US economy, call them apparel and aircraft. Workers and professionals can work in either sector. If this sounds unrealistic, remember that this is a story about what matters over a reasonably long period of time. While people obviously do not lose an apparel job on Monday and begin working at Boeing on Tuesday, in the relatively fluid American economy, people do switch across many economic sectors throughout their working lives.

Lastly, assume that producing each \$1 of apparel takes a *ratio* of workers to professionals twice as high as producing each \$1 of aircraft—that is, apparel is the more *labor-intensive* business.

Now, say that falling trade costs (a tariff cut for example) reduces the price of apparel imports. Since domestic producers must compete with imports, this means that the price of *domestically produced* apparel falls as well. Fewer domestic producers are then willing to make apparel, as falling prices make this a less attractive business. Imports rise to replace this lost domestic production. Lastly, and importantly, aircraft exports rise as domestic investment once ploughed into apparel looks for new opportunities and as US trading partners' greater specialization in apparel leads them to demand more aircraft from the US.

As domestic apparel production contracts, too many workers are displaced to be absorbed in the expanding aircraft sector *at the going wage for workers.* Remember that the ratio of workers to professionals was higher in the apparel sector, so each \$1 of apparel production abandoned releases "too many" workers relative to professionals to be absorbed by a \$1 increase in aircraft production. Even after absorbing *all* of the professionals released from the declining apparel sector, there will still be many former apparel workers not finding work in the aircraft sector *at the going wage.*

If these unemployed workers want a job, they must agree to a wage cut. Further, it is not just the *unemployed* labor that takes a wage cut—*it is all workers economy-wide.*

Any incumbent worker in either aircraft or apparel not agreeing to this wage cut would be replaced with those unemployed workers. The process works in reverse for professionals, with the apparel sector not shedding *enough* of them at the going professional wage in order to meet the demands of the expanding aircraft sector. This imbalance bids up professional wages.

Essentially, by changing the structure of what an economy produces, globalization changes the relative demand for different kinds of labor, skill, and capital. In the example above, globalization pushed the domestic economy into demanding fewer workers and more professionals by tilting the structure of domestic production away from labor-intensive apparel and towards professional-intensive aircraft.

The most well-known outcome of this process is that the *gross gains* for professionals outweigh the *gross losses* of workers, hence the national economy sees *net* gains from trade[2]. It is these net gains (which are much smaller than either the gross gains or gross losses) that constitute the argument in favor of global integration. However, it is (obviously) the gross losses that worry many workers about globalization, and this fear is *utterly rational* in light of economic theory[3].

It should be noted that the (slim) majority of US imports come from countries that are not that much poorer than the United States. This sort of trade (call it rich/rich trade) is not necessarily inequality-inducing in the way described above. However, a significant (and the fastest growing) portion of US trade is with nations that are significantly poorer than the United States, and as such, the scenario sketched out above is (and should be) a real and growing concern to US workers.

Wage Cuts Without Tariff Cuts?

While it is easiest to explain in terms of falling trade costs, one can get similar wage results even without a change in trade costs. Using the previous example, if the prices of apparel and aircraft are flexible, an increase in the quantity of the factor (say labor) intensively used in a given sector (say apparel) will lead to a declining price for that sector's output. This sparks an adjustment in the wages of workers and managers, driving down workers' wages as before[4].

This idea was initially developed for a closed economy, but one can look at it as a prediction of what will happen when labor-abundant nations (such as China and India) are integrated into the world economy, increasing the global labor pool. In this case, theory predicts that the price

Contd...

Contd...

of labor-intensive commodities will fall as a result of the increase in the global labor pool, and these falling prices will harm labor in professional-abundant nations like the United States.

To test the reasonableness of this, think of the price of DVD players, apparel, and the price of call center operations and whether or not the expansion of the global labor pool has reduced their prices. Given these price reductions, resources in the United States will move out of producing these commodities and into the production of professional-intensive goods. This move sets off the chain of causation described above, leading to a fall in labor's wage and a rise in professional wages. Hence, wage adjustments occur *even without changing trade costs*—labor earnings in the United States fall resulting from the integration of labor-abundant economies into the global trading regime. This is surely one of the more intuitive aspects of the economics of globalization.

Globalization's Real Costs: Not Just Unemployment or Adjustment

Some readers may think these results are obvious. Nobody, for example, denies that, say, US steel workers displaced by import competition face hardship from trade. These costs, however, are often thought to be small and manageable with temporary government assistance.

This is, however, a radical understating of globalization's costs. Note that the above example did not take into account the *adjustment cost* of workers' unemployment spell between jobs. These adjustment costs are, of course, real and should be of concern to policy makers, but they are not the first-order costs of globalization to American workers[5].

Rather, the losses identified above are *permanent* wage-loss suffered by labor in this simple economy. Empirical studies in the trade and wages debate have generally used *production* and *non-supervisory labor* as a proxy for labor in the United States, and *non-production* and *supervisory* labor as a proxy for professionals. Occasionally, workers with a 4-year college degree stand in for professionals, with the rest of the workforce standing in for labor.

Production workers constitute roughly 75% of the entire US workforce, and workers without a four-year college degree constitute roughly 70% of this workforce. Hence, while gross *gains* may exceed gross *losses* in the US as global integration proceeds, it is not necessarily the case that *winners* outnumber *losers*. Global integration, in short, has the potential to inflict *permanent* harm to *most* American workers, and, as later sections of this paper demonstrate, the scale of this harm is much larger than commonly realized.

This basic axiom of economic theory is all too often ignored, or, even actively hidden. For example, Bradford, Greico, and Hufbauer (2005), in what they bill as a comprehensive accounting of the gains and losses attributable to trade liberalization, count only the costs of *direct displacement by imports* as a debit in the balance sheet of globalization, and do not even acknowledge the possibility of permanent wage losses through a broader labor market. Failing to count the largest cost of globalization is, of course, an excellent way to make the cost/benefit analysis of integration come out well to those favoring the *status quo*.

The Impact of Globalization on Today's Wages...

During the trade and wages debate of the early 1990s (see text box on page 174 for more on this), Krugman (1995) used a simple *computable general equilibrium* (or, CGE) model to examine the issue of international trade and wage inequality. CGE models are a series of equations that capture the economic relationships between and within nations. They can be incredibly complex, consisting of hundreds of equations and needing substantial computing power to solve, or they can be quite simple, representing what Krugman (1995) calls "glorified back of the envelope estimates."

This section uses the Krugman (1995) model to get exactly such a "back of the envelope" estimate of how much offshoring has impacted American wages and inequality to date, and how it could possibly impact it in the future. The mechanics and assumptions behind the model are described more fully in Bivens (2007).

The essential features, however, can be described as follows and follow directly from the example above. The United States is assumed to be abundant in professionals offering specialized skills, capital, and credentials relative to the rest of the world, but relatively deficient in labor. The US consequently exports goods that are professional-intensive and imports goods that are labor-intensive. As labor-intensive industries are shed and replaced with professional-intensive industries in the US economy, the relative demand for labor falls, while the relative demand for professionals rises, leading to greater inequality.

The relevant parameter for assessing the US labor market impacts of globalization is the volume of trade conducted with lower-wage trading partners (know in the jargon as less-developed countries, or LDCs for short). This paper uses the average of imports and exports from non-OECD countries (as OECD countries are generally rich, and trade with them will not necessarily follow the predicted patterns regarding the labor-intensity of imports and exports that drives the inequality-inducing effects of trade), non-OPEC countries (as oil is not generally thought to compete with US production), and Turkey and Mexico (the two poorest OECD nations) for this parameter.

Table 1 presents the results. The first row shows this LDC import-share expressed as a percentage of GDP for 1995 and 2006. The second row shows the resulting outcome on relative wages from the Krugman (1995) CGE model[6].

Table 1: Results – Past and Present

	1995	*2006*
LDC Share (data input)	3.5%	4.9%
Relative Wage Change (CGE output)	4.8%	6.9%
Absolute Change in:		
Raw labor	-2.8%	-4.0%
Skills	2.0%	2.9%
Change in representative household income	-$1,325	-$2,135
Annual federal income tax, middle quintile	$2,603	$1,495

Source: author's calculations as described in the text. Trade shares as a percentage of gross domestic product are derived from data obtained from the United States International Trade Commission (USITC) and the Bureau of Economic Analysis (BEA). Data on tax rates for middle-income households are from the congressional budget office. Data on income of prototypical households derived from Mishel, Bernstein, and Allegretto (2006).

The third and fourth rows translate these changes in *relative* wages into the absolute change in earnings implied by these results in each year. Again, the mechanics behind this translation are described in some detail in Bivens (2007). The fifth row looks at the results from the perspective of a representative household consisting of a married couple each earning the median wage and working the average hours for married-couple households. Taking the average hours worked for this representative family type, globalization would have cost them over $1,000 annually by 1995. By 2006, the costs from globalization for this representative household have risen to more than $2,000.

The last row of the table suggests an alternative benchmark for deciding whether or not these losses from globalization are "large" or "small": the average federal income tax payment for families in the middle quintile of the income distribution.

The 1990s Trade and Wages Debate

A common argument in the globalization debate grants the point that trade theory argues that American workers have something to fear from global integration but minimizes the *empirical* relevance of globalization's costs. By now, all serious people concede that the United States has seen a sharp increase in inequality over the past 25 years; the *de minimus* argument scales the impact of trade against this wider march toward a less-equal economy.

In the early 1990s a flurry of studies addressed this issue. The resulting estimates are spread widely, but most indicated that trade could account for roughly 10-40% of the total rise in inequality that occurred in the 1980s and early 1990s. The observation that "most" of the rise in inequality was generated by factors other than trade was often emphasized to allay anxieties about globalization. This is true but uncomforting; a significant minority of a very large number is a large number. (To put it another way, if threw myself into a chasm that was "only" a fifth as deep as the grand canyon, I'd still be dead.)

Further, findings from this first round of the trade and wages debate are now a decade old, yet are still often invoked in contemporary debates. Academic interest in the topic essentially waned after 1995 as wages for all workers began rising; a tight labor market trumped all other influences. However, this does not mean that trade stopped dragging on some workers' wages. There are lots of determinants of wage growth, and just because the net outcome of them all is positive does not mean that all are benign. In fact, as soon as the momentum from the red-hot labor market of the late 1990s dissipated, wage growth decelerated and then turned negative. This begs another question that can be answered with a model from the earlier round of the trade and wages debate: *how much has trade dragged on wages in the very recent past?*

By 2006, the costs of globalization rival those from taxation for this group. One imagines that none of these households consider federal income taxes a trivial cost (although they are much smaller for this group than commonly realized, as payroll and other taxes constitute the major taxes paid by families in the middle of the income distribution). Politicians make a lot of hay about income taxes, but these taxes purchase something useful for middle-income households: "civilization," as Oliver Wendell Holmes memorably said. The globalization tax largely buys higher incomes for the already better-off.

It should be noted that the original Krugman (1995) results were often presented as an argument for the relatively benign impact of trade flows on American wages, as they were on the low-end of results in the first round of the trade and wages debate. A disaggregated (and much more computationally complex) version of this model was used by Cline (1997), who found that trade's wage impacts were almost four times as great as the Krugman (1995) results[7].

...And the Potential Impact on Tomorrow's Wages?

An interesting, though still speculative issue concerns the issue of service-sector offshoring and the future of globalization's impact on American wages. The ability of US companies to import work that was traditionally considered untradeable (call center operations, software programming, and various business process services) has led to anxieties over job security spreading to a much wider swath of the American workforce. The rise of service-sector offshoring essentially gives globalization a much larger lever with which to impact US labor markets. Put simply, if offshoring doubles the number of workers who are employed in industries that are now tradeable, then it will (at least roughly) double the impact globalization has on American labor markets.

In the next section of this paper, the same model used to examine globalization's past and present impact on inequality is fed forecasts of offshoring's future reach to assess its potential impacts on American inequality and wages. (See Offshoring: Raising the Ceiling on p.177 for more on why economists think offshoring is big news.)

Forecasts of Offshoring's Reach

Obviously, nobody knows for sure what will happen in the future. However, a number of economic researchers and observers have made forecasts as to the number of jobs that could be potentially "up for grabs" in the future, as technology, policy, and the introduction of billions of workers from China, India, and the former Eastern Bloc countries into the capitalist global economy make more jobs internationally contestable, particularly through service-sector offshoring.

The estimate with perhaps the best pedigree comes from Alan Blinder, Princeton professor and member of the Council of Economic Advisors under President Clinton. Blinder wrote in a now-famous *Foreign Affairs* article that offshoring's impact could mean that "two to three times" as many jobs could be internationally contestable as are presently in the manufacturing sector (which supplies the vast majority of contestable jobs today). In a follow-up piece with substantially more data-crunching behind it, Blinder scaled back his original estimate, rating 22-29% of the US workforce as *potentially offshorable* over roughly the next one or two decades.

Table 2 compares many of these forecasts of offshoring's potential reach (including Blinder's) and also provides a rough baseline of the number of jobs potentially tradeable *today*.

Table 3 presents results from plugging these forecasts into the same model used previously to glean the impact on the relative earnings of labor and skills. Plugging in the highest estimate of offshoring's future reach (from Jensen and Kletzer (2005)) leads to trade flows increasing the returns to professionals *vis-à-vis* labor by 25% over the coming decades. The low-end estimate, from McKinsey Global Institute (2004), yields an impact of just under 12%. Results from using the Blinder forecast essentially splits the difference, with trade flows leading to a 17% increase in relative earnings.

An increase in relative earnings of 17% is, it should be noted, an amount equal to (roughly) half of the *total* increase in the inequality of wage incomes between college graduates and all other workers that occurred between 1979 and 2006. Offshoring, in short, has the potential to wedge apart incomes to a huge degree in a short time.

Table 2: Jobs Currently Offshorable and Forecasts for the Coming Decade

	Offshorable Jobs	**Trade Share**	**LDC Trade Share**
Current	14,500	14.2%	4.9%
Forecast for Newly Offshorable Jobs by:	**(New) Offshorable Jobs *(thousands)***	**Implied Trade Share**	**Implied LDC Share**
Forrester Research	20,000	29.8%	10.9%
Bardhan and Kroll (2004)	14,850	25.4	9.3
Kletzer+ and Jensen + (2005)	36,800	44.4	16.2
McKinsey Global Institute (2005)	12,029	22.9	8.4
Van Welsum and Vickery (2005)	18,100	28.2	10.3
Blinder (2006)	21,275	30.9	11.3
Average	**20,509**	**30.2**	**11.0**

Sourrce: Author's calculations as described in the text. Trade shares as a percentage of gross domestic product are derived from data obtained from the United States International Trade Commission (USITC) and the Bbureau of Economic Aanalysis (BEA). Data on tax rates for middle-income households are from the Congressional Budget Office. Data on income of representative households derived from Mmishel, B Bernstein, and Allegretto (2006).

Table 3: Offshoring's Projected Impact on the Returns to Raw Labor and Skills			
	Ratio	*Labor*	*Skills*
High (Jensen/Kletzer)	25.0%	15.0%	10.0%
Low (MGI)	12.0%	-7.0%	5.0%
Blinder	17.0%	-10.1%	6.9%
Average	**16.0%**	**-9.4%**	**6.6%**

Sourrce: Author's calculations as described in the text. Trade shares as a percentage of gross domestic product are derived from data obtained from the United States International Trade Commission (USITC) and the Bbureau of Economic Aanalysis (BEA). Data on tax rates for middle-income households are from the Congressional Budget Office. Data on income of representative households derived from Mmishel, B Bernstein, and Allegretto (2006).

Table 3 also translates these relative income results into *absolute* values for changes in earnings of labor and skills. It is, again, a fundamental finding of trade theory that a country's "scarce" factor of production (labor in the United States) loses in *absolute*, not just relative terms, as trade expands.

Offshoring: Raising the Ceiling

While past and present rounds of the trade and wages debate reached no firm consensus on the precise contribution of trade to rising inequality, there was widespread agreement that trade's impact had a natural ceiling: the (relatively) low share of US. workers employed in tradeable industries[8].

"In 1993, roughly 15 percent of American workers were employed in manufacturing. The vast majority of unskilled workers were employed producing nontraded goods, such as retail trade and various services. In such a world, it is hard to see how pressures on wages emanating from traded goods can determine wages economy-wide." (Freeman 1995)

"In particular, imports of manufactured goods from developing countries are still only about 2 percent of the combined GDP of the OECD. The conventional wisdom is that trade flows of this limited magnitude cannot explain the very large changes in relative factor prices that have occurred..." (Krugman 1995)

"...when the large portion of the economy that is nontradeable and the limits of international specialization imposed by home orientation in consumption and production are taken into account, there is much more limited scope for trade to affect relative factor prices." (Cline 1997)

As these words were written roughly a decade ago, substantially fewer than 15% of American workers could be plausibly identified as being in direct competition with workers around the globe. This was still enough to have allowed trade to put downward pressure on some workers' wages, but it did mean that there was a natural ceiling on this impact.

The average of the forecasts indicates that the future reach of offshoring will lead to an absolute decline of 9.4% in the returns to labor and a 6.6% increase in the return to skills. To put this into some historical perspective, earnings for workers without a college degree rose by just 2.2% between 1979 and 2005. It took the full-employment boom of the late 1990s to finally push these earnings (in 2001) above the 1979 level. The implied loss due to offshoring would push these wages well below the 1979 levels, completely undoing (and then some) the entire increase in these wages over the past three decades.

Conclusion

These calculations allow us to go one step further and provide a measure of the magnitude of compensation that would be needed to alleviate the harm done by globalization. In debates over trade and globalization, the trade adjustment assistance (TAA) program is often mentioned as a way to compensate globalization's victims in the United States. In 2006 TAA allocated $655 million in income supports for workers harmed by globalization, and, another $200 million for training. A key weakness of this program is that it only aids workers for a limited period of time; mainstream trade theory, conversely, teaches that the harm done by trade to incomes is *permanent*, as the pattern of production that holds for following global integrations leans against the labor earnings of domestic workers now in competition with similar workers around the world.

The results in Table 3 call for a hugely more ambitious response to offshoring than has been provided so far. Taking the numbers on offshoring's potential reach seriously means that current TAA income supports would replace less than 0.2% of the potential income loss to American production workers by the end of the next couple of decades.

The potential level of redistribution caused by offshoring is vast, and so should be the policy response. The best way to fashion redistribution of the scale implied by this paper's findings is through large-scale social insurance programs and public investments that insure a baseline level of economic security for American families: universal health care, stable pension income, disability and life insurance, and a lifetime of access to high-quality public education. Offshoring and trade are, of course, not the only rationale for such social insurance programs, but they do starkly illustrate the fundamental fact underlying the need for them: your economic lot in life is not wholly your own making, and in the new economy, it is less under your own control than ever before.

The failure of the economics profession to educate the larger public (including the policy-making and pundit-class elites) about this too-little known aspect of trade theory explains much of the chasm between elite and popular attitudes toward globalization. A serious understanding of what globalization means for the US economy and its workers—and what must be done to hold the broad American working- and middle-classes whole in the face of global integration—requires this failure be corrected.

(L Josh Bivens is associated with Economic Policy Institute. The author can be reached at lbivens@epinet.org).

Endnotes

1 See Appendix 1 for a couple of representatives of this view.

2 It is taken for granted in this paper that the arguments for expanded trade increasing national incomes are well-known and generally agreed-upon. There are, of course, exceptions to this scenario. The larger point of this paper is that even when integration of trade does indeed lead to national gains, the redistribution caused by trade can still lead to harm for the majority.

3 For those interested, it should be noted that this is a very crude formulation of the Stolper-Samuelson Theorem.

4 This is the implication of the Rybczynski Theorem (RT), an important complement to the Stolper-Samuelson Theorem.

5 Note that these adjustment costs may actually be greater for rich/rich trade, as the cost differentials between rich nations are thin, and, production may shift back and forth between rich and poor countries more readily because of this.

6 The 1995 results are slightly larger than that found by Krugman (1995), but show that the current model results are in line with past findings on trade and wages. This is a result of the LDC income share in this paper being higher—Krugman (1995) measured the LDC import share of the entire OECD, not just the United States.

7 The Cline (1997) results were often reported as finding wage impacts only twice as large as the Krugman (1995) results. This was because the benchmark the wage impacts were compared to was different than the one Krugman (1995) used. Based on the more commonly-used benchmark cited in Krugman (1995), Cline's results indicated that trade could explain almost 40% of the rise in relative earnings throughout the 1980s and early 1990s. See Bivens (2007) for more detail on this point.

8 Note that these quotations are not meant as illustrations of myopia on the part of the authors: these were (and are) some of the smartest authors writing on trade's labor market impacts. What they illustrate is the sea change in perceptions about trade's potential impact on the US economy in the era of offshoring.

References

Bardhan, Ashok Deo, and Cynthia A. Kroll (2003) "The New Wave of Outsourcing, Research Report", Fisher Center for Real Estate and Urban Economics, University of California at Berkeley, Fall.

Bivens, L. Josh. (2007). "Globalization, American Wages, and Inequality". Economic Policy Institute Working Paper. Washington, D.C.: EPI.

Blinder, Alan. (2006). Offshoring: The next Industrial Revolution. Foreign Affairs magazine.

Blinder, Alan. (2007). "How Many US Jobs Might Be Offshorable?" Unpublished Working Paper.

Bradford, S., and P. Grieco and C. Hufbauer. 2005. "The Payoff to America from Global Integration." In Bergsten and the Institute for International Economics (IIE), (eds.,) *The United States and the Global Economy: Foreign Economic Policy for the Next Decade.* Washington, D.C.: IIE Press.

Cline, William. (1997). *Trade and Income Distribution.* Washington, D.C.: Institute for International Economics.

DeLong, Brad. (2006). Comment to Martin Wolf forum on *Financial Times* blog, available at: *http://www.rgemonitor.com/blog/setser/144955/*

Freeman, Richard B. (1995). Are your wages set in Beijing? *journal of Economic Perspectives*, Vol. 9, No 3. Summer, pp. 15-32.

Forrester Research. (2004). *3.3 Million US Services Jobs To Go Offshore.* Research Brief.

Jensen, J. Bradford, and Lori Kletzer. (2005). Tradable Services: Understanding the Scope and Impact of Services Offshoring," in Lael Brainard and Susan M. Collins, eds. *Brookings Trade Forum 2005*, Offshoring White-Collar Work—The Issues and the Implications Forthcoming.

Kirkegaard, Jacob. (2004). *Outsourcing—Stains on the White Collar?* Institute for International Economics, available at: *http://www.iie.com/publications/papers/kirkegaard0204.pdf*

Krugman, Paul. (1995). *Growing World Trade: Causes and Consequences.* Brookings Papers on Economic Activity, Volume I.Washington, D.C.: Brookings Institute.

McKinsey Global Institute. (2003). *Offshoring: Is it a win-win game?*

Mishel, Lawrence, Jared Bernstein, and Sylvia Allegretto. (2006). *The State of Working America 2006/2007*. An Economic Policy Institute Book. Ithaca, N.Y.: ILR Press an imprint of Cornell University Press.

Rodrik, Dani. (1992). "The Rush to Free Trade in the Developing World: Why So Late? Why Now? Will It Last?" National Bureau of Economic Research (NBER) Working Paper #3947. Cambridge, Mass.: NBER.

Rogoff, Kenneth. (1995). "Paul Samuelson's Contributions to International Economics." Prepared for volume in honor of Paul Samuelson's 90th birthday, ed. Michael Szenberg. Avaiable at: *http://www.economics.harvard.edu/faculty/rogoff/papers*

Samuelson.pdfSamuelson, Paul. (2004). "Where Ricardo and Mill rebut and confirm mainstream economists supporting globalization". *Journal of Economic Perspectives*. Volume 18(3).

Van Welsum, D. and G. Vickery. (2005). *New Perspectives on ICT Skills and Employment*. Organization of Economic Cooperation and Development (OECD) Information Economy Working Paper.

Appendix 1: Quotes on Costs/Benefits of Globalization

"In the United States, at least, the problem is that most beneficiaries from globalization don't really know that they are beneficiaries, or how much they benefit. Feckless congressmen and congresswomen don't understand that the American economy is cushioned from their fiscal policy stupidities by the ability of the US government to sell bonds internationally on a jaw-droppingly unbelievable scale. Home sellers in California don't realize that they got such a good price because of financing from across the Pacific. Walmart shoppers see the "made in China" stickers, but don't understand what a good deal they are getting because the rulers of the PRC are desperate to sell the products that their workers make at always low prices in order to stay as close as possible to full employment. The task is primarily one of making perceptions agree with reality, and only secondarily one of changing reality."

– J Bradford DeLong

"While the gains from increased trade generate a permanent rise in income, the associated losses are temporary. Nevertheless, they are very real, and are concentrated on a small fraction of Americans."

– Bradford, Grieco, and Hufbauer

12

Trade, Jobs, and Wages: Are the Public's Worries about Globalization Justified?

L Josh Bivens

Job loss is by far the most visible and easily understood way that international trade can affect American living standards. The effect of trade flows on American jobs is actually pretty complicated and so requires a bit of untangling.

A wide gulf exists today in American politics. On one shore are voters increasingly anxious about globalization and its effect on their jobs and communities. On the other are economists, policy-makers, and pundits who maintain that trade is good for the economy, that the wider public is simply misguided about its benefits, and that politicians who sympathize with those concerned about globalization are pandering to special interests at the expense of the wider economy. This latter group relies heavily on the suggestion that "all economists believe" globalization is good for the vast majority of American workers.

This reliance is odd given that mainstream economics actually argues that there are plenty of reasons for concern about globalization's effect on the majority of American workers. This primer highlights two issues in particular that should worry American workers about globalization: job losses stemming from growing trade

Source: EPI Issue Brief # 244, May 6, 2008 (www.epi.org). *© Economic Policy Institute. Reprinted with permission.*

deficits; and downward wage pressure for tens of millions of American workers. These problems are not unexpected consequences of expanded trade; quite the opposite, they are exactly what standard economic reasoning predicts.

Trade and Jobs

Job loss is by far the most visible and easily understood way that international trade can affect American living standards.

The effect of trade flows on American jobs is actually pretty complicated and so requires a bit of untangling. First, trade creates new jobs in exporting industries and destroys jobs when imports replace the output of domestic firms.

Because *trade deficits* have risen over the past decade, more jobs have been displaced by imports than created by exports.

The Trade Deficit and Future American Living Standards

In a sense, a trade deficit is the difference between a country's production (exports) and its consumption (imports). Each year that the United States runs a trade deficit is a year that it must borrow from abroad to finance this excess of consumption over production. This borrowing leads to growing foreign debt that must be paid, with interest. In 2007, US borrowing was on the order of $2 billion *every day*.

Australia provides a cautionary tale on the consequences of such borrowing. In recent years, the Australian *trade* deficit has averaged around 2% of gross domestic product, yet Australia's *total* deficit of international credits over debits reached 6% of GDP. The 4% gap between the trade and total deficit was debt service (i.e., interest) paid on the borrowing to cover previous years' accrued trade deficits. This large income flow leaving Australia to pay interest on accumulated foreign debts should be a red flag for the future of the US economy.

There are, however, some possible off sets to this job loss resulting from trade flows. As the trade deficit grows, dollars piled up by our trading partners come back to the US economy, and this increases the supply of funds available for US business and households to borrow. This increase drives down the price of borrowing (interest rates), just as an increase in supply in any other market drives down prices. Lower interest rates spur job growth in interest-sensitive industries (like housing); and these can off set some of the job losses from trade.

Can these jobs created through capital inflows completely balance jobs lost to growing trade deficits? It is possible, but unlikely. Of course, other macroeconomic influences may push an economy to full-employment even in the face of trade deficits. In the late 1990s, for example, manufacturing jobs were lost to trade while construction jobs (at least partially spurred by foreign capital inflows) boomed. In the early 2000s, conversely, manufacturing hemorrhaged jobs due to trade faster than any other industry (even interest-sensitive industries) could replace them.

The Economic Policy Institute and other researchers have examined the job impacts of trade in recent years by netting the job opportunities lost to imports against those gained through exports[1]. One criticism of these studies is that they do not try to estimate the jobs gained from capital inflows. However, this criticism misses the point of these studies: estimates of jobs displaced by growing trade deficits are not a declaration of *exactly how many* more jobs the economy would have today if these deficits had *not grown*. Rather, they are a conservative measure of the involuntary job displacement caused by these growing deficits and an indicator of imbalance in the US labor market and wider economy. These studies also provide an indicator of how trade has affected the *composition* of jobs in the US labor market.

Economists may cheerfully label it a wash when the loss of a hundred manufacturing jobs in Ohio or Pennsylvania is offset by the hiring of a hundred construction workers in Phoenix, but in the real world these displacements often result in large income losses and even permanent damage to workers' earning power[2].

Lastly, and importantly, even if trade deficits and capital inflows were to fight to a draw and there was no effect on the *total* number of jobs, job *quality* could still suffer. Manufacturing jobs (disproportionately lost to trade) tend to pay more and have better benefits, especially for workers without a four-year degree.

Trade and Wages

While job-loss caused by rising trade deficits is the most visible effect of globalization, its impact on wages is a concern to an even much larger number of workers. Even if trade flows begin to balance and there is less job loss in the future, the integration of the US economy with those of its low-wage trading partners will pull down wages for many American workers, and will contribute to the ever rising inequality of incomes in the US economy.

While global integration is usually "win-win" *between countries*, it can still translate into steep losses for tens of millions of workers in the US economy. Crucially, this wage-loss is not restricted to just workers in sectors exposed to trade, but is experienced by *all workers who resemble* those displaced by imports in terms of education, skills, and experience. Many of these workers probably *do not even know* that they are being affected by globalization, but they are. Landscapers may not get displaced by imports, but their wages do indeed suffer from job competition with import-displaced apparel workers.

Trade Agreements and American Jobs

The ongoing dispute over the effects of the North American Free Trade Agreement (NAFTA) on the US economy raises a narrower issue than addressed above: do trade *agreements* (and not just trade *flows*) impact American jobs and wages?

As described in this overview, increased trade *flows* affect jobs and wages in the United States. Given that a key *purpose* of trade agreements (like NAFTA) is to increase these trade flows—and all evidence indicates that they have succeeded—it is safe to say that trade agreements have indeed increased pressure on American jobs and wages by increasing trade flows.

It is, however, hard to disentangle the precise influence of trade agreements apart from all other economic influences. Given this difficulty, researchers (and editorialists) frequently compare trade levels and other economic outcomes in periods before and after the implementation of trade agreements to assess their impact. While these "before-and-after" comparisons are assessments of the impact of *increased trade* generally, not trade *agreements* alone, this general method of assessing the outcomes of trade agreements is essentially an industry standard employed by nearly all commentators in the debate over trade agreements[3].

Take the case of China and the United States. Reducing trade barriers allows each to specialize in what they do more efficiently, and this specialization generally leads to *national-level* gains for both countries—that is, increased efficiency, worldwide production, and total consumption. This is essentially chapter one in trade textbooks.

However, a later chapter in the textbook points out that, when the United States exports financial services and aircraft while importing apparel and electronics, it is implicitly exchanging the services of capital (physical and human) for labor. This exchange bids up capital's price (profits and high-end salaries) and bids down wages for the broad working and middle-class, leading to rising inequality and wage pressure for many Americans. In the textbook's index, this is called the Stolper-Samuelson Theorem. (For those more convinced by appeals to authority, the text box *Interpreting Wage Impacts* provides some quotes from standard economics texts.)

How big is this impact on wages? A reasonably cautious estimate is that between 1973 and 2006, global integration lowered the wages of US workers without a four-year college degree (the large majority of the US workforce) by 4%. College-educated workers saw 3% gains from trade, so inequality increased in this time as well[4].

Four percent might not sound like that big a deal, but to put it in some perspective, wages of workers without a college degree rose by only 2% over the *entire* 1973-2006 period. If not for the effects of trade, then this group's wage increase could have been 100% larger.

Interpreting Wage Impacts

The first thing to note is that the losses described above are *not* the unemployment spells suffered by workers displaced by imports. These unemployment costs are not even considered in most trade theory, although in the real world they obviously should be. Rather, the biggest losses are the *permanent* wage cuts resulting from America's new pattern of specialization made possible by globalization. These wage losses, it should be reiterated, are suffered by *all* workers who resemble import-displaced workers in education, skills, and experience.

Second, the wage losses discussed in this overview factor in the ability of all workers to buy cheaper imports or find new job opportunities in expanding export sectors. Too often even professional economists imply or even state outright that cheaper imports or expanding opportunity in export sectors make the net outcomes of globalization for American workers impossible to predict. This is wrong.

Third, the channels described above are, of course, not the only way trade affects US wages. Just the *threat* of substituting foreign labor and imports for US workers (made more credible as global integration proceeds) reduces the bargaining power of US workers—even of high-wage, high education workers who are generally helped by the effects described above (e.g., college-educated accountants buying cheap imported shirts at Wal-Mart). These *threat effects* are all but impossible to measure, but are nevertheless important.

Finally, for those more convinced by appeals to authority on the issue of trade and wages, below are two quotations, one from Kenneth Rogoff, economics professor at Harvard and former chief economist for the International Monetary Fund (IMF), and another from a standard undergraduate international trade textbook authored by Paul Krugman and Maurice Obtsfeld:

> *"From a policy perspective, the major result of [the SST] was to confirm the intuitive analysis of Ohlin about who wins and who loses when a country opens up to trade. The answer, as we now well understand, is that the relatively abundant factor gains, and the relatively scarce factor loses, not only in absolute terms but in real terms. Thus if capital is the relatively abundant factor (compared to the trading partner), then an opening of trade will lead the return on capital to rise more than proportionately compared to the price of either good, whereas the wage rate will fall relative to the price of either good."*[5]

> *"....International trade has a powerful effect on income distribution.... This means that international trade tends to make low-skilled workers in the United States worse off—not just temporarily but on a sustained basis."*[6]

An Honest Debate on Globalization

American workers are perfectly rational to worry about what globalization means for their living standards, and actually have a much better grasp of the underlying economics than do the elite policy making class who routinely tells them otherwise. Furthermore, the globalization *status quo* is at least as stingy to the poor trading partners of the United States as it is to American workers. It is time we had a national debate that acknowledged these facts and treated views dissenting from the elite consensus on globalization with the respect they deserve. This debate needs to include responses to globalization that match the scale of the economic insecurity, the wage losses, and the re-distribution it leaves in its wake. Simply put, this scale is not appreciated or acknowledged in today's globalization debate, and policy responses reflect this failure.

(L Josh Bivens is associated with Economic Policy Institute. The author can be reached at lbivens@epinet.org).

Endnotes

1 The latest such report from EPI is: Scott, R. Bruce Campbell, Carlos Salas, and Jeff Faux (2007), *Revisiting NAFTA: Still not working for North America's workers.* Economic Policy Institute Briefing Paper #173. Other reports using the all-but-identical methodology include: Groshen, Erica, Bart Hobijn, and Margaret M. McConnell (2005); US Jobs Gained and Lost through Trade: A Net Measure, *Current Issues in Economics and Finance*, Federal Reserve Bank of New York; and, Bailey, Martin N. and Robert Z. Lawrence (2004), *What Happened to the Great US Jobs Machine: The Role of Trade and Electronic Off shoring*, Brookings Papers on Economic Activity, Volume (2). Further, it should be noted that pundits use this implicit logic of counting jobs embodied in trade flows *all the time.* The April 10 editorial of the *Washington Post* argued for passage of the US/Colombia Free Trade Agreement partly on the basis of jobs created in the US through exports to Colombia: "The trade agreement would...give US firms free access to Colombia for the first time, *thus creating US jobs.*"

2 In fact, one study (Philip Oreopolous, Marianne Page, and Ann Huff Stevens (2005), *The Intergenerational Effect of Worker Displacement.* NBER Working Paper No. 11587) has actually shown that involuntary job displacement leads to lower lifetime income for the displaced worker's *children*. Involuntary job-loss, in short, is costly to workers in the real-world.

3 EPI, for example, is careful to identify just what is being measured. For example, the EPI report referenced above (Scott *et al.,* (2007) notes that "Growing trade deficits with Mexico and Canada have displaced production that supported 1,015,291 US jobs since NAFTA took effect in 1994" [emphasis added].

Some recent examples of this "before and after" assessment of NAFTA's effect from pro-NAFTA sources follows: *Trade Distortions,* Washington Post Editorial, 12/3/2007, "...*[T]he impact of NAFTA seems to have been both larger* and more positive in Mexico.... Mexico's gross domestic *product...more than quadrupled since 1987.*" (It should be noted that this particular "before and after" snapshot is wrong in almost every way: Mexican GDP has not quadrupled since 1987, and NAFTA took effect in 1994, not 1987.

NAFTA – Myth vs. Facts, Office of the United States Trade Representative, March 2008, "*Myth* #2: NAFTA has cost the US jobs...Fact: US employment rose from 110.8 million people in 1993 to 137.6 million in 2007."

4 For this number, see Bivens, L. Josh (2007), *Globalization and American Wages: Today and Tomorrow.* Briefing Paper, Economic Policy Institute, Washington, D.C.

5 Rogoff , Kenneth (2005), "Paul Samuelson's Contributions to International Economics," chapter in volume edited by Szenber in honor of Paul Samuelson's 90th birthday.

6 Krugman and Obstfeld (1994), 6. *International Economics: Theory and Policy.* 3rd Edition. Harper-Collins.

13

Globalization and the Least Developed Countries
Issues in Trade and Investment*

Though the relationship between trade and development is the subject of contentious debate in the literature, there is little doubt that trade can be a powerful source of economic growth. International trade can expand markets, facilitate competition and disseminate knowledge which can catalyze economic growth and human development. Trade can also raise productivity and increase exposure to new technologies, which can also drive growth. However, none of this is automatic or inevitable.

Introduction

Globalization has been associated with rising world income. Many countries and people have benefited from this, but some countries and people have been left out.

* This issues paper was prepared for the Ministerial Conference "Making Globalization Work for the LDCs", Istanbul, Turkey, July 9-11, 2007 by the Division for Africa, Least Developed Countries and Special Programmes (ALDC) United Nations Conference on Trade and Development (UNCTAD) Geneva, Switzerland. The paper is based on UNCTAD (2004 and 2006) and includes significant inputs from the Inclusive Globalization Cluster of the Poverty Group in UNDP's Bureau for Development Policy. Comments were provided by staff in the Office of Development Studies of UNDP and by the Executive Office of UNDP. Issues raised by UNDP Country Offices have also been included as appropriate.

Source: www.un.int/turkey/3.pdf © United Nations. Reprinted with permission.

Amongst the latter are many Least Developed Countries (LDCs), and a relatively large share of the population of the LDCs. Many LDCs have been marginalized in the world economy although they have undertaken far-reaching economic reforms.

In the past decades, many LDCs have pursued extensive liberalization and today have relatively open trade regimes. The considerable trade liberalization of LDCs is sometimes overlooked as LDCs have typically pursued trade liberalization in the context of structural adjustment programmes rather than multilateral trade negotiations. Today, the central question for LDCs is not so much how they may achieve a further liberalization of their trade regime; rather it is how they can effectively promote development with a relatively open trade regime.

This paper argues that while each country will need to identify a "post-liberal development strategy" that is most suitable to its particular circumstances, the various "post-liberal development strategies" are likely to have common features regardless of the specific context[1]. In particular, regardless of country context, they should include a shift in focus from trade-led development to development-led trade, with a complementary broadening focus from supply-side capacities to productive and economic growth capacities at the national level. At the international level, it is important to look beyond further trade liberalization to strengthening the export capacity and performance of LDCs in a sustainable manner and ensuring effective market access.

The Impact of Past Reforms and the Challenges Ahead

The majority of LDCs have participated extensively and intensively in structural adjustment reform programmes. According to a recent World Bank study many low-income countries, including LDCs, have sound macroeconomic policies in place[2], and according to the IMF index of trade restrictiveness, many low-income countries, including LDCs, have relatively open trade regimes. Despite decades of reform, the LDCs remain marginalized in the world economy. While some LDCs, mostly in Asia, have managed to increase their share in world trade and income, and have also managed to reduce their high incidence of extreme poverty, most LDCs – mainly in Africa – have seen decreasing shares in world trade and income, and increasing

1 UNCTAD, 2004, pp.282-283.

2 World Bank, 2002.

incidence of extreme poverty[3]. The trends that can be observed for the different groups of LDCs, based on their geographic location, are closely related with trends that can be observed for different groups of LDCs classified by their export specialization. The Asian LDCs that have done better have typically managed to diversify into manufactures and/or services while the African LDCs which have done less well continue to specialize in non-oil primary commodities[4].

Despite Reforms, LDCs Remain Marginalized in the World Economy

In the thirty-year period between 1960 and 1999, the income gap between the world's 20 richest countries and the LDCs continued to widen[5]. Weighted by population, the average income per capita of the 20 richest countries was about 16 times as high as that of non-oil commodity exporting LDCs in 1960, while it was 35 times as high by 1999. As such, this gap more than doubled by 1999. By contrast, the income per capita of the 20 richest countries was 8 times as high as that of manufactures and/or services exporting LDCs in 1960 and 12 times higher than that of this subgroup of LDCs in 1999. While the income gap between the richest countries and all LDCs continued to increase, the gap with non-oil commodity exporting LDCs increased at a much more rapid pace by the late 1990s compared with the income gap between the richest countries and manufactures and/or services exporting LDCs, which increased by much less[6].

A similar difference between the LDCs can be observed with regard to poverty incidence[7]. While LDCs that continue to specialize in non-oil commodities have seen an increase of extreme poverty in the past decades, the LDCs that specialize in

[3] Karshenas, 2001.

[4] UNCTAD, 2002, pp. 49-61, 124.

[5] UNCTAD estimates based on Summers and Heston International Comparison Programme and World Bank, *World Development Indicators 2001,* CD ROM (UNCTAD, 2002, pp. 122-123). The income gap is the ratio of the weighted by population average GDP per capita (in 1985 PPP dollars) in the world's 20 richest countries to that in the LDCs and LDC subgroups. The sample of the world's 20 richest countries varies over time.

[6] UNCTAD, 2002, p. 123.

[7] There is a lack of poverty data for the LDCs that makes it difficult to monitor poverty trends in these countries. The most comprehensive and latest figures on the incidence and depth of poverty in the LDCs are derived from UNCTAD's *The Least Developed Countries Report 2002* database (for further references and methodological notes, see UNCTAD 2002, pp. 39-100, particularly pp. 62-64). While this paucity of data is very unfortunate, and has been highlighted by UNCTAD on various occasions (LDC Report 2002, LDC Report 2004 and background papers to both reports), very little had been done to rectify this lacuna till very recently. UNCTAD is now seeking to update its poverty estimates. This paper will be updated with the new data once this is available and before it is finally published after the Istanbul Conference.

manufacturing have seen a decrease of extreme poverty. Between the late 1980s and the late 1990s, extreme poverty in non-oil commodity exporting LDCs rose from 67 percent to 69 percent, an increase from the early 1980s, but it fell in manufacture exporting LDCs (even if Bangladesh is excluded) from 48 percent to 44 percent[8]. The unfavourable poverty trends are particularly pronounced in LDCs which specialize in extractive industries, and the positive poverty trends are particularly pronounced in Bangladesh which has successfully increased its specialization in low-tech manufactures. Incidence of extreme poverty between the late 1980s and late 1990s also increased in LDC exporters of services from 41 percent to 43 percent[9]. If past trends persist, extreme poverty in the LDCs will increase rather than decrease in the coming decades. While the developing world as a whole is on track to achieve the objective of reducing extreme poverty by half between the base year 1990 and the target year 2015, the group of LDCs as a whole will not achieve this objective[10].

Because of these trends, policy makers in LDCs are concerned that they should be better integrated in world trade, that their share of world trade should be larger, and that they should manage to sustainably reduce the incidence of extreme poverty. In this context, recent literature has placed great emphasis on further trade liberalization[11]. It is argued that a further liberalization of trade will increase trade flows, that this will stimulate growth, and that higher rates of economic growth will reduce poverty. However, empirical evidence shows that past trade liberalization had ambiguous effects on growth and poverty reduction in the LDCs, and that further trade liberalization is unlikely to bring about the desired effects on growth and poverty reduction without a strong complementary policy package that changes the direction of development[12].

---

8 Using the same poverty estimate and including Bangladesh, poverty in manufacture exporting LDCs fell from 28 percent to 25 percent during the same period. UNCTAD, 2002, Chart 36 "The incidence of poverty in LDCs grouped according to export specialization, 1981-1983, 1987-1989 and 1997-1999" based on a $1 per day poverty line, p. 124.

9 Ibid.

10 UNCTAD, 2002, pp. 124.

11 See Sachs and Warner, 1995; Dollar and Kraay, 2000.

12 See Rodriguez and Rodrik, 2001; Helleiner, 2000; Helleiner, 1994.

Non-Tariff Trade Barriers, Commodity Dependence and Phase-out of Trade Preferences

Today, tariff barriers to trade affect fewer LDC exports than non-tariff barriers to trade. In 1999-2001 environment-related trade barriers affected 20 percent of the merchandise exports of other developing countries, but no less than 41 percent of the merchandise exports of LDCs.

In the same period, 28 percent of LDC exports suffered from commodity price decline, compared with 15 percent in other developing countries. More recently, however, the resurgence of global commodity prices has helped lift many commodity-dependent countries out of a prolonged period of economic stagnation. This is partly due to increased demand for commodity exports from the LDCs in the most dynamic developing economies, particularly China and India. Strong demand for raw materials from these countries has had a remarkable impact on commodity prices and volumes of trade. For instance, there has been a considerable improvement in the terms of trade of sub-Saharan African countries (some 30 percent) between 1999 and 2004, far higher than in any other region[13]. Also, the trade volume of rice was up 67.5 percent in the decade between 1993-1995 and 2003-2005, while cotton increased by 48.8 percent, fresh and chilled vegetables by 69.7 percent, and cut flowers by 72.9 percent during the same period[14]. Nevertheless, such price increases do not cover all commodities and their real magnitude has been diminished by exchange rate movements, especially the US dollar. Furthermore, while markets are likely to remain buoyant in the medium term, the secular trend of declining real commodity prices may eventually reassert itself. Price movements, moreover, are not the only disadvantage for countries specialized in commodities, since commodity production is not associated with the technological externalities and 'learning by doing' which characterizes much of manufacturing and the technology-oriented service industries. The challenge for these countries is to sustain or accelerate the growth momentum over the coming years by gaining ground in more knowledge based activities whilst simultaneously upgrading the quality of their commodity production[15].

Furthermore, LDCs, more than other developing countries, are affected by challenges associated with the specialization in extractive industries, and LDCs, more

13 UNCTAD, 2005.

14 UNDP, UNCTAD, ACP and CFC, 2007.

15 Global Initiative on Commodities, Outcome Document, Brasilia, May 7-11, 2007.

than other developing countries, are negatively affected by the phasing-out of preferences on textiles and clothing[16]. While the EU has essentially compensated both African and Asian LDCs for phasing-out market access preferences in textiles through the introduction of wider GSP preferences (i.e., EBA), the US has compensated only African LDCs for the phasing-out of market access preferences with the introduction of wider GSP preferences (i.e., AGOA). Market access to the US has thus eroded for many Asian LDCs, especially in textiles and clothing. This affects some of the largest exporters of textiles and clothing amongst the LDCs[17]. Bangladesh's export-oriented Ready-Made Garment (RMG) exports account for 76 percent of total export earnings; the US is the destination of 42 per cent of RMG, yet clothing is excluded from the GSP. Furthermore, Nepal is deprived from the US duty-free quota-free treatment to apparel, which is a major export product to overseas markets[18].

Implications for Trade Policies: From Trade-led Development to Development-led Trade

Though the relationship between trade and development is the subject of contentious debate in the literature, there is little doubt that trade can be a powerful source of economic growth. International trade can expand markets, facilitate competition and disseminate knowledge which can catalyze economic growth and human development. Trade can also raise productivity and increase exposure to new technologies, which can also drive growth. However, none of this is automatic or inevitable[19].

Much policy advice in the 1990s advanced the argument that trade liberalization "as such" is the engine of economic growth and that it is also a driving force for poverty reduction[20]. As a result, many developing countries and development partners have focused on trade liberalization. However, the trade integration policies of most LDCs has been characterized by two types of problems: (i) the projected trade expansion is delinked from the prescribed trade policies; and (ii) the prescribed trade policies are characterized by a very narrow focus. At the international level, trade

16 UNCTAD, 2004, pp. 230-239.

17 UNCTAD, 2004, p. 232.

18 UNDP Bangladesh Country Office and UNDP Nepal Country Office.

19 UNDP, 2003, p. 21.

20 See Sachs and Warner, 1995; Dollar and Kraay, 2000.

policies focus on the benefits of further trade liberalization, while at the national level they concentrate on the benefits of trade capacity building. However, as indicated, trade liberalization had ambiguous effects on economic growth and poverty reduction in the LDCs.

The experience of LDCs has belied the belief that trade liberalization automatically promotes growth and alleviates poverty. According to UNCTAD[21], available evidence shows that trade liberalization has so far not been closely associated with poverty reduction[22]. Poverty appears to be increasing in the LDCs with both open and closed trade regimes. Between these extremes, poverty increased less in countries that have pursued moderate trade liberalization. While this does not imply that trade liberalization increases poverty, it does show that liberalization has not helped reduce poverty.

On the other hand, LDCs that experienced economic growth in the 1990s became more export oriented. However, increased export orientation was not necessarily associated with growth, as 'GDP per capita declined or stagnated in 8 of the 22 LDCs with increasing export orientation between 1987 and 1999; and in 10 of these countries poverty actually increased'[23]. A key lesson, therefore, is that increased exports alone do not result in poverty reduction. In this context, sustained economic growth[24] and institutional innovations, many requiring policy space, have been crucial to ensuring sustainable economic and human development for the LDCs.

Benefits for LDCs Derived from Further Multilateral Liberalization are Overestimated

Sustained economic growth can be accelerated by increasing both imports and exports; however, since there is no automatic relationship between growth and poverty reduction, whether and the extent to which this happens will depend on household choices and broader government policies and spending. At present it appears that the benefits that LDCs may derive from further multilateral trade liberalization are likely to be

21 UNCTAD, 2002, Chapter 3.

22 Among the LDCs, trade varies greatly and depends on whether their main exports are primary products, non-oil primary products, or manufactured goods. Primary products exporters exhibit the highest poverty levels. More than 80 percent of the people in mineralexporting countries lived on less than $1 a day at the end of the 1990s, compared with 43 percent in service exporting LDCs and 25 percent in manufactured goods exporting LDCs (excluding Bangladesh) (UNCTAD, 2002, p. 115; UNDP, 2003).

23 UNDP, 2003, p. 34.

24 Sustained economic growth in 14 LDCs with rising GDP per capita led to a fall in poverty in them between 1987 and 1999 (UNDP, 2003, p. 34).

overestimated and are actually rather small because, today, most LDCs have very open trade regimes. The LDCs will therefore derive relatively small benefits from a reduction of their own tariffs. Furthermore, LDCs benefit from many tariff-related market access preferences. They will therefore also gain relatively little from further tariff reductions by developed countries. LDCs could, however, derive relatively high gains from (i) better market access to the more industrialized developing countries, (ii) the reduction of non-tariff barriers in developed countries, and (iii) from a less restricted movement of natural persons. For instance, in 2005 official remittance inflows were approximately four times higher than net aid flows and nine times higher than FDI in Bangladesh[25]. Currently, however, multilateral trade negotiations under the Doha Round do not promise meaningful progress in these areas.

Support Needed at the International Level

At the international level it is necessary to look beyond further trade liberalization and prioritize the strengthening of LDC export performance. Three types of policy measures are particularly important in this respect[26]:

- *Generally applicable support:* which should focus on all developing countries and would (i) help countries cope with commodity price instability and decline; and (ii) help them address challenges associated with the management of mineral resources and mineral revenues. Specific measures under the former could include the establishment of an export diversification fund, strengthening the capacity of developing country financial institutions to provide credit to small producers and small and medium enterprises and the creation of regulatory environments enabling national stakeholders to use modern finance and risk management instruments[27].
- *LDC-specific support measures:* which should focus on (i) strengthening special and differential treatment provisions, (ii) strengthening market access preferences, and (iii) the introduction of supply-side support measures. The policy instrument of market access preferences will inevitably erode, and it is therefore necessary to design new instruments to stimulate exports. But while market access preferences continue to have bite, it is essential to make the best

[25] UNDP Bangladesh Country Office.

[26] UNCTAD, 2004, pp. 239-263

[27] Global Initiative on Commodities, Outcome Document, Brasilia, May 7-11, 2007.

possible use of them. To this end, market access preferences should not be undermined by the exclusion of sensitive products, the escalation of tariffs, overly complex rules of origin, or overly stringent product standards in developed countries.

For instance, despite promising signs for export of agro based products such as tea and herbal and aromatic plants, Nepal has not been able to exploit international market access opportunities due to strict technical requirements[28]. Market access preferences should provide complete duty and quota-free access for all products for LDCs, and they should be granted on a mandatory basis by all developed countries and more industrialized developing countries. The introduction of Economic Partnership Agreements between the EU and many LDCs do not promise to improve market access preferences. An enticing feature of these arrangements is that LDCs are promised aid for the strengthening of trade capacities. Nevertheless, another feature of the arrangements is that many LDCs will need to comply with relatively stringent intellectual property rights and investment regulations, which go beyond current regulations in the multilateral trading system, and will effectively set a minimum standard for future multilateral trade negotiations.

- *South–South cooperation:* South–South trade has significantly increased and many developing countries have benefited. But the LDCs, which are marginalized in North–South trade, are also increasingly marginalized in South–South trade. While the share of LDC imports that originate in other developing countries has significantly increased, the share of imports of other developing countries that originate in the LDCs has decreased. Today, other developing countries import a smaller share from the LDCs than they did in the early 1980s. To counteract these developments it is necessary that other, more industrialized developing countries open their markets to exports from LDCs. An important instrument in this context is the Global System of Trade Preferences among Developing Countries (GSTP), of which countries should make more use.

National Level Priorities

Today, the focus on trade liberalization at the international level is accompanied by a focus on trade capacity building at the national level. Efforts to strengthen trade capacities

---

28 UNDP Nepal Country Office.

typically (i) help countries implement appropriate trade policies and regulations and/or (ii) help producers comply with product standards. There is also an increasing recognition of the need to develop transport-related infrastructure such as roads and storage facilities as part of the current priority being placed on 'Aid-for-Trade'. The development of appropriate transport infrastructure is a particularly great challenge for landlocked developing countries. For instance, difficult routes both internally and through Tanzania and Kenya further slow down and restrict Rwanda's access to markets[29] and the landlocked status of Malawi is a major handicap for its highly competitive sugar industry[30]. But while all of this is important, none of this is sufficient. The weak export performance of LDCs is not only related to trade barriers at the international level, and it is not only related to inability to ship products. The weak export performance of LDCs is more fundamentally related to their inability to compete internationally in terms of product prices and quality. In order to support efforts of LDCs to increase their world exports, it is insufficient to focus on a narrow conception of supply capacities. Instead, there is a need to broaden the focus to address productive capacities more generally. The analytical shift from trade-led development to development-led trade thus needs to be complemented by a shift from a narrow focus on supply constraints to a broader focus on productive capacities.

Current trade strategies comprise a prominent part of development strategies. While it may be an exaggeration to suggest that trade strategies have replaced development and poverty reduction strategies, trade strategies have certainly conditioned the development and poverty reduction strategies (PRSPs or otherwise) of an increasing number of countries. A more balanced relationship between trade and development will require a shift from trade-led development strategies; which bank on quasi-automatic positive effects of further liberalization of trade for growth and poverty reduction, to development-led trade strategies which instead focus on the ways in which the development of productive capacities can contribute to sustained economic growth with poverty reduction, with increased trade as a valuable instrument of development, but not an objective in itself.

From Supply Capacities to Productive Capacities

During the past decades many LDCs have not been able to effectively increase their exports. This fact shows that market access opportunities are distinct from market

29 UNDP Rwanda Country Office.

30 UNDP Malawi Country Office.

entry requirements. Although market access can be improved, and many market access preferences should be significantly strengthened, the LDCs already benefit from market access preferences to many developed countries, but so far only a few of them have been able to effectively use such preferences, as indicated by low levels of effective utilization. The ability of LDCs to make better use of market access preferences does not only depend on an improvement of supply capacities, in the narrow sense, but requires rather an improvement of productive capacities in the broadest sense.

In particular, the development of productive capacities will require an expansion, but also a better utilization, of the following three factors[31]:

- *Productive resources:* These refer to the factors of production, which include human, physical, financial and natural capital.
- *Entrepreneurial capabilities:* These are essentially the core competencies and technological capabilities that entrepreneurs ought to have in order to effectively use productive resources to convert raw inputs into internationally competitive outputs.
- *Production linkages:* These refer to backward and forward, and horizontal and vertical linkages between small and large enterprises, informal and formal enterprises, and domestic and foreign enterprises. They also include various linkages beween the informal and formal sectors and the agricultural and non-agricultural sectors.

Productive capacities are closely associated with three economic processes, namely (i) the process of capital accumulation[32], (ii) the process of technological progress[33] and (iii) the process of favourable structural change, characterized by an increasing specialization in high value added activities and an increasing number of productive employment opportunities[34]. On the one side, productive capacities influence these three economic processes, but on the other hand, productive capacities are also influenced by these economic processes. However, this potentially virtuous relationship

---

31 UNCTAD, 2006, pp. 59-81.

32 Akyüz and Gore, 1996.

33 Knell, 2006.

34 UNCTAD, 2006, pp. 85-189.

in the LDCs is constrained by three factors, namely (i) an underdeveloped infrastructure, (ii) weak institutions[35] and (iii) weak external and domestic demand[36]. It is therefore necessary to overcome these three constraints in order to develop productive capacities.

Implications for Investment

A key implication of the analysis above is that the LDCs need to increase investments related to the development of productive capacities (namely productive resources, entrepreneurial capabilities and production linkages). They also need to significantly step up investments which are related to productive capacities (especially in infrastructure and institutions). Only if LDCs overcome these constraints and successfully develop productive resources, will they benefit from a more favourable process of capital accumulation, technological progress and structural change. The necessary investments to develop productive capacities and to relieve constraints on them are a formidable challenge for any country, but especially the LDCs, which are resource-stripped economies. It is important to emphasize that these investments go beyond the current investment foci of many countries. Investment in entrepreneurial capabilities goes well beyond the current focus on universal primary education (it should include investment in technical and vocational training, secondary and tertiary education, research and development and extension schemes); investment in institutions goes well beyond an exclusive focus on anti-corruption measures and a favourable investment climate (with good governance and anti-corruption, it should also include the development of effective business support institutions and banks); and investment in physical infrastructure should go beyond current efforts to close the digital divide (it must include large investments in electricity grids and transport networks). According to World Bank estimates, LDCs require infrastructure investment equivalent to about 7 percent of their GDP annually[37].

External Resources for Development Financing

The significant resource needs of the LDCs cannot be covered by their domestically available resources in the near future. This resource gap can only be financed by external resources, especially official development assistance (ODA), but also foreign

---

35 Kozul-Wright, 2000.

36 UNCTAD, 2006, pp. 193-280.

37 Briceno-Garmendia, Estache and Shafik, 2004.

direct investment (FDI). Between 1999-2003, net FDI inflows to LDCs were about 2.6 percent of GDP, while in 2004 net ODA disbursements to LDCs were about 9 percent of GDP.

These figures indicate that the LDC group has benefited from rising FDI and ODA inflows during the past few years. Nevertheless, many LDCs have been excluded because FDI is highly concentrated in a few countries (namely countries that benefit from oil, metals and minerals) and a few sectors (namely extractive industries). Moreover, ODA is also concentrated in selected countries (especially conflict-affected countries), and a few areas (namely the social sectors, emergency assistance and debt relief). In order to finance the investment necessary in LDCs it is essential that:

- *Aid is further increased:* In order for aid to play a more effective role in underpinning progress towards the MDGs, the commitments made in 2005 on increasing aid quantity must be met. In 2005, G8 summit leaders agreed to increase aid to developing countries by US$50 billion a year by 2010, with at least $25 billion a year going to Africa. A few months earlier member states of the European Union resolved to reach the internationally agreed target of 0.7 percent of GNI in ODA by 2015 with an interim target of reaching 0.51 percent by 2010. Donors should meet their stated commitments and do so in a manner that channels real additional resources to development. An increase of aid effectiveness will also depend on the untying of aid and further exploring opportunities for OECD countries to provide additional resources beyond those freed through debt cancellation through new innovative sources of finance (such as the International Finance Facility for Immunization (IFFIm), the solidarity Air Transport Levies (ATLs) for drugs facilities, and Advance Market Commitments for vaccine investments), some of which have the potential to deliver benefits for the LDCs. Due attention should also be directed to the growing volume of aid provided by emerging economies and measures that ensure ownership should be reinforced[38].
- *There should be a better balance between the productive and social sectors:* Much more aid needs to be committed to the development of infrastructure and the productive sectors than was the case in past years. Between 1992-1994 and 2002-2004, the share of ODA from OECD/DAC countries to LDCs committed

[38] UNDP Senegal Country Office and UNDP Mauritania Country Office.

to social sector development, emergency assistance and debt relief increased from 35 per cent to 62 per cent. By contrast, over the same period, the share of ODA from OECD/DAC countries to LDCs committed to infrastructure development and the productive sectors decreased from 48 per cent to 24 per cent.

- *Aid should be more effectively deployed:* In order to strengthen the development effectiveness of aid, it is important for donors to achieve greater policy coherence. For example, it is necessary that trade policies, which protect the agricultural sector in developed countries, do not undermine aid policies, which promote rural and agricultural development in developing countries. Furthermore, donors must achieve greater coherence in their reporting procedures, and both donors and recipient countries should use aid in a more transparent and accountable manner. With agreement in principle on the Paris Declaration, the OECD countries have already begun reforms in this area based on the principles of harmonization, alignment, ownership and mutual responsibility[39]. The speedy and comprehensive implementation of the Paris Declaration is necessary for an increase of aid effectiveness and it can effectively promote progress towards development objectives including the MDGs. Finally, aid given for military purposes should not be included in ODA. Such an inclusion could be a fatal mistake since it will serve to undermine the development orientation of ODA.

Domestic Resources for Development Financing

Although the LDCs have limited domestic resources and will continue to depend on high levels of aid, they can and should raise additional domestic resources to complement aid inflows. The LDCs have opportunities to raise resources for public investment through an improved tax collection system. Furthermore, they have an opportunity to make more resources available for private investment through an improved banking system.

Banks are more important than financial markets for credit provision at low levels of development. The weakness of the banking sector in LDCs is highlighted by the fact that (i) in 2003, money supply was 80 per cent of GDP in other, more

[39] UNDP Mauritania Country Office.

industrialized developing countries, but just 31 percent of GDP in LDCs; and that (ii) between 1980 and 2003, the share of domestic credit to the private sector doubled from 30 percent to almost 60 per cent for low- and middle-income countries, but stagnated at around 14-15 percent in the LDCs[40]. Contrary to common perceptions, the problem in LDCs is not so much that banks do not have the liquidity to make loans; it is rather that the potential borrowers do not have the collateral that banks require. In Senegal, for example, 80 percent of loan applications by small and medium-sized enterprises were rejected because of lack of collateral[41].

Lending by microfinance institutions does not effectively compensate for the lack of activity by commercial banks, or the weakness of many national development banks. This is because microfinance institutions typically provide relatively small credit volumes at relatively high interest rates for relatively short durations, whereas real-sector investments require relatively large credit volumes at relatively low interest rates for relatively long durations. In order to ensure that the domestic private sector, especially small and medium sized enterprises, have access to loanable funds and are able to conduct necessary investment, it is essential that commercial banks as well as development banks become more effective in fulfilling their core functions.

Conclusion

Poverty reduction may be achieved through either the creation of productive employment opportunities for the poor or through different types of transfer payments in cash (e.g., payment of welfare) or in kind (e.g., provision of complimentary social services) to the poor. While these two approaches to poverty reduction might be considered contradictory, they are in fact complementary. However, the creation of productive employment opportunities is the only proven sustainable, long-term measure to reduce poverty, even though the provision of transfer payments is an important short-term measure to alleviate poverty. Despite this, and while both approaches are important, the latter approach has gained dominance in recent years. The understandable desire for quick results has encouraged developing countries and their development partners to focus more and more on "high-impact actions", which are associated with transfer payments. Today, poverty reduction efforts are mainly associated with the provision of social services; in this context, they are mainly

[40] UNCTAD, 2006, pp. 230-246.

[41] IMF, 2005.

concentrated on basic health and education. While the provision of social services is important for short-term poverty alleviation, it cannot by itself help to ensure long-term, sustainable poverty reduction. Moreover, if donors decrease their aid for social services, many poor countries will find themselves unable to provide these services to the poor. The only way for LDCs to decrease their high and sustained dependence on aid money and to sustainably invest in their social sectors in the long-run is for them to promote high and sustained rates of economic growth and employment.

While economic growth is not the ultimate objective of development, it is a necessary means. It is necessary (although not sufficient) for government revenues and essential government expenditures to increase. Furthermore, it is necessary (although not always sufficient) for the creation of productive employment opportunities and an increase in household incomes. Accordingly, this paper has argued for a productionoriented approach to poverty reduction in the LDCs. The development of enhanced productive capacities should assume centre stage in national development and poverty reduction strategies. It should also be a key concern of international development assistance.

References

Akyüz, Y. and Gore, C.C. The Investment Profit Nexus in East Asian Industrialization, *World Development*, 24(3), 461-470, 1996.

Briceno-Garmendia, C., Estache, A. and Shafik, N. Infrastructure Services in Developing Countries: Access, Quality, Costs and Policy Reforms, World Bank Policy Research Working Paper 3468, Washington, DC, 2004.

Dollar, David and Aart Kraay, *Trade, Growth and Poverty,* Policy Research Working Paper 2615, World Bank, Washington, DC, 2000.

Helleiner, Gerald, *Trade Policy and Industrialization in Turbulent Times,* Routledge, New York, 1994.

———, *Markets, Politics and the Global Economy: Can the Global Economy be Civilized?* Tenth Raul Prebisch Lecture, UNCTAD, Geneva, 11 December, 2000.

IMF. *Senegal: Financial Stability Assessment Update.* IMF Country Report No. 05/126, Washington, DC, 2005.

Karshenas, M., Measurement and Nature of Absolute Poverty in Least Developed Countries, background paper to *The Least Developed Countries Report 2002,* UNCTAD, Geneva, 2001.

Knell, M., "Uneven Technological Accumulation and Growth in the Least Developed Countries", Background paper to *The Least Developed Countries Report 2006*, UNCTAD, Geneva, 2006.

Kozul-Wright, Z., The Firm in the Innovation Process. In: Singer *et al.* (eds). *Technological Diffusion in Third World*, Delhi, 2000.

Rodriguez, Francisco and Dani Rodrik, "Trade Policy and Economic Growth: A Skeptic's Guide to Cross-National Literature", In Ben Bernanke and Kenneth Rogoff (Eds.), *National Bureau for Economic Research Macro Annual 2000,* MIT Press, Cambridge Massachusetts, 2001.

Sachs, Jeffrey and Andrew Warner, *Economic Reform and the Process of Global Integration,* Brookings Paper on Economic Activity 1: 1-118, Brookings Institution, Washington, DC, 1995.

UNCTAD, *The Least Developed Countries Report 2002: Escaping the Poverty Trap.* Geneva and New York, 2002.

———, *The Least Developed Countries Report 2004: Linking International Trade with Poverty Reduction.* Geneva and New York, 2004.

———, *Trade and Development Report 2005,* New York and Geneva, 2005.

———, *The Least Developed Countries Report 2006: Developing Productive Capacities.* Geneva and New York, 2006.

UNDP *et. al., Making Global Trade Work for People,* Earthscan, London and Sterling, Virgina, 2003.

UNDP, UNCTAD, ACP and CFC, *Open Editorial on The Commodity Problematique, "If you will not pay us reasonable prices for our exports, we will export ourselves"*, May 2007.

World Bank, *Globalization, Growth and Poverty*, Policy Research Report, Oxford, 2002.

Index